I0815481

Many critics of the Bible misunderstand what the Bible is all about. John Marriott and Shawn Wicks address a number of commonly held false assumptions about the Bible in an intelligent, accessible, and friendly way. I enthusiastically recommend this book not only for skeptics but also for those of us who love the Bible, to make sure that we don't share some of those false assumptions ourselves.

Tremper Longman III, PhD, distinguished scholar and professor emeritus of biblical studies, Westmont College

Whatever the causes—and they are many—the Christian church in the West is losing members. Some think the Bible is irrelevant, unscientific, anti-intellectual, or simply obsolete. In *Is It Really the Good Book?* John Marriott and Shawn Wicks challenge this thinking by showing what the Bible really is and how it should be read and understood. This is a timely and much-needed book. I highly recommend it.

Craig A. Evans, distinguished research professor, The Bible Seminary, Katy, Texas

Something has been happening in the Western world on an unprecedented scale in this new millennium—people "deconverting" from apparent Christian faith because of problems created for them from close reading of the Bible. None of these problems are new; all have been discussed in detail with good answers suggested throughout history. What *is* new is the internet and its ability to spread misinformation as effectively as genuine information. As a result, this book is needed more than ever before. What kind of "book" was the Bible intended to be? Which negative critiques of Scripture largely or entirely miss its point? Why have a much larger number of people throughout history responded more positively, even with belief in Jesus, after reading its pages? This wonderful, succinct work debunks a whole raft of misunderstandings about the Bible and explains why it truly is good news!

> **Craig L. Blomberg,** distinguished professor emeritus of New Testament, Denver Seminary, Littleton, CO

In recent years, the Bible has come into increasingly hard times. It is no longer the book that is highly revered in society but is fast becoming an object that is criticized and dismissed. It is treated with increased skepticism and seen as out-of-date. Tragically, this is often happening because people do not understand it for what it is. Marriott and Wicks address this confusion by uncovering faulty assumptions made about the Bible and its message. With clarity, warmth, and compelling insight, they invite readers to discover what the Bible truly says and why its contents are attractive and compelling.

> **Clinton E. Arnold,** research professor of New Testament, Talbot School of Theology (Biola University)

It is easier for a camel to go through the eye of a needle than for modern persons to recognize their interpretive assumptions. This isn't a Bible saying, but it is a saying about why so many contemporary Christians find it difficult to make sense of their Bibles. *Is It Really the Good Book?* provides a service to both apologetics and hermeneutics in identifying common but mistaken interpretive assumptions and challenging readers to ask themselves, *Am I really reading the Bible the right way?*

> **Kevin J. Vanhoozer,** research professor of systematic theology, Trinity Evangelical Divinity School

This book by Marriott and Wicks will be beneficial for people of every affiliation, whether they consider themselves to be among the converted, the unconverted, or the deconverted. This is an important book about the proper interpretation of the Good Book.

Douglas S. Huffman, PhD, dean of the School of Theology and Ministry and special advisor to the president at University of Northwestern–St. Paul, MN

John Marriott and Shawn Wicks have given the church—and its honest skeptics—a gift. *Is It Really the Good Book?* doesn't paper over the Bible's thorny passages; it investigates them with historical savvy, pastoral warmth, and intellectual courage. By exposing the unspoken modern assumptions that so often sabotage faith, the authors invite readers into a richer, contexthonoring engagement with Scripture's grand story. The result is neither a naive defense nor cynical deconstruction but a thoughtful road map toward resilient trust—one that respects both scholarship and lived experience. Anyone wrestling with doubt, guiding students, or preaching to a disenchanted generation will find this volume indispensable.

Michael R. Licona, professor of New Testament studies, Houston Christian University

Is It Really the Good Book?

IS IT REALLY THE GOOD BOOK?

Restoring Your Faith *in the* Bible by
Questioning Your Assumptions About It

John Marriott & Shawn Wicks

Visit Tyndale online at tyndale.com.

Is It Really the Good Book?: Restoring Your Faith in the Bible by Questioning Your Assumptions About It

Cover design by Faceout Studio

Interior design by Cathy Miller

Published in association with the literary agency of Mark Sweeney & Associates, Carol Stream, Illinois.

For information about special discounts for bulk purchases, please contact Tyndale House Publishers at csresponse@tyndale.com, or call 1-855-277-9400.

Library of Congress Cataloging-in-Publication Data

A catalog record for this book is available from the Library of Congress.

ISBN 979-8-4005-0325-2

Printed in the United States of America

32 31 30 29 28 27 26
7 6 5 4 3 2 1

To Carson Tremper, Matthew Balos, and the 2025 Graduating Class of Whittier Christian High School

—John

For all those who never stop asking questions and want to understand. For Patrick, Lydia, Julia, and Cassia, may you grow to love and cherish the Word of God, and may it be your guiding light throughout life. For Cari, Owen, and David, the Lord knows.

—Shawn

Contents

Foreword *xiii*

Introduction *1*

PART 1 **PRELIMINARY MATTERS**

CHAPTER 1 Never Judge a Book by Its Cover *17*

CHAPTER 2 The Legacy of the Bible *33*

CHAPTER 3 The Church's Book *49*

PART 2 **FALSE ASSUMPTIONS**

CHAPTER 4 Once Upon a Time . . . *71*

False Assumption #1: The Bible Is an Ancient Fairy Tale

CHAPTER 5 To Err Is . . . Divine? *89*

False Assumption #2: The Bible Must Be Error-Free

CHAPTER 6 Easy-Peasy Lemon Squeezy *109*

False Assumption #3: The Bible Is Simple

CHAPTER 7 The Case of Mistaken Interpretation *121*

False Assumption #3: The Bible Is Simple, Part 2

CHAPTER 8 A Fish out of Water *137*

False Assumption #4: The Bible Is Written to Me

CHAPTER 9 Doing the Right Thing *153*

False Assumption #5: The Bible Is a Rule Book

CHAPTER 10 Behind the Times *173*

False Assumption #6: The Bible Is a History Book

CHAPTER 11 It's Not Rocket Science *187*

False Assumption #7: The Bible Is a Science Book

CHAPTER 12 Truth, Justice, and a Better Tomorrow *205*

False Assumption #8: The Bible Is a Social Justice Book

Conclusion *225*

Notes *229*

Discussion Guide *261*

About the Authors *265*

Foreword

Some three hundred years ago, one of the world's most famous skeptics of Christianity was the French writer and intellectual Voltaire. He is reputed to have said that "one hundred years from my day, there will not be a Bible on earth except one that is looked upon by an antiquarian curiosity-seeker."

Of course, that is not what happened. In fact, the great irony of Voltaire's prediction is that, a century after his declaration, Voltaire's own home in Geneva, Switzerland, had become a storehouse for Bibles and tracts produced by the Evangelical Society of Geneva. Likewise, the same printing presses that had been used to print Voltaire's anti-religious pamphlets were being used to print their Bibles.

The Bible has always had a habit of outliving its critics and remains the bestselling book of all time, bar none. Nevertheless, criticisms of Scripture have become increasingly common in our present online age. Many skeptics of the "New Atheist" variety have dismissed the Bible as immoral, unreliable, and irrelevant.

However, the experience of hosting hundreds of radio and

podcast debates between Christians and skeptics has led me to realize that the most prominent critiques of Scripture are often mistaken and misplaced. As John Marriott and Shawn Wicks show in this helpful and timely book, modern culture is dominated by faulty assumptions about what Scripture is and what it is for.

For instance, in chapter 4 the authors pick up on a memorable conversation I hosted on whether the science of the universe provides evidence for God with Oxford professor Peter Atkins. An outspoken atheist scientist, Atkins announced that the Bible might be able to authenticate its divine credentials if it contained an unmistakable scientific hypothesis, such as the second law of thermodynamics, saying, "If I were looking in the Bible, heaven forbid, I would expect to see maybe 'increase in entropy is equal to Q reversible divided by temperature.' If there was an equation in the Bible rather than all this wishy-washy elastic writing."

How generations of readers would have made any sense of these unintelligible words before nineteenth-century physicists came along to explain them is left unclear! Yet this idea—that the only way the Bible should be taken seriously by modern people is if its ancient writers had been inspired to include predictions about contemporary scientific theories and modern technology—is surprisingly common. Likewise, skeptics often accuse the Bible of failing to live up to modern standards of ethics, morality, human rights . . . the list goes on.

However, what these contemporary critics often forget is that the Bible is arguably the foundation for the development of modern science. Its story inspired the work of the great pioneers of the scientific revolution—all of whom were Christians. Similarly, our modern beliefs in equality, freedom, progress, and compassion are all inextricably bound up with the Bible.

Starting from page one of the Bible, when God creates human

beings in his own image, humans were invested with a dignity and value that could never be derived from science or reason alone. Likewise, when God came in person in Jesus to lay down his life for his creation, his teachings recorded in Scripture and his example lived out in the lives of his followers began a movement that changed the world for good, leading to the development of the rule of law, human rights, hospitals, charities, public education, and much more.

That's not to say there aren't plenty of challenging passages in the Bible—especially when it comes to slavery, warfare, and violence in the Old Testament. We must all be careful students of Scripture as we navigate the history and context of these passages. However, it's somewhat ironic that the Bible's most vociferous critics are usually judging its morality on the basis of a twenty-first-century Western moral framework that derives from the Bible itself.

The fact that the books of the Bible weren't written in a way that satisfies the somewhat arbitrary level of contemporary scientific or moral knowledge demanded by critics like Atkins is hardly a valid objection to a God who may have a much bigger picture in mind than only the concerns of early-twenty-first-century skeptics. This shortsighted approach to Scripture reminds me of a phrase coined by C. S. Lewis. He described the "chronological snobbery" of those in his own age who regarded the thought and philosophy of the era they had been born into as the only one worth listening to.

The reason many of these critiques of the Bible are so shallow is because they are based on a fundamental misunderstanding of the purpose of Scripture. If we start out with faulty assumptions about the Bible, then we shouldn't be surprised if it doesn't live up to our unrealistic expectations.

However, when we take the Bible on its own terms, seek to

interpret it in context, and understand the bigger story that is being told through the whole sweep of Scripture, we will soon discover a book that defies a purely naturalistic explanation.

What really marks the Bible as unusual is that, despite being the end product of many different authors writing in times and places very different to each other and our own, it still tells a historically coherent and thematically unified story.

Perhaps even more remarkably, it has been able to unfailingly communicate the meaning and wisdom of that story to multiple generations in diverse parts of the world. Whole swaths of people whose lives have been soaked in the words of the Bible have consequently been able to locate themselves and their purpose within a grand narrative of what it means to be human.

This is the miracle of Scripture—not some parlor trick of finding a scientific equation predicted in its pages (as Peter Atkins might wish), nor some magical ability to exist hermetically sealed off from the normal processes of time and history (as even some Christians might like to believe). The miracle of Scripture is that it has spoken, and continues to speak, to every generation, place, and time it encounters. In doing so, its message has transformed individuals, nations, and empires.

I'm grateful for the work of scholars like John Marriott and Shawn Wicks. In this book you will find clear, thoughtful, and honest responses to the contemporary challenges aimed at Scripture. Most importantly, you'll discover why the Bible continues to outlive its critics and remains the bestselling and most influential book of all time.

Justin Brierley
Speaker, broadcaster, and author of Why I'm Still a Christian
and The Surprising Rebirth of Belief in God

Introduction

Bible-believing Christians, those who see the Bible as the perfect word of God, would be horrified to know how often loss of faith is triggered by someone deciding to read the good book and discovering the long litany of slavery, incest, misogyny, genocide, or scientific absurdities there.

VALERIE TARICO

On a warm, end-of-summer afternoon, four of us sat in my (Shawn's) backyard, shooting the breeze and talking about anything that came to mind. The conversation included a discussion about socialism and capitalism, the Bill of Rights, and the current state of the education system. It was at this time that a close friend of mine since childhood leaned in and pointedly asked my younger cousin, Brad, whether he still believed in God. You could have heard a pin drop.

My friend did not ask this question out of the blue. He asked it because Brad, who had once professed to be a Christian, was espousing opinions that were clearly no longer grounded or informed by God or the Bible.

I knew Brad had been drifting away for some time. It was his habit to drive down and visit our family during Thanksgiving, and it seemed without fail he would want to talk about God or the prevailing culture. However, as each holiday came and went, I saw the light of his faith gradually dimming. It was also during this time that he walked away from church. He told me he could no longer stomach the hypocrites and the intolerance he encountered there. He found the people he worshiped with to be judgmental and prejudiced. Despite this, he somehow still clung, albeit precariously, to his belief in God and Jesus for another year. But I could see doubts were growing and festering. It was during this season that I noticed a paradigm shift in his thinking. Catalyzed by several major events in his life, he started denouncing the "sin language" of the Bible as harsh and oppressive. He explained that he preferred the terms *ignorance* and *unenlightened* to *sin* and *evil.* He consumed articles and books that attacked Christianity.

The candor of my friend's question genuinely caught my cousin off guard. Once he had recovered from the initial shock, though, he slowly shook his head as if gathering the nerve to confess out loud what he and the rest of us already knew. He no longer believed in God. But he did not stop there. He added that he could not understand how any intelligent person could believe in such nonsense.

His words still echo in my heart. "The only evidence we have about God or Jesus comes from the Bible," he said. "And don't get me started on the Bible. How can any thinking person believe in the Bible? When we read Grimms' fairy tales, we don't think they're true, right? For me, the Bible is just that. Nothing more than a bunch of fairy tales."

I pushed back. "You don't really believe the Bible is a bunch of fairy tales, do you? I mean, fairy tales are a specific genre. When you pick up a newspaper or a history book and read it, you don't think it is *just* a collection of fairy tales, do you? Of course not. Because it's not. And neither is the Bible."

The conversation paused there, so I stood up to get a drink. As I made my way to the ice chest, I noticed Brad was following me. While I grabbed some ice for my drink, he revealed that he could never believe in a book that condones slavery. He even wondered how anyone, including myself, could choose to believe in such an antiquated, immoral book. These, of course, were loaded statements, and I knew better than to respond to him without carving out time to discuss them at length. But Brad was family, and alas, I did not heed my own wisdom.

My first shortcut response was to confront my cousin's accusation with proof texts. I knew the slavery he had in mind was a certain brand of slavery—rooted in human trafficking and racism and reflected especially in pre–Civil War America. I knew I would not get far explaining that ancient customs and institutions do not correspond directly to the modern world, so instead I pointed him to Exodus 21:16 and Deuteronomy 24:7, old covenant laws against human trafficking. Next, I showed him 1 Timothy 1:9-10, which condemns "enslavers" as "unholy and profane" and associates them with murderers. But I could tell my proof texts barely left a mark. So I asked him, "Where did you get the idea that the Bible condones slavery? It's actually quite the opposite."

"Well, if it doesn't condone it, it certainly tolerates it," he countered. "Doesn't it tell slaves they should obey their masters? I get that slavery was accepted back then, but you believe this is God's Word, right? So why doesn't God just say, 'Hey, everyone! Slavery is wrong! Stop it!' Instead, it tells slaves to obey their masters."

It was at this moment that I had an epiphany of sorts. My intelligent, college-educated, well-read cousin, who once claimed to be a Christian and regularly attended church, was working from some faulty assumptions and expectations about the Bible. Not only did he not understand the historical context of this verse, but he was also, based on faulty interpretation, drawing wrong conclusions as to what it was communicating. This left me dismayed and grieving.

The thing is, if I believed what he believed about the Bible, I would think it was nonsense too.

Time to Raise the Red Flag

Shawn's cousin isn't an outlier. Research shows that large numbers of people who once identified as Christians are shedding that label. They have left the church, denied the faith, and stopped identifying as believers. Some identify as atheists, others as agnostics, and still others as spiritual but not religious. When asked on surveys what their religious affiliation is, they select the only option available to them: "none." As a result, sociologists have taken to referring to them as the nones. And the data shows the percentage of individuals who once identified as Christians but who now identify as nones is increasing at a stunning rate. For example, in the 1990s 90 percent of Americans identified as Christians and only 5 percent identified as nones. Today those numbers are radically different, with 64 percent of Americans identifying as Christians and 30 percent as nones.[1] Studies also show that the vast majority of those identifying as nones—nearly 80 percent—were made, not born.[2] They're not the products of secular homes but rather grew up in religious homes and later deconverted from their faith. To get an idea of the magnitude of this shift, consider the Pew Research Center's claim that for every one person who converts to Christianity four depart.[3] Pew also says that if current deconversion rates continue, within one generation those who identify as nones in the United States will outnumber those who identify as Christians. If that's not enough to raise a red flag, then consider the conclusion of a study conducted by the Pinetops Foundation, which found that within the next thirty years, thirty-five million people who once identified as Christians no longer will.[4] We could cite more studies, but these should be sufficient to make the case that the church in the United States is hemorrhaging the faithful at an alarming rate.

We should acknowledge that the above studies don't do a good job of distinguishing between those who had a robust faith that was central to their life and those for whom Christianity was only a box they checked on a survey. We suspect that many—possibly even the majority—of those leaving the faith were box-check believers. Regardless, there are *significant* numbers who did display a vibrant faith but who no longer identify as Christians.

Consider Gregg. One morning I (John) opened my email to find a message from Gregg, a middle-age Christian man struggling to hold on to what he believed. Gregg asked if I would be willing to chat with him because before he renounced his faith, he wanted to make sure he had turned over every stone in his search for answers. I responded that I was happy to talk with him and asked if he could share with me before our meeting what was causing him to suspect Christianity was a sham. Here's what he said:

> I am still very pro-Christian and believe it is the best religion (or tradition?) in its current state for society. . . . I still go to church as I enjoy the preaching and the music and even participate. I also go to a small group meeting every other Sunday and watch much Christian programming on TV. But when I attend or watch these religious presentations, I just marvel at what they actually believe. I am convinced now that after fifty years of being totally immersed in the "faith" and "apologizing" for it, the religion is demonstrably false. . . . But unlike most

> atheists and agnostics I wish the salvation gospel was true. Amazing how euphoric and giddy one would be if they really believed there was a God who knew their name before the foundation of the world and that there was a purpose and plan in this veil of tears on earth and someday, they would get to live in eternal bliss, reunited with family and friends in a heavenly city with streets lined with gold.

Far from being a box-check believer, Gregg both was well-versed in the faith and demonstrated sincerity in his actions and desires. I assumed Gregg was local to Southern California and asked him when and where he wanted to meet. To my surprise he said he would have to check for the most convenient flight to Los Angeles. "You're not local?" I asked him. "No, I live in Tennessee, but I want to meet with you face-to-face, and I'm willing to pay you $200 an hour to talk with me." I told him I couldn't take his money, but if he was willing to fly across the country, I would give him all the time he wanted. I met Gregg on the campus of Biola University, where I teach. He was soft-spoken, kind, and thoughtful. As we talked, it became apparent what was causing him to have serious doubts about Christianity. You guessed it: the Bible.

Both Christians who have shown little serious engagement with their faith *and* folks like Gregg, who are willing to do almost anything to retain it, often share something in common: The very book that should have strengthened their faith has undermined it. For them, the Bible being called the Good Book is the height of irony. How, they wonder, could a book filled with so many problems ever be good?

The B-I-B-L-E, That's *Not* the Book for Me

If you spend any time reading deconversion narratives, you'll find many stories from people like Gregg. While the details differ, the general contour of their stories remains the same. Often raised in a Christian home, they took for granted that the Bible is God's Word and learned many of the major stories in Sunday school and through sermons. But they were largely unaware of the less-popular parts until they read the Bible for themselves. Surprised by the apparent contradictions they discovered, dismayed by the miracle stories they had never given much thought to, and troubled by the violence commanded by God, they began to suspect the Bible wasn't what they were told it was. How could a book from God legislate slavery, get basic details of history wrong, conflict with established science, command genocide, and warn of eternal separation from God for not believing the right things? It's as though a light bulb went on causing them to ask, *Why haven't I ever thought about this before? Do I really believe this stuff?* Should *I believe this stuff?*

These are all questions David asked himself. Standing in the baptismal tank at his church, David was ready to identify as a disciple of Jesus. Recently converted and active in the youth group and church worship band, David believed he had found the meaning of life. As he stood in the cold water waiting to be dunked, the pastor whispered to him, "You know, Son, you can't just say you believe—you have to *know* it to be true to your heart." David thought,

> I don't know it. I have so much research to do. This is weighing over my head, I do not deserve this team [the church]. I better go figure this stuff out. And I ran

> home, grabbed a bottle of water, flipped open the Bible, and I read, and read, and read. I was probably the only fifteen-year-old on the planet reading Genesis to Exodus. Reading entirely the Bible! And in every little step, stuff was falling apart for me. My goal honestly was to get so close to God that I could defend him. But I got so close I saw there wasn't one.[5]

David's story is a good example of what Rodney Wilson, professor and coordinator of the history and political science department at Mineral Area College, discovered when he surveyed nearly 1,600 former conservative evangelical and fundamentalist Christians about why they had left the faith. The catalyst for the clear majority was reading the Bible for themselves. Here are what a few respondents had to say:

- "Reading the Bible through in a year is what led to my deconversion."
- "Honestly what made me change my views was simply reading the Bible! Now, I believe it is a document that is very much a product of its culture and time period, like the *Epic of Gilgamesh* or any other ancient/old document. I think it was created by humans (men, to be precise), and was in no way influenced by any god."
- "I sat down and read the Bible from cover to cover out of genuine interest and the desire for something more. Little-by-little it became impossible for me to believe in the mythology I was raised with."
- "While reading it from cover to cover, I began to discover that the character Yahweh and I had some pretty strong disagreements on morality. I didn't like his jealous,

murderous nature and so the doubts were born. Then it hit me. 'Talking snakes and donkeys?!? Every species of animal from every continent on a ship?!? For real?'"
- "Once I started really reading the Bible, my faith started to wane heavily. Too many contradictions, too many unbelievable things. The more it was pressed as God's truth, the more I questioned it."
- "After reading a bit more I realized there were so many fairy tales and inaccuracies in the Bible and that there is no way they could be the product of some all-knowing God."[6]

The above quotes are representative of thousands of similar ones you'll find on the internet.

What is it about the Bible, the so-called Good Book, that so many former Christians discovered and that caused them to leave their faith? While we don't deny the Bible is a complex book with a lot of challenging passages, we're convinced that the problem for many former Christians lies not so much with the content of the Bible but with the assumptions they brought to it. Specifically, assumptions about what the Bible is and how to understand it.

Assumptions about the Bible act like eyeglasses. They're the conceptual lenses through which we see the Bible. In the same way that glasses with the wrong prescription will distort our vision of the physical world, wrong assumptions about the Bible will distort our understanding of what it is and how to read it well. The main difference between eyeglasses and assumptions is that when it comes to glasses, we're aware that we have them on and how they affect our vision. But we are almost entirely unaware of our assumptions. That's because we don't really think about them. We take them for granted because they allow us to think in the first place. Assumptions are like deep ocean currents that are undetectable on the surface but whose power determines the destination of anything caught in their flow.

We're convinced the assumptions that many Christians—current and former—have about the Bible tend to distort rather than clarify its message. When the Bible is left on the shelf or passively heard preached on Sunday mornings, it doesn't matter what glasses we have on. If we don't personally interact with it, those wrong assumptions go unnoticed. But if we take the Bible off the shelf and seriously read it, the incompatibility between our mistaken assumptions about the Bible and what the Bible actually is becomes painfully evident. It's no coincidence that a significant theme in former Christians' stories is that when they got serious about reading the Bible, their crisis of faith began.

We want to be crystal clear: We are not blaming former Christians for their faulty assumptions. In fact, many Christians in the United States share those faulty assumptions. We did, too, and they caused us great frustration as we tried to be faithful to Jesus and at the same time maintain intellectual integrity as we wrestled with the Bible. We share the sentiment expressed by the son of a pastor who needed to have his view of the Bible corrected: "Reading about the Bible . . . and the ways in which it's helpful to read it . . . saved me from walking away from the faith altogether. . . . I had to go outside the Bible to understand what the Bible was to save me from ditching the whole thing."[7]

We're not promoting some novel way of reading the Bible, nor do we claim to possess any secret knowledge that unlocks its "real" message. Rather, when we suggest that a new set of lenses will help you read the Bible, we mean that by reading resources like the one you have in your hands, you will recognize the ways in which you are imposing your own mistaken assumptions on the Bible and instead allow the Bible to be what it is on its own terms.

The Church's One Foundation Is . . . ?

The place and role of the Bible in the Christian faith can't be overstated. Well, actually, it can be. Sometimes it's said that the Bible is the foundation of Christianity, but that's not quite true. The foundation of Christianity is Jesus Christ. Christianity is centered on a person, not a book. Theologian Greg Boyd puts it this way:

> We do not relate to a book, or a list of doctrines that are rooted in that book. We relate to, and our faith is founded upon, Christ and his love for us. Participating in this love that is centered in Christ is the end to which all beliefs about the Bible point. This relationship is what gives significance to everything else the Bible teaches.[8]

While Boyd is correct, there's no denying that we learn about Jesus from a book. Perhaps a more accurate way of stating the roles of Jesus and the Bible is to say that Jesus is the foundation of the faith, and the Bible is the foundation for what we know about Jesus. Because of that, Christians have placed a high priority on believing what it says. Unfortunately, the church hasn't always done a good job of communicating what the Bible is and how to read it well. Some common misunderstandings Christians have about the Bible are that it is . . .

- A lawbook, a source of commands that believers must follow.
- A book of blessing, a collection of stand-alone promises that can be claimed by believers to make their lives better.
- A puzzle to be solved, a metaphysical riddle that, when cracked, will provide truth about the nature of reality.

- A storybook, full of comforting stories about people interacting with God in a warm, fuzzy way.
- A how-to guide, a manual on how to live a life that God blesses.
- A contemporary book, one that ought to align with current moral sensibilities and scientific knowledge.

These problematic views lead to assumptions and expectations about the Bible, which in turn set believers up for a crisis of faith when the Bible doesn't meet those expectations.[9]

What to Expect from This Book

This book is not so much a defense of the Bible as it is our attempt to provide you with a new set of lenses for looking at it. It's a guide to help you truly understand what it is saying (and not saying) so you can evaluate its claims fairly and appropriately. We do this by identifying eight faulty assumptions that lie at the heart of many deconversion stories:

1. The Bible is an ancient fairy tale
2. The Bible must be error-free
3. The Bible is simple to understand
4. The Bible is written to me
5. The Bible is a rule book
6. The Bible is a history book
7. The Bible is a science book
8. The Bible is a social justice book

We don't claim this book solves all the problems people have with the Bible. However, we do think that when the Bible is seen for what it is, many of those problems get resolved on their own. We believe that when the Bible is approached in the manner outlined in this book, it stands on its own merits. Blaise Pascal once observed that "we are generally better persuaded by the reasons we discover ourselves than by those given to us by others." We could not agree more. So if you are someone struggling with doubts about the Bible, or know someone who is, it is our hope that after reading this book, you'll have the foundation necessary to discover your own good reasons to trust it as a source of divine wisdom, power, and goodness and be able to pass on that foundation to others. But before we address the eight faulty assumptions that often lead to a faith crisis, we need to address three preliminary matters: what the Bible is, what the Bible has done, and who the Bible belongs to. We turn to those matters now, in part 1.

PART 1

PRELIMINARY MATTERS

CHAPTER 1

Never Judge a Book by Its Cover

The Bible. It's just not working for me. I wish it was. Wouldn't it be great if it did work for me and I had the peace one gets when knowing the universe is just and kind and guided by eternal intelligence? Maybe I'm reading it wrong.

JUDD APATOW

Almost everyone is familiar with the saying "Never judge a book by its cover." It expresses the idea that we should not judge someone or something based upon what we see on the outside only. It's an appeal to give someone or something a chance before completely dismissing them because they might surprise us. Actually, there are several English idioms that express this sentiment. For example, "Clothes don't make the man" or "Looks can be deceiving" or "Things are not always what they seem." There is great wisdom here. When I (Shawn) talk to my teenage son about girls he is attracted to, I am constantly reminding him it is what is on the inside that matters. I warn him regularly of the dangers of being shallow-minded and encourage him to get to know someone or something before passing judgment. This wisdom, of course, is not only for freshman boys. It is suitable for everyone, for we are all prone to pass judgment without truly appreciating and valuing something first.

Stating the Problem

Sadly, many people today have judged and dismissed the Bible without truly getting to know it. They have tossed it aside without hearing what it actually has to say. Considering the bad experiences some have had with Christianity, the slew of strange and embarrassing verses skeptics have passed around the internet, and a rising secular culture that pushes against the Bible's core values, it is not difficult to see why this is the case. There are, of course, those who have genuinely *studied* the Bible and concluded there is nothing holy or sacred about it, but in our experience, this is the exception, not the rule. Many people—being products of a culture that is averse to thorough, in-depth study, especially when it comes to exploring and investigating religious thought and expression—have dismissed the Bible not because of meticulous research, insightful articles, or compelling arguments but because of something they saw in a meme, or read in a book, or heard from a so-called expert. The problem with this approach, besides the obvious dangers of being manipulated and misled, is that it is not concerned about the truth. It is judging something without truly getting to know it.

Making things more complicated is that this view of the Bible has become trendy, spreading like wildfire through social media. It is far easier to mock and discredit an idea or belief system than it is to explain or appreciate it, especially if we think we won't agree with it or don't understand it fully. Combine that with the ability to spread (mis)information from one person to the next through a simple click of the mouse, and you can see how distorted views of the Bible might develop. The result? People have come to see the Bible at best as a strange, unenlightened curiosity and at worst as a weapon from the past used to bully others. Even though this view of the Bible is neither fair nor accurate (which we will make plain throughout this book), it has proved rather effective at rattling the faith of many Christians.

Unfortunately, some preachers and Bible teachers have unwittingly contributed to this perception. One of the primary reasons why so many Christians and ex-Christians have only a surface knowledge of the Bible is that the majority of sermons, Bible studies, and Sunday school lessons are geared to be inspirational or moralistic in nature. Preachers cherry-pick what passages they share from, often ignoring the more scandalous and less flattering stories. When those struggling with their faith later become aware of these passages, they feel shocked and betrayed, concluding that either their pastors are not aware of them or are hiding them.[1] Thankfully, many preachers and teachers are realizing that skipping over these troublesome passages is no longer prudent. They are seeing that their failure to preach the entire Word of God from cover to cover has left a generation of Christians vulnerable to the attack of modern skeptics.

Open and Sincere

If your faith in the Bible has been shaken, we invite you to read this book with an open mind and a sincere heart. If you have come to associate the Bible with fantasies and horror novels or see it as a book of bigotry, violence, and superstition, we ask you to rethink your assumptions. If you are settled in your unbelief, our book is unlikely to persuade you, but it might help you see ways you are misrepresenting the Bible or unfairly condemning it. A sincere critic who cares about their integrity should always want to properly represent what they are critiquing. And if your faith in the Bible is sound and unshakable, this book will help you present the Bible in such a way that you do not needlessly push others away from it by spreading poor or misleading information about it.

We should say from the outset that what you will not find in this book is a robust study of the Bible and its doctrines. And though we will use many Scriptures throughout the book as examples, this is not a reference book where you can quickly look up specific Bible difficulties and find easy solutions. Instead, we believe your nagging doubts about the Bible are worthy of a foundational response—one that addresses the core issues and gives you the tools to properly interpret the Bible. As the old adage goes, "Give a man a fish, feed him for a day; teach him to fish, feed him for life." We will do this by first reacquainting you with the Bible (chapters 1, 2, and 3) and then sharing many of the faulty assumptions and unwarranted expectations people have placed on it (chapters 4 through 12). We will show how those have led to skewed interpretations that have wrongly (and unfairly) put the Bible in a bad light. We believe if you are a sincere Christian with honest doubts about the Bible, your appreciation for it will be renewed and your faith in it will be restored. We believe this because we have experienced it ourselves.

What Is the Bible?

We all have an idea of what the Bible is. For many, the Bible is the written Word of God and the ultimate guide to life. For others, it is a human work full of made-up stories and teachings that people use to justify bigotry and condemn others. Some of these assumptions are rooted in our upbringings. Some of them are rooted in what we have learned about the Bible from school, books, or other people. Wherever we got our ideas about the Bible, though, it is important to put aside our assumptions. We will come to see that some of our beliefs about the "Good Book"—whether positive, negative, or indifferent—are true and accurate, some are mistaken or erroneous, and some are imprecise or incomplete. But if we aren't intentional about letting the Bible speak for itself, our preconceived ideas will have a way of overruling or dismissing new information.

The first step to becoming reacquainted with the Bible, then, is to gain a right understanding of what it is. How we answer the question "What is the Bible?" determines how we will approach and apply it.[2] Determining what it is will also help us answer what it is about, what purpose it serves, and what role it should play in the lives of Christians and even the world. And once we have reacquainted ourselves with the nature and purpose of the Bible, we will be free to explore it at a deeper, more insightful level. Only in doing this will we expose our wrong assumptions about it and unravel the seemingly bizarre, antiquated, and troublesome verses.

The English word *Bible* has its roots in the Greek word *biblos*. This word was used to describe a scroll made of Egyptian papyrus that was imported to Greece through the Phoenician port city of Byblos.[3] The plural form of the word *biblos* is *biblia*. The word *biblia* was adopted into Latin and gradually became specifically associated with the collection of Christianity's holy texts. It was during this time that the word gradually transitioned from a plural word into a singular word, referring to the collection of books as a single unit

From the origin of this word, we quickly discern that the Bible is not merely one book but a collection of books. These books were written in several languages—Hebrew, Greek, and Aramaic (though loanwords from other languages are not uncommon).[4] The Bible is an anthology of texts compiled by God's historical people over a span of roughly 1,800 years (1400 BC–AD 400). It is composed of sixty-six books, written by over forty authors of disparate cultures and backgrounds. By design it incorporates a variety of literary genres, including creation stories, genealogies, history and biographies, laws and customs, liturgies, poetry and songs, wisdom, parables, prophecies, and letters (among others). These genres are usually grouped together, but multiple genres can be located within individual books.

The Bible as a whole is divided into two major sections, which represent two epochs in salvation history. The first section is referred to as the Old Testament; the second is the New Testament. Ancient Jews broke the Old Testament into three sections: the Law, the Prophets, and the Writings. In English Bibles, the texts are grouped according to genre into four subsections (Law, History, Poetry, and Prophecy). The New Testament is grouped according to genre into three subsections: History (the Gospels and Acts), Letters (written by the apostle Paul and others), and Prophecy (Revelation).[5]

To refer to the Bible as a simple anthology, though, is misleading. God's people believe it is more than that. Yes, it is a collection of books, but it is a collection of books that are connected in such a way that they are often treated as one unit. The common threads that bind the books together as a unified collection are the divine character Yahweh (usually translated "Lord" in most English versions of the Bible) and his covenant bond with humankind, especially his people.[6] While Yahweh is not mentioned by name in every portion of Scripture (for example, there is no direct mention of him in the book of Esther), his unmistakable presence looms over every story and verse. His bond with humankind is rooted in *hesed*, a Hebrew term often translated as "mercy," "steadfast love," or "lovingkindness." It is what moves Yahweh to act on behalf of his people and all humankind. Specifically, he acts in order to bring about peace and salvation.

So then, for God's people, the Bible is more than an anthology. It is a collection of sacred texts. They are sacred because they reveal God's nature, plan for salvation, and will for his people. They are sacred because they share through a variety of genres how people have experienced God throughout history. These texts have been widely recognized and accepted as such by the community of faith, though not always immediately.[7] The process by which they were accepted was more organic and less formal than most Christians today realize, but this should not lead us to think the Bible was formed without thought or rationale. And while it is outside the scope of this book to detail or defend this process, it is worth noting that while Jesus disagreed with the Pharisees (religious leaders of his day) about many things, he never disagreed with them about what Old Testament books should be recognized as sacred texts.[8] Not only did he recognize them as sacred texts, but he also claimed they were ultimately about him.[9]

Jesus also gave his disciples the authority to pass on his message. This message is recorded in the New Testament. He promised to give them the Holy Spirit to guide them in remembering, understanding, and sharing his words.[10] The fulfillment of this promise was later confirmed "by signs and wonders and various miracles" (Hebrews 2:4). This provides Christians with a firm theological basis for accepting the books of the Old and New Testaments as Scripture.

So, what is the Bible? It is an anthology of sacred texts that record how people in the past have experienced or encountered Yahweh (the God of Israel and the early church). Of course, not everyone discovers God in the exact same way, but the majesty of the Scriptures is that people have been "finding God" in them throughout history. It is for this reason Christians recognize and honor these texts as sacred and holy even today. They refer to them as prophecy and revelation because they bring to light things about God and his plan of salvation that people would otherwise not be able to discern on their own.

What's It All About?

> God has now revealed to us his mysterious will regarding Christ—which is to fulfill his own good plan. And this is the plan: At the right time he will bring everything together under the authority of Christ—everything in heaven and on earth.
>
> EPHESIANS 1:9-10, NLT

When we survey the collected works of the Bible from a bird's-eye view, we are able to see its overarching, unifying story. The Bible is the story of God's redemption of humankind, rooted in his deep desire to commune with his creation—the men and women he made in his image for that express purpose. This story is not a children's tale or some Hollywood movie. It is a story acted out in history with real people, real circumstances, real experiences, and real events. From creation to the fall, from the fall to redemption, from redemption to the final consummation, it is the story of how God saves those he loves.[11]

That the God of the Bible is identified as a historical figure whom people of diverse backgrounds and cultures come to know intimately and worship makes the Bible unique among sacred texts. While other holy books speak about god or gods, none of them describe God primarily in that way. So what is the Bible about? It is about God's desires, plans, and actions to make peace with (fallen) humanity for all eternity. We call this salvation history.[12] This idea is key to understanding the heart of every chapter and verse. This idea is clearly seen in passages like Psalm 105 and the speeches recorded in Acts given by Peter, Stephen, and Paul.[13] Of course, salvation history finds its greatest realization and expression in the person of Jesus Christ.[14] So then, when we call the Bible sacred revelation, we are saying that it is a unique and trustworthy source by which a person can encounter Yahweh, the God of Israel and the church, and draw close to him.[15]

Interpreting the Bible

Whether you believe in the Bible or not, everybody has a method or way of interpreting it, even if they are not aware of it. Some people say, "I don't interpret the Bible. I let it say what it says." But this is a way to interpret the Bible. When someone picks up the Bible and starts reading it as if it were written to them yesterday by a friend, without any further context, this is a method (albeit an unsound one) of interpreting the Bible. When someone uses this approach, they are not avoiding reading into the text at all. They are actually doing the opposite. They are imposing their own context and meaning onto the text (this is akin to the psychological phenomenon of projecting, where a person unconsciously attributes their thoughts, feelings, or behaviors to another person). This is true whether their interpretation leans more progressive or traditional. When this happens, they end up reading the Bible through their own self-made glasses, and this often leads to misreading and misunderstanding the text, despite the perceived purity of their method and intentions. If we are to truly grasp what the Bible is saying, we must work to avoid this imprecise and inconsistent method of interpretation. We must replace it with a more reliable and scientific approach (yes, there is a science to interpretation; this science is called *hermeneutics*).

The desire of any student or fair-minded critic of the Bible should be to adopt the best interpretive method in order to comprehend, apply, analyze, synthesize, and evaluate what they are reading in a dispassionate and accurate manner. This is especially important when trying to decipher controversial or contradictory passages.[16] Indeed, the reason why particular verses and passages seem strange, out-of-date, vindictive, or petty is usually because we modern-day readers are so out of touch with the context and heart in which they were originally written. It is a goal of this book to address biases and false assumptions about the Bible that poison the well and taint the way we interpret it.

For example, in the introduction, I (Shawn) talked about how my cousin Brad understood the Bible to condone, or at least tolerate, slavery. He came to this conclusion after reading the following verses:

> Slaves, obey your earthly masters with deep respect and fear. Serve them sincerely as you would serve Christ.
>
> EPHESIANS 6:5, NLT

> Slaves, obey your earthly masters in everything you do. Try to please them all the time, not just when they are watching you. Serve them sincerely because of your reverent fear of the Lord.
>
> COLOSSIANS 3:22, NLT

It is easy to see how he interpreted the Bible the way he did, especially considering our modern sensibilities. The United States has experienced the horrors of slavery. We have seen the ugliness of racism and cringe when we encounter people who are ignorant to its evils. And although ancient customs and institutions do not correspond directly to the modern world, no one can deny that slavery in the ancient world could still be cruel and dehumanizing. So we ask, *Why doesn't the Bible simply say slavery is wrong instead of telling slaves to "obey [their] earthly masters"?* That is a fair question, so long as we are open to understanding the Bible in its historical, literary, and theological context. If we don't, we will likely misunderstand what the Bible is saying.

It is *not* saying that God endorses or condones slavery. How do we know this? Because this interpretation contradicts everything else the Bible has to say about the value and dignity of all human beings, regardless of their race, gender, abilities, and social status. For example, look at what Paul—the same person who wrote the verses quoted above—had to say elsewhere:

> There is no longer Jew or Gentile, slave or free, male and female. For you are all one in Christ Jesus.
>
> GALATIANS 3:28, NLT

> In this new life, it doesn't matter if you are a Jew or a Gentile, circumcised or uncircumcised, barbaric, uncivilized, slave, or free. Christ is all that matters, and he lives in all of us.
>
> COLOSSIANS 3:11, NLT

> He [Onesimus, Philemon's runaway slave] is no longer like a slave to you. He is more than a slave, for he is a beloved

> brother, especially to me. Now he will mean much more to you, both as a man and as a brother in the Lord.
>
> So if you consider me your partner, welcome him as you would welcome me.
>
> PHILEMON 1:16-17, NLT

Clearly, we have misunderstood something in the first set of verses if we think they condone slavery. To get to the heart of the "slave" passages cited above, then, we need to ask several other probing questions. Who is Paul referring to when he mentions "slaves" and "masters"? How does this passage fit into the rest of Paul's letter? Why does he bring up this subject at all? What are we reading into the verses that might be causing us to walk away with the wrong message? But for now, we'll point you to the key to understanding many passages like this. It comes by answering this essential question: How does this text fit in with the overarching theme of salvation history?

The answer might surprise you in its simplicity. Paul wants *Christian* slaves to obey their masters for the same reason Jesus wants his followers to "not resist an evil person," and turn the other cheek, and go the extra mile (Matthew 5:39-42, NLT). When Jesus said these words, he was not saying it is permissible for someone to slap another person on the face or compel them to walk a mile. Rather, he was teaching his followers how to win over others by loving and respecting them. And they would do this by doing what Jesus said: "Do good to those who hate you. Bless those who curse you. Pray for those who hurt you" (Luke 6:27-31, NLT). As Martin Luther King Jr. once commented, "Love is the only force capable of transforming an enemy into a friend."[17] He also famously said, "Darkness cannot drive out darkness; only light can do that. Hate cannot drive out hate; only love can do that."[18] Jesus and King are by no means approving or tolerating the behavior of their abusers or enemies here. Neither is Paul condoning, or even tolerating, the institution of slavery. We know Paul has something more subversive in mind, because only a few verses after exhorting slaves to obey their masters, he writes these revealing words:

> Pray for us, too, that God will give us many opportunities to speak about his mysterious plan concerning Christ. That is why I am here in chains. Pray that I will proclaim this message as clearly as I should.
>
> Live wisely among those who are not believers and make the most of every opportunity. Let your conversation be gracious and attractive so that you will have the right response for everyone.
>
> COLOSSIANS 4:3-6, NLT

What Paul is saying is that the right and proper response of a Christian slave is to obey their master, not because God condones slavery, but because in choosing this approach, they are planting the seeds that will eventually uproot the evil of slavery that marred the Roman Empire—and they are doing it without raising a single sword.[19]

It should be clear now that these verses found in Paul's letters do not condone the institution of slavery, nor do they ignore it. Rather, they subvert it. They show a Christian how to live the good news of Jesus in such a way that they could win over even their enemies. Of course, you might ask, *Why does he tell masters to be "just and fair to your slaves"* (Colossians 4:1, NLT) *instead of simply commanding them to set their slaves free? Great question!* We will discuss this later in the book.

You Be the Judge

The origin of the quote "Never judge a book by its cover" is typically credited to George Eliot, author of *The Mill on the Floss.*[20] In the novel, the character Mr. Tulliver, while discussing the book *The History of the Devil* by Daniel Defoe, says, "And there's a lot more of 'em,—sermons mostly, I think,—but they've all got the same covers, and I thought they were all o' one sample, as you may say. *But it seems one mustn't judge by th' outside.* This is a puzzlin' world."[21]

He says this to explain how he came to possess the book—he purchased it accidentally because he didn't look inside but judged it by its cover.

This scene and quote are far more profound than most casual readers realize. In context, Mr. Tulliver's daughter, Maggie (the novel's protagonist), is presented as an inquisitive and impetuous girl who loves to read. And when the opportunity presents itself to discuss Defoe's book with one of her dad's friends, Mr. Riley, she engages in a lively discussion with him about it. Mr. Riley is taken aback by her "cleverness," and his response is reflective of the times: "I advise you to put by the 'History of the Devil,' and read some prettier book. Have you no prettier books?" Obviously, the quote "But it seems one mustn't judge by th' outside" takes on added meaning, as Mr. Riley has wrongly judged the girl in front of him. He has judged her without getting to know her. This scene takes on *even more* added meaning when we understand that the name of the author, George Eliot, is a pseudonym for Mary Ann Evans. Evans had several reasons to hide her identity as the book's author. Without a doubt, one of them was that she wanted to avoid the stereotypes associated with women's writings at the time. She wanted her book to be judged on its merits. More specifically, *she* wanted to be judged on her merits as an author, not on her gender.

It is in the spirit of Maggie Tulliver and Mary Ann Evans, then, that we sincerely invite you, no matter where you are on your spiritual journey, to do the same with the Bible. Judge it on its merits. Get to know it before you dismiss (or embrace) it. Put aside for the moment your feelings about religion and sacred texts. In fact, we encourage you to start reading it as a sacred text and a witness to salvation history (even if you doubt its veracity). Read it as revelation—an ancient text by which people even today claim to encounter God. See it as a collection of various texts written by diverse authors of every kind of background that tell the story of redemption. This will mean letting go of some major assumptions, but in doing so, you will slowly grasp what the Bible teaches.

CHAPTER 2

The Legacy of the Bible

One cannot be literate in our society without an intimate familiarity with the Bible.

SAM ARMATO

Sam Armato, professor emeritus of the University of Southern California, developed several courses during his tenure at the school, including one called "The Bible as Literature." According to Armato, it was "the first such course in the country." This course, which he taught for ten years, was a great success, attracting about a hundred students each semester. To complement his class, he authored a book called *The Bible and Western Culture*. Amusingly, he dedicated this book to his students who joined him for a seven-week study abroad in Italy, because, as he says in his own words, "When we visited museums and monuments each afternoon during the course, except for representations of David and Adam and Eve, the students had difficulty identifying any other biblical figures." From this he realized that a "comprehensive course" to better acquaint his students with the Bible was necessary if they "were to achieve cultural literacy of the western world."[1]

While Armato's experience with his students is surprising, it is not uncommon. If you asked most young people today what the single most important influence on the Western world is, the Bible would likely not come to mind.[2] Its positive influence is often underestimated or overlooked. The result is a populace that is perilously unaware of its own cultural heritage. People today are growing less and less acquainted with the Bible, and what they think they know about it is usually inaccurate, which fuels antagonism toward it.

If these inaccurate, antagonistic beliefs about the Bible were the whole story, we would expect to see them reflected in the Bible's history. But when we objectively study the history of the Bible, we discover that it has, for the most part, had the opposite effect. It has a legacy of inspiring and promoting the values that many of us cherish most today. Vishal Mangalwadi, described as "India's foremost Christian intellectual," calls the Bible "the soul of Western Civilization." Why? "Because it propelled the development of everything good in the West: its notion of human dignity, human rights, human equality, justice, optimism, heroism, rationality, family, education, universities, technology, science, culture of compassion, great literature, heroism, economic progress, political freedom."[3] In a nutshell, the Bible has provided the framework and environment where the greatest innovations benefiting humankind have flourished. It has promoted advancement in these areas in ways no other sacred book or religion has or likely ever will. This is not insignificant, for as the old proverb goes, "Wisdom is justified by her children."[4]

Unfortunately, when we talk to people today about the Bible, they often discount it as archaic, unenlightened, and oppressive, even though they are largely living in the world founded upon its teachings and stories. Ironically, they are usually oblivious to the fact that the moral and educational foundation they use to criticize the Bible comes from the Bible itself.

The topic of the Bible's impact on history is complex and cannot be covered exhaustively in a single chapter. Our aim here is to acquaint you with a portion of the unique legacy of the Bible and its unmatched, enduring impact. In doing so, we believe you will see why people of faith trust it as God's Word.

The Bible's Impact on the World

> I saw another angel flying through the sky, carrying the eternal Good News to proclaim to the people who belong to this world—to every nation, tribe, language, and people.
>
> REVELATION 14:6, NLT

Whether you are aware or not, if you are living in the Western world (which includes the United States), you are under the influence of the Bible. Any person who seriously studies art, literature, music, law, science, philosophy, ethics, politics, economics, history, warfare, anthropology, education, or any other branch of learning will quickly be made aware of the impact of the Christian Bible on their field of study.[5] It has left an undeniable, permanent mark on the West. Its influence in these areas is so far-reaching that its presence throughout culture has no rival. For example, it has inspired and guided many of the world's greatest pioneers in their respective fields: Michelangelo, Leonardo da Vinci, Rembrandt, Van Gogh, Isaac Newton, Blaise Pascal, Francis Bacon, John Locke, Thomas Jefferson, Abraham Lincoln, Florence Nightingale, William Shakespeare, Charles Dickens, Emily

Dickinson, Dante, Milton, Chaucer, Wordsworth, John Newton, Harriet Tubman, Frances Willard, Dietrich Bonhoeffer, C. S. Lewis, J. R. R. Tolkien, Martin Luther King Jr., Beethoven, Bach, Mozart, Haydn, Handel, Isaac Watts, Fanny Crosby, T. S. Eliot, Charlemagne, Theodore Roosevelt, and Queen Victoria, to name only a few. This abbreviated who's who intentionally excludes the countless history-changing preachers, evangelists, and missionaries it has produced as well.

In addition to inspiring incredible leaders and innovators, the Bible has been the foundational and prevailing force behind most compassion organizations the world has to offer today, including hospitals, orphanages, prison ministries, hospices, and hostels. Through these charitable organizations, Christians since the days of the Roman Empire have brought relief all over the world to millions of hungry, ill, oppressed, neglected, and afflicted people. The Bible is also the prevailing and foundational force behind many of the West's most prestigious universities—Oxford, Cambridge, Harvard, Yale, Princeton, Paris, Prague, Heidelberg, and Wittenberg. George Lindbeck, former professor of theology at Yale University, locates the peak of the Bible's influence during post-Reformation America, when the Bible was for the first time in history being mass-produced and read and studied by the common person:

> Its stories, images, conceptual patterns, and turns of phrase permeated the culture from top to bottom. This was true even for illiterates and those who did not go to church, for knowledge of the Bible was transmitted not only directly by its reading, hearing, and ritual enactment, but also indirectly by an interwoven net of intellectual, literary, artistic, folkloric, and proverbial

> traditions. . . . There was a time when every educated person, no matter how professedly unbelieving or secular, knew the actual text from Genesis to Revelation.[6]

Despite how influential the Bible was (and still is) in the West, this has not limited its reach to a specific region of the world. The Bible truly belongs to no particular nationality, ethnicity, or social class, and wherever it has been taught and allowed to flourish, it has changed the world around it. One need only consider the histories of South America, India, South Korea, the Philippines, Hong Kong, and sub-Saharan Africa to see its enormous impact. The Bible's influence can still be seen all over the world. It is inscribed and read in the poorest villages and in the richest palaces. It is invoked by both scholars and the working classes. Many thousands of brilliant writers have written masterpieces, only to have them soon forgotten, but the Bible endures from one generation to the next, comforting and confronting those who read it. Many leaders in history, even those who did not believe in the historicity of the Bible, still spoke of its unparalleled ability to console the human soul. For example, transcendentalist Theodore Parker once wrote, "The timid man, about awaking from this dream of life, looks through the glass of Scripture and his eye grows bright; he does not fear to stand alone, to tread the way unknown and distant, to take the death-angel by the hand and bid farewell to wife, and babes, and home."[7]

The reason the Bible has affected the world so extensively is because of the profound revelations it has disclosed to humankind. Of these revelations, the four related to salvation history (creation, fall, redemption, consummation)[8] have left the most profound mark. For now, we will focus on creation because of its extraordinary impact on so many fields of study.

Image Bearers

> God created human beings in his own image. In the image of God he created them; male and female he created them.
>
> GENESIS 1:27, NLT

The doctrine of creation teaches that God created the world *and* made all human beings (male and female) in his image.[9] This essential doctrine (referred to as *imago Dei*) communicates that all human beings have incalculable worth, regardless of their age, sex, race, or national origin. And because they are made in the image of God, they deserve to be treated with dignity, regardless of their station in life or their past indiscretions. It also means the rest of creation is good and beautiful and should be cared for properly. The skies, oceans, plants, and animals—they are all gifts from God.

To be made in the image of God also means we are moral creatures, and as such, we are *morally* responsible for how we interact with the world and treat fellow image bearers.[10] It is for this reason that the biblical doctrine of *imago Dei* has been the foundation of human rights, such as the rights to life and liberty. While Thomas Jefferson declared these rights as "self-evident" in the Declaration of Independence, the historical evidence suggests otherwise. One need only look around the world to where the Bible's transformational power has not been fully realized to see that these truths are *not* self-evident. In history, we can see what this looks like. For example, in ancient Greece, women, children, and non-Greeks were treated primarily as property (they had few to no rights). This kind of dehumanization was true of Rome too.[11] And while we admittedly see hints of this in the Bible, when the doctrine of *imago Dei* was realized to its fullest extent in the person and work of Jesus Christ, these cultural barriers were eventually overcome (albeit over thousands of years in some cases). In many non-Western cultures, infanticide, especially female infanticide, was (and still is) routine. Yet where the doctrine of *imago Dei* has been adopted, women's rights have flourished. Why? Because it openly rebukes and counters many patriarchal practices accepted in places where it is not believed. These practices include specifically infidelity, divorce, incest, polygamy, infanticide, honor killings, and abortion. These practices are rooted in a failure to account for a woman's equal status as an image bearer of God. The idea that men and women are created in God's image, when informed and broadened by Jesus' work of redemption, has inspired some of the greatest social justice movements in history, including women's suffrage and the Civil Rights Movement.

Being made in the image of God does not inspire people just to advance social justice but also to explore the world of science and the arts. Scientists like Isaac Newton expected the world to be full of order and design, not chaos and randomness, because they believed it was created by a loving God. And that is what he found, leading to some of the greatest discoveries about how the world works.[12] As for artists, the idea that they are created in the image of God inspires them to follow in the footsteps of their Creator and to craft imaginative works that are good, true, and beautiful. It is in this particular field of study that some say the Bible has had its greatest impact on the world.

Dee Dyas, professor of history and culture and director of the Centre for Pilgrimage Studies at the University of York, and her research associate, Esther Hughes, have put together a book that introduces the Bible's most important stories and themes, including background information on key characters and concepts as they have been traditionally understood. This background information is then followed by a short list of specific works of art, literature, and music that were inspired by the passage. The authors confess that "due to limitations of space, these examples can only be illustrative rather than comprehensive." Glancing at the first few pages of the book (which examine the creation story), you can get a feel for just how impactful the Bible has been, finding works by Michelangelo, William Blake, John Milton, Gerard Manley Hopkins, and others. Even the abbreviated list, based on a single passage, includes some nineteen masterworks (including *The Creation of Adam* in the Sistine Chapel and *Paradise Lost*).[13]

Needless to say, the Bible has been one of the most, if not *the* most, significant forces for good in the world.

The Bible's Impact on the Individual

The Bible has not only transformed nations and empires, but it has also transformed individual lives. From our experience as pastors and camp directors, we could share hundreds of stories of people who have been drastically changed (for the better) by reading the Bible. Ask almost any Christian, and they can tell you multiple stories of how the Bible has brought clarity to people's lives, including their own. But while we could share many personal stories, we want to highlight the testimony of the "napalm girl," who was in headlines in the 1970s. We think her story epitomizes the ability of the Bible to positively transform lives.

During the Vietnam War, Nick Ut won a Pulitzer Prize for a photograph he took on June 8, 1972, of terrified children running from a nearby napalm attack.[14] The photo was so haunting and surreal that some at the time, including President Nixon, doubted its authenticity (which is no longer in question). The most stunning part about the photo is a naked girl running away from the attack, her clothes having been burned off from the napalm. The girl's name is Kim Phuc. In 2008, she shared her essay with NPR titled "The Long Road to Forgiveness." In it she tells her story of how she came to faith in Jesus Christ:

> Although I suffered from pain, itching and headaches all the time, the long hospital stay made me dream to become a doctor. But my studies were cut short by the local government. They wanted me as a symbol of the state. I could not go to school anymore. The anger inside me was like a hatred as high as a mountain. I hated my life. I hated all people who were normal because I was not normal. I really wanted to die many times. I spent my daytime in the library to read a lot of religious books to find a purpose for my life. One of the books that I read was the Holy Bible. In Christmas 1982, I accepted Jesus Christ as my personal savior. It was an amazing turning point in my life. God helped me to learn to forgive—the most difficult of all lessons. It didn't happen in a day and it wasn't easy. But I finally got it. Forgiveness made me free from hatred. I still have many scars on my body and severe pain most days, but my heart is cleansed. Napalm is very powerful but faith, forgiveness and love are much more powerful.[15]

Kim Phuc's moving testimony has left an indelible mark on us. It reminds us of the Bible's uncanny ability to redeem and transform lives.

Cultural Christianity

Speaking of transformation, one of the foremost atheists of our day, Richard Dawkins, author of *The God Delusion*, recently rattled the unbelieving world by proclaiming himself a "cultural Christian." The man who once condemned all religions as equally oppressive and divisive is now singing a different tune. What has brought on this unexpected shift? Dawkins and others like him have started to experience how dangerous and miserable a world without faith, hope, and love really is. As a result, they are coming to appreciate what the Christian faith has provided for them. In an interview with Rachel Johnson on *Leading Britain's Conversation* (LBC) radio, Dawkins announced,

> [Britain is] culturally a Christian country. And I call myself a cultural Christian. I'm not a believer, but there is distinction between being a believing Christian and being a cultural Christian. And so, you know, I love hymns and Christmas carols, and I sort of feel at home in the Christian ethos. I feel that we are a Christian country in that sense. It's true that statistically the number of people who actually believe in Christianity is going down, and I'm happy with that, but I would not be happy if we lost all of our cathedrals and our beautiful parish churches. So, I count myself a cultural Christian. I think it would matter if . . . we substituted any alternative religion. That would be truly dreadful. . . . If I had to choose between Christianity and Islam, I'd choose Christianity every single time. It seems to me to be a fundamentally decent religion in a way that I think Islam is not.[16]

As I (Shawn) watched this interview, I couldn't help but smile. It seems Dawkins wants to have his cake and eat it too. He enjoys the *fruit* of Christianity and its teachings—its music, ethics, and architecture—but not the *tree* it grows on. Unfortunately, if you cut down the tree, the fruit dies as well. Unfortunately for Dawkins and other cultural Christians, there really is no other tree—neither naturalism, secular humanism, nor another religion—that has yielded anything close to what the Bible and Christianity have given to the world.

The reason is rather straightforward: Our ideas, beliefs, and values matter. They make us who we are. And without the Bible, all grounds for equality, human rights, and human dignity are lost. As the nihilist Nietzsche once quipped, "If you give up Christian faith, you pull the *right* to Christian morality out from under your feet."[17] Vishal Mangalwadi explains it like this:

> Species, races, and individuals do not evolve equal. Evolution does not bestow any rights upon any animal. Western notions of human dignity, equality, and inalienable rights are the Bible's unique contribution to the modern world. Pico della Mirandola (1463–94) articulated the Bible's case for human dignity in *Oration on the Dignity of Man*. His case rested upon (a) creation of man in God's own image and (b) God's incarnation in Jesus of Nazareth. God became man in order to save man, because man was made in God's image—precious and immortal. Full implications of these doctrines are still being worked out. Yet, much of our future will be shaped by the question: Is man merely another animal (organic intelligence) or is he uniquely God's image—so precious to God that He would come to this earth to save him?[18]

But What About . . . ?

Of course, there is a dark side to the history of the Bible, and we would be remiss if we didn't discuss it here. The Bible's legacy, as expressed through Christianity, is not spotless. History is replete with those who have misused the Bible to incite violence, start irrational wars, oppress women and foreigners, swindle the naive, defend slavery, excuse hate, tolerate abuse, and justify nearly any heinous sin you can imagine. And it is because of these past misapplications of Scripture that it is popular today to blame the Bible for many of the atrocities we have endured as human beings.

There is no doubt these actions stain the reputation of the Bible and make it more difficult to trust it as the Word of God. And while we accept these criticisms as legitimate and agree that this has happened far too many times in history, there are a few things we would say in response.

First, many criticisms leveled at the Bible are rooted in the Bible's morality that we have unwittingly absorbed by living under its influence. This should give us pause that maybe we are missing something. Second, for those criticisms not rooted in biblical morality, we ask, Who is deciding what is right and wrong, and what gives them the authority to do so? It is a dangerous thing to judge the ancient world simply because we fancy ourselves more sophisticated than they were.[19] Third, when anyone (past or present) uses the Bible to justify attitudes or behaviors that do not line up with the character of God as revealed through salvation history, the issue has more to do with them and their own ignorance and impiety than it has to do with the Bible itself. In other words, just because someone *claims* to be following the Bible does not mean *they actually are*—even if they quote some verses that seem to support their position. Chances are they are interpreting those verses through the distorted lens of cultural bias, misguided motives, or incorrect assumptions.

This final point reminds us of a film that came out over a decade ago.

Wisdom from *The Book of Eli*

In 2010, Warner Bros. Pictures released a postapocalyptic, neo-Western action film titled *The Book of Eli*, which explored the effect of the Bible on humankind.[20]

The film's protagonist, Eli (played by Denzel Washington), is on a mission to protect and deliver a "book" somewhere out West. It is later revealed that this book is a Bible—the last one known in existence. In the process, he runs into a formidable adversary, Bill Carnegie (played by Gary Oldman), who wants a Bible of his own. He does not desire it for spiritual reasons but for the power and sway it holds over people. Carnegie eventually steals the book from Eli. Eli and a companion press on, though, and eventually make it to the West Coast, where they find a colony of survivors who are collecting notable literature and other valuable artifacts. The colony lets them in, but only after Eli tells them he has a copy of the King James Bible. It is then revealed that even though he lost the book to Carnegie, he knows it by heart. He recites the entire Bible to the curator, who writes down every word precisely as dictated. Ironically, it is also revealed that the Bible Carnegie stole is written in braille (making it useless to him).

One of the major themes of the movie is the power the Bible has to influence and control others. For Carnegie, it is a way to get rich and prosper, and also a means to exercise authority and power over others. He says, "It's a weapon! A weapon aimed right at the hearts and minds of the weak and the desperate. It will give us control of them. If we want to rule more than one small . . . town, we have to have it. People will come from all over. They'll do exactly what I tell them if the words are from the book. It's happened before and it'll happen again. All we need is that book."[21] Carnegie represents those today who would use the Bible for evil purposes like gaining power over others.

Eli, on the other hand, represents those who embrace the Bible for what it reveals and teaches about God. But he is not flawless. Indeed, at the beginning of the movie, Eli so zealously prioritizes protecting the book that he chooses not to help others in need. Later on, he refuses to share it with others, even his traveling companion who is genuinely interested. In this he represents some modern evangelical Christians who are so concerned about protecting the Bible that they fail to live out its message of love, compassion, forgiveness, and self-sacrifice. But eventually Eli does part with the Bible—in order to save his friend. When his friend asks him why he did it, knowing how important it was to him, he responds, "In all the years I've been carrying it and reading it every day . . . I got so caught up in keeping it safe I forgot to live by what I learned from it."[22]

One question the movie asks viewers is whether the Bible is ultimately a force for good or for evil. It answers that question by showing it depends on who is using it and what their motives are. Gary Whitta, the movie's writer, explains it best:

> A lot of people who see the movie assume that I'm a Christian. I'm not at all. I'm an atheist. But I'm fascinated by the way that religion and spirituality and faith does motivate people. It's clearly one of the great social forces in the world and has been for thousands of years. . . . And I was really attracted to this idea of having this conversation

> about whether or not religion [the Bible] is a positive or a negative force. The idea that I arrived at is that I think it's essentially down to whoever's hands it's in.[23]

For Christians, we can agree with Whitta's analysis even if it comes from a place of skepticism. Why? Because the Bible itself on more than one occasion records instances where it is misused and misapplied. For example, Satan quotes the Bible to Jesus in an attempt to trick him into testing the Lord. The Pharisees repeatedly use Scripture to justify not helping someone in need and to excuse their mistreatment of women, by abusing their "right" to divorce. Peter claims there are those who twist the Scriptures to say something they were not intended to say. Finally, the apostle Paul reports in his letter to the Philippians that there are those who preach the gospel not from pure motives but from a place of envy, rivalry, and selfish ambition.[24] So it should not surprise us that people have used the Bible to promote and justify their own agendas and evils, such as bigotry, racism, and oppression.

A Force for Good

A few days before he was crucified, Jesus prophesied that the "gospel of the kingdom will be proclaimed throughout the whole world as a testimony to all nations" (Matthew 24:14).[25] For roughly the last two thousand years this prophecy has continued to be fulfilled. It has left a testimony for all to see and judge. And while some accuse the Bible of being a force of evil, history tells us a different story. It tells us that the Bible has been an incredible force of progress and goodness in the world, despite the attempts by some to twist and abuse it and use it for their own gain. Despite misinterpretations and misapplications, wherever the Bible has gone, it has *eventually* liberated slaves, empowered women, and strengthened the weak and marginalized. Wherever it has gone, it has promoted justice and forgiveness and spread the message of Christ—a message of humility, compassion, and love.[26] Wherever it has gone, it has been a facilitator of reconciliation and redemption and has promulgated both human rights and respect for authority. Wherever it has gone, it has inspired art and literature of the highest caliber and allowed for scientific progress. Simply put, there is no other book—even among religious books—that holds a candle to its light. In the end, whether someone personally concludes that the Bible has had a positive or negative effect on them, it is impossible to deny its incredible influence and transformational effect on history and culture. This fact alone should encourage us to not toss it aside or stash it away on the bookshelf, but to get to know it—*really know it*—and let it speak for itself.

CHAPTER 3

The Church's Book

All accounts of Scripture are inseparable from accounts of the church.

ANGUS PADDISON

For our honeymoon, I (John) surprised my wife, Nancy, with a Hawaiian Islands cruise. Seven days of luaus, waterfalls, snorkeling, and beautiful beaches, not to mention the amazing food and entertainment provided by the cruise line. If you've ever been on a cruise, you know that a staple of many of them is the midweek art auction. Passengers can bid on works of art the gallery describes as "spectacular," "classic," and "breathtaking." With nothing planned on Wednesday, Nancy and I found ourselves in the gallery with the other passengers. Not knowing much about art, we had no intention of buying anything. But then something caught my eye—a Salvador Dalí painting. Eccentric, bizarre, and flamboyant, Dalí is one of the most famous figures in the art world. His work is exhibited all over the world, some pieces selling for millions of dollars.

So you can imagine my excitement when the gallery salesman told me we could have our very own *original* Salvador Dalí painting for the low, low price of only seven hundred dollars! My wife did not share my excitement. Why, she wondered, was an original Dalí being sold on a cruise ship for such a "low, low" price? I insisted this was a once-in-a-lifetime chance. It would surely go up in value over time, and it would be a great reminder of our honeymoon. Against her better judgment, we bought it and became owners of an original Salvador Dalí painting.

Or did we?

Not long after we returned home, I began to google our painting, which I soon regretted. As I did, I came across sites about cruise ship art auctions and was immediately struck by the words *scam*, *fraud*, *beware*, and *scheme*. But what troubled me most was a story about a fake Salvador Dalí that was purchased on the same cruise line we bought ours on! I kept searching and found another story, and another after that. I soon got the sinking suspicion that maybe *we* had been scammed too. But how could we know?

I suppose there were any number of ways I could have gone about trying to find out if the Dalí was a fake. I could have sought the collective wisdom of a Salvador Dalí Facebook group, posted a question on a Dalí subreddit, or watched a YouTube channel hosted by a disgruntled cruise ship art "expert." But would those really have been the best sources to authenticate the painting? I suspect your answer is no. None of them are Dalí experts. At best, all they would have been able to do is offer their less-than-authoritative opinions.

If I really wanted to know if our painting was legitimate, wouldn't it be best to consult the organization that Salvador Dalí himself put in charge of authenticating his work? Without question it would. That organization is the Gala-Salvador Dalí

Foundation. Dalí entrusted it with guarding his legacy. It possesses the most intimate knowledge of the man and his art. It oversees his estate and the official Dalí museums. The Dalí Foundation has been studying, interpreting, and advancing his art for more than forty years. If anyone would know if our painting was authentic, it would be the Dalí Foundation. That's not to say they can't be mistaken, or that I might not get some helpful advice from amateurs on the internet. But it is to say that when evaluating a Salvador Dalí work of art, the first source I should listen to is the one that is closest to and has the most intimate relationship with his work. To put it neatly, when evaluating or interpreting a work of art, it's wise to first consult those who are genuine experts on it.

God Lives Where?

We think a similar principle ought to be followed when interpreting sacred religious texts. When seeking to understand what the text means, we ought to give priority to those who are most familiar with it. For example, who knows the Book of Mormon better than the Church of Jesus Christ of Latter-day Saints? If we want to understand and interpret the Book of Mormon well, it's hard to imagine doing so without listening to what the LDS Church has to say about it. They've been studying, interpreting, and applying it for nearly two hundred years.[1] I (John) should know, because I made the mistake of not doing that and ended up looking foolish.

Years ago, I worked at a Christian bookstore. One day, two missionaries from the Church of Jesus Christ of Latter-day Saints came into the store. After looking around at the books, they began to talk with me. Eventually the conversation turned to matters of faith. I arrogantly let them know I wasn't a candidate for conversion because I knew a lot about Mormonism and was convinced it was a false religion. To make my point, I told them I thought it was unbelievable that the Book of Mormon teaches that God lives on a planet called Kolob. Who could believe such a ridiculous claim? After I finished insulting my LDS guests, they looked at each other and in unison said, "We don't believe that!"

"Yes, you do," I said. "It's a standard Mormon belief."

"No, it's not," they replied. "It's a standard Christian misunderstanding of what Mormons believe." They then explained to me what Mormons really believe about Kolob. First, they told me that the Book of Mormon doesn't teach God lives on Kolob. Kolob is mentioned in the Book of Abraham, not the Book of Mormon. Second, they informed me that Kolob isn't a planet but a star. Finally, they explained that the Book of Abraham doesn't say that God lives on a star but that Kolob is the closest star to God's throne. In the passage where it's found, the Kolob discussion is intended to teach Abraham that there is a hierarchy to all things, not that God dwells on a giant celestial gas orb.

I still cringe when I think of that conversation. Where did I get the idea that the god of Mormonism lived on a planet named Kolob? I'm embarrassed to say I got it from a film I watched that was produced by a Christian apologetics ministry. I trusted a source that in hindsight was highly questionable. But at the time, I trusted that they were giving me the truth about Mormonism. I never once thought to double-check *with Mormons* that the film represented the beliefs of Mormonism. I was happy with the distorted view because it confirmed what I already believed. I was quick to take the word of an uninformed critic with a clear bias because I *wanted* Mormonism to be foolish. That way I could easily write it off.

It's important to note that although I changed my understanding of Mormonism because I was willing to listen to authorities on Mormonism—actual Mormons—I did not change my view of Mormonism itself. There is a difference between gaining a better understanding of what Mormons believe by listening to them and determining if their religion is true. Mormons determine what Mormons believe, but Mormons do not determine whether Mormonism is true. What determines that is whether the claims of Mormonism correspond with the facts of reality. To find out if they do, we should seek out the best arguments Mormons offer for why Mormonism is true and evaluate them against the counterarguments.

When it comes to attributing erroneous religious beliefs to others, we suspect John isn't the only one who has taken the word of questionable sources. In fact, we know he's not because we see it all the time when critics evaluate Christianity. Whether it be videos, social media, or subreddits, misinformation about what the Bible teaches abounds online. But it's important to consider the source. Yes, the Bible speaks about slavery, just as the Book of Abraham speaks about the star Kolob. But to really understand what the Bible teaches about slavery, we encourage you to seek the wisdom of those within the historic Christian church who are qualified to speak on such issues before taking the word of an internet skeptic.[2]

Does that mean that what Christians say the Bible teaches is above criticism from those outside the church? No, not at all. The church isn't infallible. We believe the Bible speaks truthfully about all it affirms, but what it affirms needs to be interpreted. While we maintain that the voice of the church should be given priority in interpreting the Bible due to its relationship with the text, that doesn't mean the church's interpretation can't be revised by other voices.[3] However, it does mean that before you accept claims such as "The Bible endorses slavery" or "God commanded genocide," you should make sure those claims are not guilty of the same distortion and ignorance as what John once believed about the god of Mormonism living on Kolob.

People of the Book

As it relates to correctly interpreting what the Bible teaches, we believe the equivalent of the Dalí Foundation is the historic community of Christians known as the church. Just as Salvador Dalí gave the Dalí Foundation authority to authenticate his work, Jesus gave the church authority to interpret his Word. But not everyone at the Dalí Foundation is equally equipped for this task. Some people work at the front desk answering phone calls and others give tours. Then there are those who have put in the time and effort to become experts in Dalí's work. Everyone at the Dalí Foundation knows something about his work, but the experts are the people qualified to speak with authority on it.

Likewise, every Christian knows something about the Bible, but there are some Christians who have dedicated their lives to the study of the Bible and to becoming experts in various matters pertaining to it. There are experts in theology, church history, biblical studies, and textual criticism. These are people who both love Jesus and are authorities in their respective fields. When we encounter a biblical difficulty that is beyond the expertise of our local church leadership, we believe these are the folks we ought to seek out in the same way the experts at the Dalí Foundation are the ones we should pay attention to about Dalí's work.[4] To put a finer point on it, here are three reasons why someone who is wrestling with the Bible should seriously consider what learned Christians have to say.

First, the texts of the New Testament were composed, edited, distributed, used liturgically, copied, transmitted, received, and interpreted by Christians. They wrote them, revised them across time, read them in public worship and private devotion, and republished them for future generations.[5] In other words, they literally wrote the book. This fact alone should be enough to give the Christian community a measure of interpretive authority.

Second, Christians have been seeking to understand the entire Bible for nearly two thousand years. In that time, they have wrestled with *all* its challenging passages, apparent contradictions, and supposed inaccuracies. Internet skeptics aren't the first people to have problems with the command to annihilate the Canaanites, with the guidelines regarding slavery, or with the stories about Jesus in the Gospels differing in some ways. Christians have thought long and hard about these things and have offered numerous helpful responses. This doesn't mean Christians always agree on how to interpret biblical difficulties, but it does mean that as a community that is thousands of years old, the church's responses and interpretations about troubling and difficult passages should be given strong consideration.

Third, although the basic message of the Bible is simple enough to grasp, the Bible itself is a complex collection of ancient books that comes to us from an array of different cultural settings, languages, and assumptions. Often it is the gap between those things and our own culture, language, and assumptions that causes us to misunderstand what the Bible says. Consulting experts who have spent years studying the Bible out of a love for Jesus can help clear up many of those misunderstandings. To be clear, we're not saying you must have a PhD to understand the Bible correctly. We are saying, however, that those folks who have, by diligent study, committed themselves to becoming experts in matters pertaining to the Bible are resources who should be given priority over the latest social media skeptic.

Just Christian Scholars?

Having said that, it needs to be pointed out that not only those who identify as Christians are experts in matters pertaining to the Bible. It might surprise you to know there are biblical scholars who are not Christians, and they don't always see eye to eye with their Christian counterparts on the reliability of the Bible or how it should be interpreted.[6] If, as we have argued, we should give priority to those who have achieved a level of expertise regarding the Bible, how should we respond when non-Christian biblical scholars disagree with Christian biblical scholars on important matters?

First, we need to be careful not to assume that non-Christian biblical scholars are more trustworthy than Christian scholars because non-Christian scholars are objective researchers, unmotivated by the need to defend their religious convictions. In other words, we should not assume that because non-Christian biblical scholars have no skin in the game, they're impartial researchers who seek the truth and follow the evidence wherever it leads. Neither should we assume that Christian scholars, by contrast, are motivated to derive interpretations that align with their Christian commitments despite where the evidence leads. The problem with this idea is that it fails to recognize that *all* interpreters have skin in the game, not just Christians. This is easy to see. Might not an atheist scholar be tempted to conclude that the book of Daniel—which predicts the reign of Alexander the Great—was written after the rise and fall of his empire, not because of an objective evaluation of the evidence, but because supernatural predictions don't align with their atheism? Or might not a Jewish scholar downplay the evidence that Jesus fulfilled numerous messianic prophecies because otherwise they would have to face giving up their current religious tradition and all that would mean personally and professionally? We think the answer in both cases is yes. Such scenarios are very possible. In saying that, we aren't being critical of either scholar. Our point is simply that when it comes to interpreting the Bible, no one is neutral. We're all influenced by our worldview commitments whether we realize it or not. Which is why instead of explaining away competing viewpoints by identifying the psychological factors that may have contributed to them (religious commitments, personal desires, and so on), we should rather evaluate viewpoints based on the arguments and evidence that support them.

Second, we need to consider the role that tradition plays in Christian biblical interpretation. German philosopher Hans-Georg Gadamer has persuasively argued against the commonly held notion that to interpret a text well someone needs to achieve a disinterested vantage point of total objectivity. Rather, he argues that being embedded in a tradition can be a *benefit* to interpreting a text.[7] Traditions provide accumulated wisdom that results from a group's sustained engagement with the text. As it applies to Christian biblical interpretation, the acceptance of the Christian tradition as a framework for meaning may give Christian scholars an interpretive advantage when engaging with theological or spiritual dimensions of the text. That's because Christian scholars may approach the text with a richer familiarity with the theological assumptions, doctrinal developments, and spiritual practices that have grown out of the biblical tradition than those outside the tradition.

Again, this doesn't mean that Christian interpreters are always right. A commitment to tradition can lead to interpretations that confirm existing beliefs that are weakly supported. And interpretations of scholars from outside the tradition can sometimes benefit from having a sense of distance from the text that provides them with insights that a purely tradition-bound approach might overlook. At the end of the day, we ought to adopt the interpretation that makes the best sense of the matter under investigation after evaluating the arguments and evidence for it. That said, as you seek answers to aspects of the Bible that have caused you to question it, we encourage you to give serious consideration to the responses offered by the people of the book, Christian scholars.

The Bible: So Misrepresented It's a Sin

When we encounter charges such as that the Bible justifies genocide, hates gays, endorses slavery, or is misogynistic, we can understand why some people say that. The Bible does have difficult passages that can seem to support those accusations. Even so, many of those who level such accusations do so for reasons that demonstrate a poor understanding of the context, composition, and content of the Bible. It is not uncommon for those who lack biblical expertise to be looked to as authorities because they have a large media platform. Despite not having the qualifications to do so, they make confident judgments denouncing the Bible as so historically unreliable and filled with contradictions that no educated person should believe it is the Word of God.

One particularly egregious example is several years ago, *Newsweek* magazine published an article by Kurt Eichenwald titled "The Bible: So Misunderstood It's a Sin." The article—a lengthy sixteen pages—argues that Christians wildly misunderstand what the Bible is and consequently, they impose their "ignorance, hatred, and bias" on it. According to Eichenwald, "The Bible is not the book many American fundamentalists and political opportunists think it is, or more precisely, what they want it to be." His article "is designed to shine a light on a book that has been abused by people who claim to revere it but don't read it, in the process creating misery for others."[8]

While Eichenwald's argument is more focused on the composition and reliability of the Bible than what the Bible teaches, we have chosen him as an example for three reasons. First, he is a good example of a person with a large platform speaking with authority on a subject when he is unqualified to do so. In this way he is like many internet personalities with massive social media footprints who criticize what the Bible teaches but are not experts on the text. Second, citing Eichenwald's claims allows us to model what we encourage you to do in the face of challenges to the Bible: seek out legitimate Christian experts on the matter before you make up your mind. We hope you will see that although Eichenwald's claims sound troubling at first, Christians who are expert authorities in ancient manuscripts and the transmission of the text of the New Testament offer powerful critiques of Eichenwald's claims. Third, in the next section of the book, we will begin to look closely at missteps in interpreting the Bible that often lead to rejecting it. But before we get there, we think it is important that you have confidence in the reliability of the text, that it reflects what the original authors wrote. In addressing Eichenwald's challenges to the reliability of the New Testament, we hope you discover that there are good reasons to be confident it is accurate.

EXPERT WITNESS?

So, who is Kurt Eichenwald? Surely a national news magazine would commission a biblical scholar, theologian, or church historian to write such an important and authoritative piece challenging the beliefs of millions of Christians, right? You would think so. But Eichenwald was a columnist for *The New York Times*, whose writing focuses on business and financial matters, Wall Street corporate takeovers, and insider trading scandals. Eichenwald is a bestselling author of multiple books, none of which are remotely related to biblical scholarship. He received a BA degree in political science from Swarthmore College in 1983. His biography at *The New York Times* lists no theological training whatsoever.[9]

Eichenwald is an accomplished journalist. But from reading his credentials you may wonder what makes him qualified to write an article in a major national magazine calling into question the reliability of the Bible. That would be a good question, because Eichenwald veers far outside his lane of expertise when it comes to the Bible. That's not to say a journalist can't write about the Bible. But one would expect that they would support their claims by citing biblical scholars, theologians, and church historians from all sides. Eichenwald cites three contemporaries, one of whom does not have a terminal degree in biblical studies (but comparative religions) and all of whom support the view he is advancing, despite his claim that "this examination—based in large part on the works of scores of theologians and scholars, some of which dates back centuries—is a review of the Bible's history and a recounting of its words."[10] Naturally, if a person were to read Eichenwald's article without input from other sources, they would conclude that it is authoritative. All of this should raise a yellow, if not a red, flag regarding how much weight to give Eichenwald's conclusion. Just because he is writing for a major magazine doesn't automatically make him a trusted authority.

Eichenwald's charge is that the transmission of the Bible has been so corrupted that for all practical purposes, the "real" Bible has been lost to history. He argues that we cannot read the Bible today, because—incredibly—it doesn't exist and never has. In his opening paragraph he says, "No television preacher has ever read the Bible. Neither has any evangelical politician. Neither has the pope. Neither have I. And neither have you. At best, we've all read a bad translation—a translation of translations of translations of hand-copied copies of copies of copies of copies, and on and on, hundreds of times."[11] Eichenwald's claim is by no means original to him. It has a long pedigree and has been asserted with authority by a wide variety of people, ranging from New Testament scholar Bart Ehrman to mega podcaster Joe Rogan.[12]

PHONING IT IN

To understand why Eichenwald thinks the Bible doesn't exist, you need to know something about the history of the Bible. To simplify things, we'll focus on the New Testament.[13] What follows may be new for you. If so, we want to warn you, it might be surprising or troubling. However, we trust if you stick with us, you'll not only be encouraged that the New Testament exists but also be confident that the copy we have today faithfully reflects what the authors wrote. You'll also possess a better understanding of how we got the New Testament.

After reading the above paragraph you might be asking, "What do you mean by 'our copy faithfully reflects what the authors wrote'? Why wouldn't it? All we need to do is check our English translation against the original Greek manuscripts of the New Testament. Doing so will tell us if our translation reflects what the authors wrote. Problem solved."

That *would* solve the problem. There's just one thing: We don't possess a single original manuscript for any book of the New Testament. They are lost to history. You may ask, "Then how do we know the original content of the New Testament? If we don't have the originals, then what are our English translations based on? And how do we know they reflect the originals?" Those are great questions.

Although we don't have any of the original manuscripts for the New Testament, we do have handwritten copies—thousands of them we have collected over the last two thousand years. It's from these manuscript copies that scholars attempt to determine the wording of the original manuscript of each New Testament book.

And this is where the problem lies for Eichenwald. He maintains that if the New Testament has been reconstructed from thousands of handwritten copies over two thousand years, then we have no reason to believe the Bible we have today accurately reflects the original manuscripts. He assumes the copying process would have so distorted the text of the original manuscripts that it is impossible to reconstruct them. And if we can't reconstruct the originals, then the Bible—or in this case the New Testament—doesn't exist. Rather, all that exists is a "bad translation . . . of hand-copied copies of copies of copies of copies."[14]

To illustrate this, he compares the process of copying the New Testament to the children's game telephone. To play telephone, one person whispers a message into the ear of another person, and they try to faithfully pass on what they've heard by whispering it in the ear of another, and so on, and so on, until the last person receives the message. Inevitably the message changes as it passes from one person to another so that when it gets to the last person, it is radically different. When the last person shares the message whispered in their ear, everyone has a big laugh at how distorted the final message is from the original.

Is Telephone a good illustration of how the New Testament was copied? To answer that, we'll enlist the help of recognized authorities in the field of textual criticism—Christians who believe the

New Testament has been reliably preserved *and* who are top-notch textual scholars.

A COMEDY OF ERRORS?

Eichenwald is not ignorant of the fact that we have thousands of manuscript copies of the New Testament. His concern is that no matter how many manuscript copies we have, there's an insurmountable problem for reconstructing the originals: Those copies have an enormous number of differences between them. Consequently, Eichenwald argues, it's impossible to recover the originals.

Before we respond to his assertion, we want to acknowledge that Eichenwald is correct. There *are* an enormous number of differences, or *variants*, between the copies we possess. It's estimated there are over 500,000 differences among the copies.[15] That sounds like a huge amount, especially when you consider there are only about 138,000 words in the entire New Testament! With so many differences, how can we have any confidence that our modern New Testament accurately reflects the original text? To answer that question, we turn to the science of textual criticism.

Textual criticism is the discipline that analyzes all the different copies of something—say, the Gospel of Matthew—to reconstruct what the author originally wrote. Textual criticism is a complex practice, but simply put, scholars compare all the manuscripts that have been discovered for a particular passage, identify where the manuscripts differ, determine where accidental or intentional changes were made by copyists, and then reconstruct what they believe the original said.

Nevertheless, doesn't the fact that the New Testament manuscripts have over 500,000 differences among them cast doubt on the ability of textual critics to represent the original correctly? If the manuscripts have that many differences, how can we be confident that scholars have reconstructed the original? While it's beyond the scope of this chapter to do a deep dive into textual criticism,[16] we can say three things in response.

First, the vast majority of the differences between the manuscripts are easily recognizable as being obvious mistakes that do not reflect the original text. Examples include spelling errors, repeated words, missing words, and nonsense errors. Textual scholar Peter Gurry notes that "the vast majority of variants, upwards of 99 percent are awfully boring for most Bible readers [and] are easily resolved."[17] Even former Christian New Testament scholar Bart Ehrman agrees that "in spite of these remarkable differences, scholars are convinced that we can reconstruct the original words of the New Testament with reasonable (although probably not 100 percent) accuracy."[18]

Second, the reason there are so many differences is because there are so many manuscripts. More copying means more chances to make mistakes. However, in this case, the source of the problem becomes the source of the solution. That's because the success of reconstructing the original is directly related to the number of manuscripts scholars have. The more manuscripts they have, the more obvious copying errors become. The late textual scholar F. F. Bruce put it this way: "Fortunately, if the great number of MSS [manuscripts] increases the number of scribal errors, it increases proportionately the means of correcting such errors, so that the margin of doubt left in the process of recovering the exact original wording is not so large as might be feared; it is in truth remarkably small."[19]

And when it comes to copies of the New Testament books, we have a massive number of them. According to Daniel Wallace, director of the Center for the Study of New Testament Manuscripts, "The wealth of material that is available for determining the wording of the original New Testament is staggering: more than fifty-seven hundred Greek New Testament manuscripts, as many as twenty thousand versions, and more than one million quotations by patristic writers."[20]

That's a huge number of copies! And it's far more than any other ancient book. So yes, there are a lot of differences among the copies, but that's because there are so many copies, and it's the large number of copies that allows textual scholars to identify the contents of the original with a high degree of confidence.[21]

Third, when scholars compare the time span between the writing of the original books of the New Testament and the date of the first copies of those books to the time span between the originals and first copies of other works from antiquity, the difference is striking. The difference is important to consider because the more time there is between the original and the first copy, the greater the opportunity for the text to be distorted. Another way of saying this is, the closer our oldest copy is to the time when the original was written, the less opportunity there is for it to become distorted by errors in copying. So how does the New Testament stack up against other ancient works? There's no comparison.

Scholars believe the Gospel of John was written near the end of the first century, approximately AD 96. The first copy of the Gospel of John that we possess is a small manuscript dated between AD 100 and 150. At most that's a gap of only 60 years. When it comes to Paul's epistles, there's a gap of only about 100 to 150 years between when Paul put pen to paper and the first copies we possess for several of his letters.[22] The Gospel of Matthew has slightly more time between Matthew's original and the first copy, approximately 200 years. Those time spans may sound concerning.

Isn't 60 years a long time, let alone 200? In a word, no, not when we consider ancient documents. Contrast those time spans with those of three well-known works from antiquity: Caesar's *Gallic Wars* (950 years between the original and the first copy), Plato's *Tetralogies* (1,300 years), and Herodotus's *History* (1,350 years). Furthermore, scholars possess nowhere near the number of manuscript copies for those works that they do for the New Testament. They aren't even close.[23]

Why does this matter? It matters because while not having the original manuscripts, having only a fraction of the copies that the New Testament does, and averaging more than a thousand years between the original and the first copy, no one denies that we have faithful reconstructions of Caesar's *Gallic Wars*, Plato's *Tetralogies*, or Herodotus's *History*. If that's the case, then why is there such skepticism from Eichenwald about the New Testament? If he's going to deny that anyone has ever read the Bible, he should make the same claim about the writings of Caesar, Plato, and Herodotus. Or for that matter, *any* work from antiquity.

Dalí or Not?

If you're wondering if I (John) ever got that Salvador Dalí painting authenticated, I'm sorry to say I haven't. The main reason is because getting it evaluated by the Dalí Foundation costs almost as much as the painting itself! I can't bring myself to spend money only to find out that it's a fake. But rest assured, if I ever do have the painting authenticated, the Dalí Foundation is where I'll send it because they are the ones who know Dalí's work best.

We hope that you will do the same when it comes to questions you have about the Bible. Instead of listening to the voices of those who neither believe nor have the expertise to judge the Bible, we encourage you to first listen to what the Christian community has to say about your questions. Specifically, those who are experts in the matter in question. They are part of the community who for over two thousand years have believed, preserved, studied, and loved the Bible. That doesn't mean they will always interpret it correctly, or that they don't have a bias in favor of it, but it does mean that at the very least, as you seek answers, you should consider how the best thinkers from the historic Christian community have answered questions about *their* book. In doing so you might just find that they have solid answers. And unlike getting a painting authenticated, it won't cost you a penny.

PART 2

FALSE ASSUMPTIONS

CHAPTER 4

Once Upon a Time . . .

False Assumption #1: The Bible Is an Ancient Fairy Tale

We cannot use electric lights and radios and, in the event of illness, avail ourselves of modern medical and clinical means and at the same time believe in the spirit and wonder world of the New Testament.

RUDOLF BULTMANN

In 2008 comedian and talk show host Bill Maher starred in *Religulous*, a documentary film exposing what Maher believed to be the absurdities of religious belief. In a particularly cringeworthy scene, Maher talks with Steven Burg, the manager of a Roman Catholic gift shop, about Burg's conversion from Judaism to Christianity. During the conversation, Maher asks Burg about his thoughts on the story of Jonah. His words dripping with ridicule, Maher asks Burg, "This man [Jonah] lived inside a fish for three days?"

"Miraculously, yes," says Burg. "You don't believe in miracles . . ."

"Of course not," Maher scornfully replies. "I'm not ten!"[1]

Maher's response to Burg leaves no doubt as to what he thinks about miracles. The very idea of them is nonsense. Children can be excused for believing in something so ridiculous. Adults, however, are no more justified in believing in miracles than believing in Santa Claus.

When it comes to skepticism regarding miracles, Bill Maher isn't alone. Thousands of former Christians say that what started their faith deconstruction was realizing how bizarre many of the stories in the Bible sound. How could any reasonable person be expected to believe such things actually happened? One former Christian puts it this way:

> In 2022 do adults really believe that an axe head floated, that Elijah was taken to heaven in a fiery chariot, that Baalam's donkey talked, that the sun stood still for a win in battle, that magically bones were resurrected when Elisha was buried, that Elijah ran faster than Usain Bolt, etc. etc.? MILLIONS of people believe these are historical facts. These stories made sense to a three-year-old, but sure sounds like fairy tales to me as an adult.[2]

In other words, the Bible reads like a fairy tale. Educated adults shouldn't believe in fairy tales. Therefore, educated adults shouldn't believe in the Bible.

What's Your Problem(s)?

It seems to us the criticism that the Bible reads like a fairy tale is the result of two different but related matters, the combined force of which makes it hard for thoughtful modern people to take it seriously. The first is that the Bible is filled with miraculous stories that are presented as historical facts, including—but not limited to—a talking donkey, a bush that burns but is not consumed, a staff that turns into a snake, a floating axe head, a man who lives inside a fish for three days, and scores of people healed of leprosy, blindness, deafness, paralysis, and all kinds of diseases, not to mention numerous people raised from the dead!

The second objection is that sections of the Bible sound a lot like . . . well, fairy tales. In both the Bible and fairy tales you find wondrous encounters, talking animals, royal family drama, far-off kingdoms, and of course the theme of good versus evil.[3] The first eleven chapters of Genesis include the formation of the first human being from the dust of the ground, the second from his rib. Not long after, the couple living in paradise is tricked by a talking snake into eating fruit from a supernatural tree that results in their being banished from paradise and having a curse placed on them. Then we are told about the existence of giants, a six-hundred-year-old man who built a boat to save all the animals from a worldwide flood, and a genealogy populated with people who supposedly lived for five hundred to nearly a thousand years!

If the above criticisms resonate with you, we can relate. How could we not? First, although miracles seem to fill the pages of the Bible, they're conspicuously absent from our daily experience. We've personally never seen a blind person receive their sight, the sun stand still, or a person raised from the dead. Second, it's a valid question as to whether people living in a world that owes so much to the advent of science are justified in believing in miracles. Our ancestors who didn't know anything about the laws of physics called all kinds of things miracles. But for us in the modern world, science has demonstrated that many of those "miracles" are merely natural phenomena.

On the one hand, it's difficult to see how one can be a Christian and deny the possibility of miracles (our faith has the resurrection of Jesus at its center). On the other hand, it's also difficult to see how an educated adult living in the modern world can believe that the Bible is the Word of God when it contains so many of them.

In what follows, we will look at two main objections to miracles: that miracles don't happen, and that the Bible sounds so much like a fairy tale that we can't take its claims seriously. The goal of this chapter isn't to make a positive case for miracles. Rather, in this chapter we'll do two things. First, we'll offer responses to two of the most popular philosophical arguments against belief in miracles. And second, we'll identify what we think is perhaps the most common and powerful—yet subtle and unconscious—reason that miracles are viewed with suspicion.

But before we discuss the topic of miracles and the arguments for and against them, we must define our terms. When we speak of a miracle, we're referring to a rare intervention in the observed regularities of nature by a supernatural force to bring about an event beyond the power of nature.[4] Notice that this definition assumes that nature is *typically* uniform, meaning it operates the same way repeatedly. For example, the sun always rises in the east and sets in the west, water freezes at 32 degrees Fahrenheit and boils at 212 degrees Fahrenheit, and light travels at 299,792,458 meters per second. Miracles occur when that regularity is disturbed. Also notice that we do not refer to miracles as violating or breaking the laws of nature. Instead, we use the term *intervention*. Why we do this will become clear below. Now that we have established what a miracle is, let's look at the objections raised against them.

Error #1: Always Bet the Odds

The most well-known argument against miracles was championed by Scottish Enlightenment philosopher David Hume, who said he wanted to set an "everlasting check" against belief in miracles.

In his immensely influential work *Enquiries Concerning Human Understanding and Concerning the Principles of Morals*, began in 1748, Hume defines a miracle as "a transgression of a law of nature by a particular volition of the Deity, or by the interposition of some invisible agent."[5] While he denied that such transgressions are possible, he argued that even if they were, there could never be sufficient evidence to justify anyone believing that a particular miracle happened.[6] Therefore, belief in miracles is irrational. Michael Shermer, editor of *Skeptic* magazine, calls Hume's treatise against miracles "a knockdown argument" that shows belief in miracles is irrational. According to Shermer, Hume's argument is so devastating that every other argument against miracles is just "a footnote" to it.[7]

Hume begins his attack against belief in miracles by pointing out that for a person to be justified in believing a miracle claim, they must first have sufficient evidence. This isn't controversial. It is widely accepted that our beliefs should be based on sufficient evidence. Where Hume's view becomes controversial is that he argues no one can ever have sufficient evidence to justify belief in a miracle. Hume maintains that the history of human experience gives us overwhelming evidence that the laws of nature can never be violated. For a person to be justified in believing that the laws of nature have been violated—that a miracle has occurred—it would require greater evidence for the supposed miracle than we have for the regularity of the laws of nature. But, asks Hume, what evidence for a miracle could ever be greater than the evidence we have for the regularity of the laws of nature? In other words, he says that the entire history of humanity shares one thing in common: We have all experienced the regularity of the laws of nature. But no one has ever experienced an exception to them.

But what about those who claim they *have* experienced an

exception and offer evidence for it? Doesn't that count for something? Not according to Hume. He argues that the evidence for a miracle is of little value compared to the certainty we have for the regularity of the laws of nature. For example, most miracle claims are not firsthand experience but are believed based on other people's testimony. But what is more likely—that the laws of nature were violated or that human testimony of a miracle is false? For Hume it's a no-brainer. We're aware of times when humans have given false testimony for a variety of reasons (they were sincerely mistaken or deceived or they lied), but according to Hume, we've never experienced the laws of nature being violated. For Hume, we can never be justified in believing a miracle claim because the evidence is overwhelmingly against it. Doing so would be irrational.

Hume's argument sounds persuasive, and it has convinced many. But it is wrong for at *least* two reasons.

First, many thinkers, both religious and nonreligious, maintain that Hume's argument commits the fallacy of begging the question. It assumes what it ought to prove. Hume bases his case against belief in miracles upon the assumption that laws of nature are supported by *exceptionless* experience. But the experience of the laws of nature can only be considered exceptionless if we rule out the possibility of miracles from the start.[8] That the laws of nature are exceptionless is what Hume needs to prove, not assume. C. S. Lewis makes the point well:

> Now of course we must agree with Hume that if there is absolutely "uniform experience" against miracles, if in other words, they have never happened, why then they never have. Unfortunately, we know the experience against them to be uniform only if we know that all the

> reports of them are false. And we can know all the reports to be false only if we know already that miracles have never occurred. In fact, we are arguing in a circle.[9]

This is no minor mistake. It undercuts Hume's entire argument. If he wants to show that belief in miracles is irrational, it will take a different argument than this one to show that it is.

Second, Hume has a mistaken notion of what a miracle is. Hume takes miracles to be *violations* of the way the laws of nature must work.[10] But today philosophers and scientists suggest that a better way to think of laws of nature is not as prescriptions of how the universe *must* operate but as descriptions of how the universe *does* operate. The distinction is crucial. With this definition, miracles are not seen as violations of unalterable laws but nonnatural interventions altering the regularity of the natural world. To help make this clear, imagine a scenario where someone drops an egg off a ten-story building. We know from our repeated experience with gravity that the egg will fall to the ground and smash upon impact. Now, imagine the same scenario, but instead of allowing the egg to hit the ground, you reach out and grab it just before impact. In this scenario the egg didn't smash on the ground—not because you violated the law of gravity but because you, an agent with the power to do so, intervened in the way the world would operate when left to itself. You altered the typical outcome but did not violate any natural laws.[11]

Something similar is the case with miracles. Just as the natural world responds to the natural intervention of your hand catching the egg, it responds to supernatural intervention by God. An egg suddenly stopping in midair by an invisible supernatural force would by all accounts be a miracle, but it would no more be a violation of the laws of nature than when you caught the egg and stopped it from falling. Miracles do not break the laws of nature. Instead, they occur when the divine hand of God reaches into our world and intervenes in the natural course of events.[12]

Hume's arguments against the likelihood of miracles are logically fallacious (they beg the question) and assume an incorrect definition of what a miracle is. The combination of these two errors fatally undermines his goal of demonstrating the irrationality of belief in the miraculous. Which is why philosopher John Earman says that far from being a knockdown argument against miracles, as Shermer claims, Hume's treatise is an "abject failure."[13]

Error #2: Extraordinary Evidence

Okay, so Hume's argument has some serious problems. Yet there is a kernel of truth in it. For a person to be rational in believing a claim, that claim needs to be supported by evidence. How much evidence does one need to be justified in believing in miracles? The answer to that question brings us to the second argument against the rationality of believing in miracles. The answer is that a claim as extraordinary as a miracle requires extraordinary evidence, and no such evidence exists for the miraculous.

The idea that "extraordinary claims require extraordinary evidence" was popularized by astronomer Carl Sagan.[14] Undoubtedly, at first glance it seems Sagan's dictum makes good sense. If I (John) tell you I saw a dog on the way to work on Monday and that on Tuesday I saw a unicorn, I suspect you'd have no problem believing the first claim but would doubt the second. That's because the claim that I saw a dog is pretty ordinary. Dogs are so common that the claim doesn't require much evidence to believe. But many people would consider the claim that I saw a unicorn to be quite extraordinary. To believe that, wouldn't you want to hear some convincing evidence? After all, aren't unicorns fictional creatures? Given the extraordinary nature of the claim, Sagan and those who follow him argue that the only way a person should believe in the unicorn is if I could provide equally extraordinary evidence. The same applies to a miracle claim. Miracles are so extraordinary that unless a person is presented with extraordinary evidence, they should refuse to believe. Yet that raises the question: What exactly does *extraordinary* mean? Unfortunately for Sagan, no matter how he defines it, his dictum runs into insurmountable problems.

On the one hand, if extraordinary means uncommon or rare, it's obvious to anyone who thinks about it that such things are claimed all the time, but we don't need extraordinary evidence to believe them. Consider Joe and Sally:

> Joe being married to someone with the specific traits and characteristics of Sally is enormously improbable—especially when one considers the numerous other couples who had to meet, and the specific sperm cells that had to meet specific egg cells, all the way back to the dawn of humanity, in order for Joe and Sally to both be living at the same time. And yet Joe would be able to offer sufficient evidence that he is in fact married to Sally—adequate evidence to overcome a low prior probability. Is the fact that Joe married Sally an extraordinary event? Well, it depends on what you mean by "extraordinary."[15]

On the other hand, if by extraordinary the skeptic means exceptional, that raises a problem for their own claims. Throughout human history belief in miracles has been the norm.

It has only been in the last few hundred years in the Western world that belief in the miraculous has come under suspicion. In fact, according to a RealClear opinion survey, in 2024, 83 percent of Americans said they believe in miracles.[16] In light of that, the skeptic's claim that miracles don't happen is quite exceptional, or to use Sagan's term, extraordinary. Therefore, the skeptic needs to provide extraordinary evidence for their claim that miracles don't happen. Yet we suspect the skeptic doesn't feel the need to do so. Nor should they, because the demand for extraordinary evidence is unclear.

Someone might respond that our definitions of extraordinary for Sagan's dictum fail to apply. But that just proves our point: What *is* the correct definition? Defining extraordinary must precede the demand for extraordinary evidence. Otherwise the demand is nothing but a conversation stopper.

Having said that, we think Sagan's claim is not completely off base. If we approach things from the angle of probability theory, we can salvage the intuitive appeal of Sagan's idea without the unhelpful use of "extraordinary." We suggest that an "extraordinary claim" is best understood as a low prior probability claim. A low prior probability claim is one that appears implausible to a person based on their background beliefs and before they evaluate any evidence for the claim. In such instances Sagan's intuition is correct: A person ought not accept the claim until they are presented with enough evidence to overcome their initial judgment that the claim is improbable. Where Sagan is wrong is in his assertion that the evidence needs to be extraordinary—whatever that means. In fact, all that is needed to overcome a low probability claim is *sufficient* evidence.[17] Instead of "extraordinary claims require extraordinary evidence," Sagan's dictum should be "initially implausible claims require sufficient evidence."

Imagine That!

As influential as David Hume's argument and Carl Sagan's dictum against miracles have been, we suspect that most people question the miracles in the Bible not so much for intellectual objections but for gut-level reasons. Namely, they have a hard time imagining the miraculous world that the Bible portrays. Consequently, they fail to take miracle claims seriously and brush them aside as relegated to a less enlightened age. We understand why. The Bible can *feel* like a myth, a primitive account of people trying to make sense of the world in which they lived. In that case, no philosophical arguments against miracles are even necessary. It's just obvious to anyone reading the Bible that it amounts to an ancient fairy tale.

Notice the above claim isn't an argument against the rationality of believing in miracles. It's a description of how we *feel* about miracle claims—and how that reaction inclines us to dismiss them. Before we even begin to think about whether belief in miracles is rational, we have a negative intuitive response that it isn't.

We're not being critical of intuitive beliefs. Intuition is how we form many of our beliefs. Intuition is a cognitive faculty that helps us draw conclusions about many things without having to deliberate about them. Imagine how exhausting it would be if we had to consciously reason through every belief we hold. For example, when you see someone with an angry look on their face, you intuitively form the belief that they are angry. You don't reason to that conclusion in the same way you do when someone asks you to solve a complex math equation. Intuition is fast, instinctual, automatic, and emotional, and it occurs outside of our conscious awareness. Intuitive beliefs are formed passively and happen to us. And when it comes to miracle claims, we have an intuitive response to them. Much as we do to an angry face, we immediately form a belief. The question is, what triggers our intuition, and why does it produce a negative response?

Our intuition is triggered to respond positively or negatively by several factors. But one of the most influential and yet unnoticed is what is known as our social imaginary. Social imaginaries are not easy to define. Simply put, they're the way ordinary people *imagine*, not think about, their surroundings.[18] Social imaginaries are not primarily philosophies of life but shared assumptions that societies are built upon. All social imaginaries contain an unspoken vision of how the world and people ought to be. They reflect how we assume the world is prior to thinking about it. Social imaginaries influence us by shaping the gut-level regions of our hearts.[19] They quietly go about their work by influencing our intuitions and moral sensibilities. In turn, they influence our reasoning processes. Because we don't adopt them by conscious evaluation but absorb them by osmosis, they're hard to detect. But one thing is certain: They squeeze us into their mold without our awareness.[20]

The point for our discussion of miracles is that if our social imaginary has space for the miraculous and we encounter a miracle claim, we'll likely be open to the possibility of it. However, if our social imaginary has no space for the miraculous, we'll likely be closed to the possibility *before we consciously evaluate it*. Yet we're also likely unaware that our response is a conditioned one, not a reasoned one. Nevertheless, we'll feel entirely justified in rejecting a miracle claim as something obviously untrue. Given the social imaginary that we inhabit, it's almost impossible for many of us to have anything but such a reaction to miracle claims because ours is a disenchanted social imaginary.

In his work *A Secular Age* Charles Taylor argues that our social imaginary is wholly disenchanted.[21] Sociologist Max Weber says that disenchantment occurs when magic and mystery are removed from society. It's the dismissal of supernatural elements and explanations from the world and replacement with naturalistic elements and explanations. Modern science is considered by Weber to be the single most important factor in causing disenchantment. Jeffrey E. Green summarizes Weber:

> Scientific methods and inventions lead to far more effective control of the world than spells, myths, and magic. Scientific rationalization means that "there are no mysterious incalculable forces that come into play." . . . Unlike primitive cultures still imbued with a sense of the magical, in the modern context "one need no longer have recourse to magical means in order to master or implore the spirits, as did the savage, for whom such mysterious powers existed. Technical means and calculations perform the service."[22]

To put it plainly, we no longer think that relics have power to heal; we know that antibiotics do. We don't think that rituals have the power to cause earthquakes; we know that tectonic forces do. We no longer believe that human sacrifice keeps the sun rising every day; we know that the laws of physics do. Such beliefs belong to those living in a pre-enlightened age, not the modern age of brain chips, genetic engineering, space travel, and AI.

Although in AD 800 belief in the miraculous was self-evident, today it is often seen as highly implausible. Our social imaginary has changed and has made belief in miracles strike us as childish at best and intellectually negligent at worst. In the disenchanted world of the 2020s, the Bible and its miracles sound like mythology.

But while our social imaginary influences our intuitive response to the plausibility of miracles, it's important to note that it's just that—an *intuitive* response based on factors that are largely outside our conscious awareness and control. Sometimes our intuition is wrong.

Consider a historical example. One of the most famous examples of an erroneous intuition is the belief in the geocentric model of the universe—the idea that the Earth is at the center of the cosmos and everything else rotates around it.

For centuries, this idea was considered intuitively obvious and widely accepted by entire societies, from ancient Greece to medieval Europe. To confirm it, all a person had to do was look, and they would see that the sun, moon, and stars moved across the sky. Philosophers such as Aristotle and Ptolemy held the geocentric view as well as early scientists Tycho Brahe and Gersonides and religious authorities Thomas Aquinas and Pope Urban VIII. No one questioned it. Until someone did.

The geocentric view was later proven false by Copernicus, Galileo, and Kepler. The heliocentric model, proposed by Copernicus and supported by Galileo's observations, showed that the Earth, not the sun, is in motion. Even though the heliocentric claim had strong mathematical and observational support, it was met with resistance because it contradicted what seemed intuitively true.[23] Eventually, though, the heliocentric model became the foundation of modern astronomy because people were willing to allow the evidence to override their intuitions.

The takeaway is, no matter how intuitively obvious something seems, that doesn't by itself make it true. That's just as true with the implausibility of miracles as with the heliocentric model of the cosmos. To adopt the heliocentric model, the collective consciousness of the early modern period had to move past what was intuitively obvious to them and weigh the arguments for and against it. They did, and the heliocentric model was adopted. Likewise, to decide if it is rational to believe in miracles, those of us living in the disenchanted age need to move past what seems intuitively obvious to us and look at the evidence. But only if we are willing to follow it where it leads.

So, You're Saying There's (No) Chance?

In his book on miracles, C. S. Lewis makes an important point about a person's willingness to believe in the miraculous. Although he agrees that evidence plays a role in changing their mind, it can be effective in doing so only if they are willing to let it. No matter how much evidence someone is presented with for a miracle claim, unless they are open to changing their mind, the evidence will be unpersuasive.

This is clearly seen in a discussion on the *Unbelievable?* podcast hosted by Justin Brierley. The guests are Hugh Ross, an American astronomer and committed Christian, and Dr. Peter Atkins, professor of chemistry at Oxford University and committed atheist. Brierley asks Atkins if he can think of any evidence that Christianity is true.

Here's part of the discussion:

> Atkins: I find that a very difficult question. If I were looking in the Bible for evidence (heaven forbid), I would expect to see maybe "Increase in entropy is equal to Q reversible divided by temperature." If there was an equation in the Bible rather than all this wishy-washy elastic writing.

Justin: So if there was something like that they discovered in the Bible . . .

Atkins: Then I'd think it was probably a forgery.

Justin: Well, exactly, that's the problem. . . . Is there any evidence in the universe? If the stars lined up to spell "Peter, please believe in me, it's about time"?

Atkins: I'd put it down to personal madness.

Ross: It sounds, Peter, like there's no evidence that would persuade you away from atheism.

Atkins: To be honest, I think that's probably the case.

Justin: Do you even have an evidence-based view if you're actually committed to atheism a priori?

Atkins: Well, I'm predicting that there will be no such evidence. It's not quite the same thing as being committed to it a priori. I'd think it's much more likely that I would have gone mad than such evidence would have been provided.

Justin: Right. So in principle it's impossible to ever persuade you that God exists?

Atkins: I didn't quite say that . . .

Ross: Well, what would persuade you?

> Atkins: I can't conceive . . . I suppose even if I died and was confronted with St. Peter saying, "Welcome to heaven," I'd probably think I was dreaming.[24]

Are you surprised at the length Atkins is willing to go to explain away the evidence for the supernatural? Don't be. We *all* have an incredible ability to rationalize away evidence for claims that we don't want to be true. Which is why we encourage you, as you wrestle with the idea of miracles, to do so with as much integrity as possible by following the evidence where it leads, even if it challenges your fundamental assumptions about the nature of reality.

Proof Positive

In this chapter we've offered some rebuttals to the argument that believing in miracles is irrational. We tried to show why the most formidable argument against belief in miracles fails, sought to debunk the popular dictum that extraordinary events require extraordinary evidence, pointed out the role our social imaginary plays in how we feel about miracles, and demonstrated how our philosophical commitments can preclude us from believing in miracles in the face of overwhelming evidence.

But is there a positive case to be made for genuine, verifiable, documented miracles? We think the answer to that is a resounding yes.[25] This may surprise you, but there exists an overwhelming number of well-documented accounts of miracles. And we are not talking about cases of people being "cured" of bad backs or legs being "lengthened" by some shady televangelist. These are medically documented cases of serious illnesses including cancer, multiple sclerosis, paralysis, blindness, deafness, arthritis, Sjögren's syndrome, epilepsy, and many more.

More importantly, a compelling case can be made for the greatest miracle claim of all, the resurrection of Jesus Christ. The trustworthiness of the Bible stands or falls on whether Jesus physically rose from the dead. If he did, that shows the Bible is the true story of the world. We might still struggle to make sense out of some of the things we read in it, but we can have confidence that its overall message of salvation history is true. So, before a person rejects the Bible as being a fairy tale, they would be wise to investigate the evidence for the resurrection. Making that case here is beyond the scope of this chapter. But many scholars have, and we encourage you to do the research and follow the evidence where it leads.[26] What you discover may change your life!

Contrary to Bill Maher, not only ten-year-olds believe in miracles, but intelligent and well-educated doctors, philosophers, historians, and scientists too. Why? Because they laid aside their preconceived notions and examined the evidence.

CHAPTER 5

To Err Is . . . Divine?

False Assumption #2: The Bible Must Be Error-Free

When we come to the Bible and try to listen to its claims, we can easily misjudge those claims if we hear them only from within the framework of our own modern assumptions.

VERN SHERIDAN POYTHRESS

On a sweltering Sunday in July, I (John) was driving home from church when I saw an elderly man lying by the side of the road in desperate need of help. The top half of his body was on the sidewalk while his legs were splayed in the street. His wheelchair was lying on its side, and his possessions were scattered all over the ground, being blown about by the wind. I could see he was homeless. He was bald, and his beard was a matted mess of thick gray hair.

I helped him into my car, put his wheelchair in the trunk, and began to drive him to a local shelter. As we drove, he told me his name was Tom and explained he had fallen out of his wheelchair when attempting to descend a steep spot on the sidewalk. Then Tom asked me a question that caught me off guard.

"So, are you a Christian?" he asked with a smile.

Surprised at the directness of his question, I told him I was.

"Me too," he said. "I got saved five years ago. Ever hear of *Mere Christianity* by a guy named C. S. Lewis? That's how I got saved. I read that book."

To say I wasn't expecting that answer would be an understatement. Excitedly, I told him that not only was I familiar with Lewis and *Mere Christianity*, but as a professor at a Christian university I had used it as a textbook for my classes.

"You're a Christian professor?" he asked. Before I had a chance to respond, Tom blurted, "Can I ask you a question that's really been bothering me? What do you think about Bart Ehrman's claims about the Bible?"

Few times in my life have I been caught so completely by surprise as when Tom asked me about Bart Ehrman. In fact, my first thought was that I was on a hidden camera show. How did this elderly homeless man know about the claims of one of the world's most prominent New Testament scholars? Their worlds couldn't have been further apart.

"How do you know about Bart Ehrman?" I asked.

"Well, I sometimes spend time at the library, and one day I was looking for a Christian book to read, and I came across one called *Jesus, Interrupted: Revealing the Hidden Contradictions in the Bible*. The title surprised me, so I picked it up and began reading it. What do you think? Is the Bible filled with contradictions? What he said really caused me to doubt my faith in the Bible. Are there answers to the things Ehrman said in that book?"

Bart Who?

Bart Ehrman's name has come up a few times in the previous chapters. If his name isn't familiar to you, don't feel bad. New Testament scholars aren't exactly household names, even the most prominent. But over the last twenty years or so, Bart Ehrman has managed to become known outside the small academic confines of New Testament scholarship. That's due in large part to several popular books he's written seeking to show the Bible is nothing more than a human book. These books have garnered him invitations to appear on NPR multiple times and on popular talk shows like *The Colbert Report* and *The Daily Show*. In fact, within forty-eight hours of his appearing on *The Daily Show*, Ehrman's book *Misquoting Jesus* skyrocketed to the top of the Amazon rankings. In three months, it had sold more than one hundred thousand copies, an astounding number for that period.[1]

What made his critique of the Bible so appealing? We suspect two things. First, Ehrman is a gifted communicator. He has the ability to take complex textual issues and make them easily understandable for those who have little background knowledge. Second, and we think most importantly, Bart Ehrman once identified as an evangelical Christian who was deeply committed to the inspiration and inerrancy of the Bible but lost his faith when he began to seriously study the New Testament.[2] While pursuing his doctorate at Princeton Theological Seminary, he became convinced that the New Testament had an error in it. One error grew into multiple errors. Shortly thereafter he concluded that the Bible wasn't inspired by God but was merely the product of humans: "This was a seismic change for me. . . . My faith had been based completely on a certain view of the Bible as the fully inspired, inerrant word of God. Now I no longer saw the Bible that way. The Bible began to appear to me as a very human book . . . a human book from beginning to end."[3]

An articulate, winsome, former high-level "insider" claiming he has evidence showing the world's largest religion is a fraud translates into the sale of a lot of books.

Tom and I eventually made it to the homeless shelter, but not before finding a quiet parking lot where we could have a meaningful conversation about Bart Ehrman and his claims. I reassured Tom that yes, there are answers—good answers—to the challenges raised by Bart Ehrman. Later I visited him at the shelter with a pizza and a book responding to Ehrman's claims.[4] He eagerly devoured both.

If you're struggling to believe the Bible, we suspect one reason might be that you, like Tom, have encountered what seem to be errors in it. And maybe you assume—either because you have been taught or have simply taken it for granted—that the existence of even *one* mistake means the Bible isn't the Word of God. Our goal in this chapter is threefold. First, to encourage you to hang in there. There are good answers to many Bible difficulties. Second, to help you rethink a problematic assumption you might be holding that is driving the struggle. And third, to identify a series of unwarranted assumptions that you might unknowingly be imposing on Scripture that creates the appearance of errors where there are none. In doing so we hope to help you see that even if you conclude there are errors in the Bible, you don't need to reject your faith.

Inerrancy: What's in a Name?

Bart Ehrman's writings challenge what theologians refer to as the doctrine of inerrancy. The doctrine of inerrancy states that because the original manuscripts of the Bible were inspired by God, they are without error. Another, more helpful way of putting it is that because God inspired the original manuscripts of the Scriptures, everything they affirm or teach is true. This applies not only to matters of faith and practice but to historical, moral, and geographical claims.

You'll notice that in that definition of inerrancy, we said, "the original manuscripts," not simply "the Bible," are inerrant. We did that for two reasons. One, technically speaking, the doctrine of inerrancy applies only to the original manuscripts because only the original manuscripts were directly inspired (or "breathed out") by God. However, we don't have any of the original manuscripts for any book of the Bible today. What we do have are large numbers of copies of those original manuscripts, and it's from these that we have reconstructed the original manuscripts with a very high degree of accuracy. (We looked at this in chapter 3.) Two, everyone agrees that there are some minor errors in the copies of the Bible we have today. Over time scribes copying the Bible made small mistakes, and because in some places we don't have enough manuscripts to determine which is the correct reading, we are left with conflicting accounts. For instance, 1 Kings 4:26 says that Solomon had forty thousand stalls for his horses, but 2 Chronicles 9:25 says he had only four thousand. This is clearly a copyist error. The consonants for the numbers forty and four are very similar in the Hebrew language. It's easy to see that a scribe accidentally miscopied.[5] Or take Genesis 10:4, which identifies a people group called the *Dodanim*, while 1 Chronicles 1:7 identifies the same group as *Rodanim*. The two passages are clearly referring to the same group, but the difference in spelling is due to a copyist error regarding the Hebrew letters ד (Dalet) and ר (Resh).[6] There are a number of these kinds of "errors" in our Bibles. None of them are of any consequence when it comes to the core doctrines of the faith.

It's important for you to know about these because sometimes well-meaning but uninformed Christians will say things like "If the Bible has even one mistake in it, then it *can't* be the Word of God." While that sounds nice and has a nugget of theological truth to it, as we have seen, it's not accurate. There are copyist errors in the Bible. When someone makes a pious-sounding claim like that, all it takes to shake that person's faith is to discover the contradiction between 1 Kings 4:26 and 2 Chronicles 9:25.

At the same time, it's important for you to know that while our Bibles have these scribal errors, they don't impact the doctrine of inerrancy because according to the doctrine, only what was inspired by God is considered inerrant. You can't hold God or the human authors of the Bible responsible for the copying mistakes made by other people years later. Having said that, we want to be clear: When Bart Ehrman says the Bible has errors, these are not the kind he is referring to. He's referring to something more consequential: what he believes are historical, moral, and geographical errors that were in the original manuscripts and are still in our Bibles today. So, what are we to make of those?

Be Encouraged

When it comes to Bible difficulties, we want to encourage you. For over thirty years we have wrestled with the numerous apparent errors in the Bible. We don't want to downplay their existence or their difficulty. In various places the Bible seems to contradict itself and be historically, morally, and geographically inaccurate, not to mention in conflict with modern science. But what we've discovered is that for most of these difficulties there are good explanations. And by good, we mean they are plausible and don't require interpretive gymnastics that end up sounding ridiculous.

We want to urge you to not give up in your search for such answers. Sometimes it takes time and effort to discover them. We believe the Bible speaks truthfully about all it affirms, even though we don't have answers to all the difficulties we're aware of. So why do we still think the Bible is inerrant? First, because as Christians, we accept what the Bible claims, and the Bible claims to be inspired by God. It seems like a reasonable assumption that God wouldn't inspire errors.[7] But that doesn't settle the issue because maybe we misunderstand what inspiration entails. So we tentatively hold the belief that inspiration leads to inerrancy and look at what the Bible claims about history, morality, and geography.

Ultimately, we need to bring our beliefs in alignment with the Bible God has seen fit to give to us, not force it to meet our expectations of what we think it should be. And when we look at the Bible God has given us, we are struck with numerous candidates for errors. Such as these:

- Were the fruit trees created before or after Adam was created? (See Genesis 1:11-13; 2:5-7.)
- Did Joseph, Mary, and Jesus go to Nazareth or Egypt after his birth? (See Matthew 2:19-23; Luke 2:22-39.)
- Did Jesus tell the disciples to take a staff or not to take a staff? (See Mark 6:8-9; Luke 9:1-3.)
- Did Jesus heal the blind man/men on the way into or out of Jericho? (See Matthew 20:29-34; Luke 18:35-43.)
- Did Jesus curse the fig tree before or after he cleansed the Temple? (See Matthew 21:10-22; Mark 11:11-26.)

Many more could be added. When we encounter these kinds of problems, we ask if anyone has offered reasonable explanations for these difficulties. In our experience the answer has been mostly yes. Not one supposed error pointed out by Bart Ehrman or any other skeptic has caught Christian scholars by surprise. In fact, Christian thinkers through the centuries have been aware of all the Bible's challenging passages and engaged with them openly.

In some cases, we haven't discovered a good answer. In those instances, we have a choice to make: We either assume there isn't a good answer and acknowledge there is an error, or we assume that an answer exists, but we have not encountered it yet. Perhaps we never will. So, what do we do? Given our assumption that God would not inspire errors in the original text of the Bible and our experience of discovering that many problem passages have good answers, we choose to give the Bible the benefit of the doubt on the ones we don't have answers for and trust that it speaks truthfully.

But what if we're wrong and there are errors in the Bible? Should we conclude that Christianity is a sham? No! First, even if the Bible isn't inerrant, we are persuaded beyond reasonable doubt that the Bible is *highly* reliable, and that is more than enough for an individual to make a rational decision to accept its major claims as true.[8] Theologian C. Michael Patton helps us see this with the following thought experiment:

> Let's assume that the Scriptures are not inerrant. (Please, at least attempt to go there with me!) Let's take it a step further and say that the Scriptures are not inspired at all. Here then is the situation: the Scriptures are a collection of 66 ancient historical records, given through various types of literature. The records, like any other record, may have errors—historical, scientific, or otherwise. Now that we are rollin', let's say that John did indeed make a mistake about the number of women who came to the tomb of Jesus after His resurrection. Does this make the testimony of John *completely* false? Does this mean that the *entire* testimony of John is now wrong at every turn? Of course not! Any historian who followed this methodology would quickly find himself out of a

> job, for he would have no sources for his research. If the Scriptures were like any other records of history with minor discrepancies, then this would not justify a total rejection of the events they record. Their credibility is based upon the assumption of *general* historic reliability as evidenced through the rules of historic inquiry—which do not include a criteria for inerrancy.[9]

Therefore, even if there are minor mistakes in the Bible, they don't take away from its general reliability in terms of its message of who God is, who we are, what our problem is, and how Jesus solves it for us. And general reliability, not inerrancy, is all that is required for someone to make a rational decision to accept that message.[10]

Second, finding an error in the Bible would only require us to rethink our view of *inspiration*, not whether Jesus rose from the dead. Suppose we're wrong in thinking that inspiration leads to inerrancy. If so, it makes much more sense to change our belief about what inspiration requires (a mistake-free Bible) than to conclude Christianity is bogus. Philosopher and theologian William Lane Craig notes,

> Suppose somebody actually *did* demonstrate an error in Scripture that really is wrong—it is a mistake. Does that invalidate the Christian faith? And I am saying no. It would mean you would have to adjust your doctrine of inspiration; you would have to give up inerrancy of the Scripture. But it wouldn't mean, as I say, that Christ didn't rise from the dead. It wouldn't even mean that you don't have good grounds for believing that Christ rose from the dead.[11]

The knee-jerk reaction of leaving one's faith due to becoming convinced of an error in the Bible only makes sense if one subscribes to an all-or-nothing view of inerrancy.

Unfortunately, many Christians *do* hold to that assumption.

Assumption #1: All or Nothing?

Tom was right to be concerned when he read Bart Ehrman. If Ehrman is correct and the Bible is filled with real contradictions, then we agree: That's a big problem. That would give us reason to doubt that God had inspired the Bible, because it would seem strange that an all-knowing, truthful God would breathe out a book filled with errors. But does it have to be without *any* errors whatsoever, no matter how minor, for us to believe it is reliable enough to trust oneself to Jesus? Although we believe the Bible does speak truthfully about everything it affirms, we don't think it *must* do so or it cannot be trusted. There is a difference between believing it is inerrant and demanding it must be. Demanding the Bible be inerrant or it cannot be the Word of God can be harmful because doing so sets up an unnecessary all-or-nothing situation. When that occurs, it takes only one unresolved error, like the one encountered by Christopher Redford, for one's faith to come crashing down.

Christopher Redford has one of the most popular deconversion video narratives on the internet. In his *Why I Am No Longer a Christian* series, Redford recounts in several episodes—with a total of over one million views—how he went from conservative Christian to active atheist. In an episode dedicated to the Bible, he explains how the assumption that the Bible *had to be* inerrant played a role in his loss of faith. In the video he dramatically describes the moment he discovered that the Bible has two different accounts of Judas's death and how it was devastating to his faith in the Bible:

> My tongue caught in the back of my throat. My chest seized up, adrenaline rushed through my body, and my heart pounded. It felt as if the very fabric of reality itself was tearing apart. It felt like the paint on the walls surrounding me would tear open to reveal an empty darkness. Everything I believed lay vulnerable on an altar, waiting to be pierced, waiting to be sacrificed to this horrifying moment of realization. . . . I braced myself to face the consequence that my entire religion was a mistake.[12]

Because of what he considered to be one contradiction, he concluded his "entire religion was a mistake"? Why would Christopher jump to that conclusion? It seems that somewhere along the way he was either explicitly taught, or he unconsciously caught, the belief that the Bible *must* be free from mistakes to be the Word of God. Naturally, when he decided it wasn't, his all-or-nothing assumption forced him to conclude that the entirety of the Christian faith was fraudulent. That's tragic, but Christopher isn't alone. A lot of Christians assume the same thing.

Dr. Craig Evans, the John Bisagno Distinguished Professor of Christian Origins at Houston Christian University, notes that the all-or-nothing approach is also characteristic of Bart Ehrman's method of engaging with the Bible:

> The problem is that, in his popular books, Ehrman is frequently guilty of the logical fallacy of the excluded middle, the idea that there are only two options—either

> we have every word of the original text or we do not; either we have harmonious accounts of the teaching and activities of Jesus or we don't. Bart Ehrman is arguing like a fundamentalist. It is an all-or-nothing approach. If the Bible is truly inspired (and therefore trustworthy), it must be free from discrepancies. But this is not how most seasoned scholars think, including evangelicals.[13]

To be clear, Evans is not saying there are errors in the Bible. He's making a different point. He's saying that even if the Bible did have some mistakes, that wouldn't mean it wasn't generally trustworthy. And for a Christian to retain their faith amid a crisis brought on by Bible difficulties, they don't need to believe the Bible is inerrant but only sufficiently trustworthy. We think that if someone takes the time to investigate it, they'll find the Bible is more than *sufficiently* trustworthy. It is *highly* trustworthy.

Although inerrancy is an important doctrine (what we believe about it will have an impact on other doctrines), it should not serve as the foundation of our faith. Once again, William Lane Craig's words are worthy of reflection: "The problem with a person like Bart Ehrman, and I think many people today, is that they have at the very center of their web of their theological beliefs, the belief in inerrancy. So if that belief goes, the rest collapses and they are really in danger of committing apostasy."[14]

Craig believes that inerrancy is an *important* but not *essential* doctrine. Essential doctrines are those that need to be affirmed for salvation. That means if a believer becomes convinced the Bible contains minor errors, then it's not their faith they should change their mind about but their belief about the foundational nature of the doctrine of inerrancy.[15] Evangelical scholar Michael Licona agrees: "The truth of Christianity is grounded in the historicity of Jesus' resurrection rather than the inerrancy of the Bible. If Jesus rose from the dead, Christianity would still be true even if it were the case that some things in the Bible are not. In fact, because Jesus rose, Christianity was true in the period before any of the New Testament literature was written."[16]

So how could an error in the Gospels nullify the truth of Christianity? Again, this is not to say the Bible contains errors. It is to say that since the truth of the Christian gospel does not hang on every word of the Bible being correct, the doctrine of biblical inerrancy is a secondary doctrine.

Does the Bible contain errors? We don't think so. But if someday we become persuaded that it does, we won't throw away our faith unless the number and severity of the errors is so great that it becomes obvious the Bible can't be the Word of God. Until then, we'll continue to trust that God has spoken truthfully in all that the Bible affirms, and we would encourage you to do the same.

Assumption #2: I Don't Mean to Impose, But . . .

Once when I (John) was a pastor, I went to the First Nations reservation near our church to visit an Indigenous Canadian gentleman. Upon arriving, I was told he wasn't home but to come in and wait in the living room for him. I sat on the sofa next to his son, who paid me no attention at all. He didn't even look at me. After sitting there for fifteen minutes being ignored, I took the hint I wasn't welcome and left. I recounted my experience to my friend Louise, a former cross-cultural missionary who was working as a nurse on the reservation. She laughed when I told her how disrespected I felt. "The son probably feels the same way about you," she said. "In his culture, you, being the older man and having a respected title, should have spoken to him first. It would have been improper for him to engage you in conversation. Since you didn't, he probably thinks you were being rude to him!" Did I ever feel foolish.

The way we interpret things depends a lot on our assumptions. In this case, my assumptions about how to express respect and social courtesy were shaped by my culture. But I didn't realize I was imposing my cultural assumptions on a situation where they were foreign. I was on the reservation, in someone else's home. I misjudged the situation, and as a result I imagined an offense that didn't exist.

We think something similar is going on when it comes to identifying errors in the Bible. One of the reasons we take something to be an error in the Bible is that we impose on it a standard for judging errors that is as foreign to it as my standard of courtesy was to the Indigenous home I visited. And yet we don't realize how culturally conditioned our standard is. We simply take it for granted that we recognize an error when we see one. But we need to pause and think about that for a minute.

For a claim to be true, it needs to correspond to a fact of reality. But what that correspondence needs to look like differs according to time and place. For example, if you and I are having a casual conversation and I tell you I was at the mall all day, but in fact I was there between 12:00 p.m. and 4:00 p.m., you probably don't think I've misled you. The setting of our conversation doesn't require precision to be truthful. But if I am speaking in a court of law and say I was at the mall all day, it's likely I will be accused of not speaking truthfully. In that context, "all day" means more than four hours. Or if you ask me how much I weigh and I say 200 pounds, you're not going to accuse me of lying if I actually weigh 208 pounds. In that context there is an unspoken understanding between us that I am speaking in generalities. Nevertheless, I am being truthful. But if we were having a weight-loss competition and the winner received a million dollars, you would expect me to give you my exact weight.

What's the point? Simply this: If we're comfortable with truth claims having flexible parameters in these situations, we should be comfortable with the idea that there might be a different set of expectations as to what counts as being truthful between our modern culture and the culture in which the Bible was written.

ACCOMMODATIONS REQUIRED

Old Testament scholar John Walton is right to remind us that the Bible "was written for us, and for all humankind. But it was not written *to* us."[17] By that he means we should recognize that the Bible is God's Word *for* us today. We ought to acknowledge it as the authority on matters of faith and practice written *for* all of God's people. At the same time, the Bible was written *to* specific groups of people living in specific times and places. Since that's the case, we should expect it would be written in a manner that would make sense to those people. Contemporary theories of knowledge recognize that any form of communication must be understood within the boundaries of the shared worldview of the author and audience. This means that God inspired the Bible in such a way that it often reflects the assumptions about the world of the people it was written to. In other words, God accommodated his communication to those he was communicating with so it would make sense to them. This doesn't mean that God inspired error or that truth is relative. It simply means truth can be reliably communicated while at the same time reflecting varied backgrounds, assumptions, and cultural settings.[18]

If communication requires accommodation and God accommodated his message to the assumptions, expectations, and beliefs of ancient peoples, it would be a mistake to apply to the Bible our modern assumptions about what it means to speak truthfully. Inerrancy, then, should not be thought of as the Bible measuring up to the kind of standard expected for truth-telling in a modern courtroom or scientific journal. It should be thought of in terms of the ancient world in which it was originally written. Craig Blomberg offers a helpful way to think about what it means for the Bible to be true. He says, "I personally believe that if inerrancy means 'without error according to what most people in a given culture would have called an error' then the biblical books are inerrant in view of the standards of the cultures in which they were written."[19] We agree.

WHOSE STANDARDS, WHICH CULTURE?

It's safe to conclude that even though there is overlap between our standard for what counts as speaking truthfully and those of the cultures in the Bible, there are also important differences. Both our culture and those of the ancient Near East and the first century hold that for a claim to be true, it must correspond with a fact of reality. But there are differences between oral cultures—like those of the Old Testament and New Testament—and the written and video culture of the modern world. Precise wording was not expected in oral cultures when recounting an event in order for it to correspond to reality. We know that in sharing a story or testimony, oral communities allow for some variation in detail without accusing the teller of contradiction.[20] And we observe this same phenomenon throughout the Gospels.[21]

A common issue raised by those who begin to read the Bible

closely is the tension they discover between the claim of the Gospels to be presenting an accurate account about Jesus' life and the differences the Gospels exhibit when recounting the same events. Without question, a close reading of the Gospels does reveal discrepancies between not only the sequence of events in Jesus' life but also the words of Jesus. Which raises the question, aren't these contradictions? But these apparent contradictions make sense when we understand how historical events and sayings were recorded in the first century. Examining these conventions will help us understand both the writer's commitment to accurate reporting and why the Gospel writers differ at times in that reporting.

Both the Jewish culture Jesus was raised in and the Greco-Roman culture in which he lived were oral cultures, meaning teaching was primarily done by way of verbally retelling stories. And although you might think an oral tradition would be unreliable due to how easy it would be to add or take away details with every retelling, that's not the case. When it came to reporting, accuracy was just as important to them as it is to us. There were safeguards to ensure the core elements of the story were kept intact in the retelling.[22] But the world of the first century had no problem with limited variation in how stories were retold if the gist of the story was conveyed accurately. One way of putting it is to say they were insistent on the *voice* of the story being reflected accurately but did not require the *wording* to remain the same. In fact, change in wording was an acceptable literary technique used to summarize or emphasize certain points of an account.[23] This variation within limits is seen throughout the Gospels, where the authors are clearly retelling the same event but report Jesus as uttering similar but different words. For example, when the rich young ruler asked Jesus what he needed to do to inherit eternal life,

Matthew has Jesus respond, "Why do you ask me about what is good?" (Matthew 19:17). But Mark records Jesus as saying, "Why do you call me good?" (Mark 10:18). One way to deal with this apparent contradiction is to say that Jesus said both, but that seems unlikely and forced. A better way to understand it is to recognize this as an example of variation within limits that would have been acceptable to the intended audience. *We* might want to know the exact words Jesus said, but the Gospels were not written to us. They were written to people in the first century, who were not concerned with such things.[24]

The same is true for events in the life of Jesus. The Gospel writers record some of the events in Jesus' life topically, not chronologically. But the accounts do not share the same topical themes, resulting in events being recorded in conflicting order. For example, the cleansing of the leper in Mark happens in chapter 1, but in Matthew it doesn't occur until chapter 8 and Luke in chapter 5. This means we cannot always know precisely when certain events occurred in Jesus' life. But that apparent problem results from our faulty assumption, not a flaw in the Gospels. *We* expect correct chronological sequence for a report to be considered accurate, but the original first-century audience didn't. We must resist the urge to claim the Bible is mistaken because it doesn't meet our culturally conditioned standard of what counts as accurate. We must take the Bible on its own terms, not demand that it meet ours.

The Error of His Ways

Bart Ehrman has caused many Christians—like Tom from the beginning of this chapter—to question their faith by charging that the Bible is filled with errors. We think Ehrman is wrong. Most supposed Bible errors have reasonable solutions. But even if a Christian were to become convinced there are some minor errors in the Bible, that doesn't mean they should feel they need to abandon their faith. The all-or-nothing assumption is both unnecessary and harmful. If a Christian does become convinced there are minor errors in the Bible, they should reevaluate what inspiration requires before rejecting their faith. To remain a Christian, all an individual needs is to be convinced that the Bible is sufficiently reliable in terms of its overall message as it relates to salvation history.

Regarding "errors," we are convinced that the majority of what have been identified as mistakes are the result of imposing our cultural assumptions on what it means to speak truthfully onto the Bible. No doubt we share with the people of the Bible a fundamental commitment that truth claims need to match with reality. But we differ from them in exactly what counts as matching. In many cases, recognizing this removes the need to find answers to specific objections because the objection itself is shown to be the result of our own unwarranted assumptions.

You might be wondering what happened to Tom. Me too. I wish I knew, but I haven't seen Tom since the events I described above. I often look for him when I'm driving, and I pray for him. I pray that what I shared with him alleviated his growing fear that the Bible was riddled with error. I pray that he still is following Jesus. And I pray that he is growing in his love for, and confidence in, God's Word.

And I pray those same things for you.

CHAPTER 6

Easy-Peasy Lemon Squeezy

False Assumption #3: The Bible Is Simple

The Word of God is obviously the most difficult writing men can read; but it is also, if you believe it is *the Word of God, the most important to read.*

MORTIMER J. ADLER AND CHARLES VAN DOREN

One of the joys of having children who currently attend public school is that I (Shawn) have acquired new vocabulary and idioms. "Delulu," "rizz," "salty," "slay," and "vibe check" are just a few of the terms I have added to my ever-expanding word list. One of my son's favorite phrases is "easy-peasy lemon squeezy," which means "very simple and easy to do." It is his go-to phrase when I assign him a task or chore, such as cleaning up the backyard or taking out the trash. But this snappy response causes me great consternation. Why? Because I know whatever job I've assigned him, he is going to do it in an "easy-peasy lemon squeezy" manner, which is not really doing the job at all and might even cause me more work in the long run. Truth be told, sometimes I'd rather hear moans and groans, because at least I would know he genuinely understands what is being expected of him.

Not a Lemon, but an Onion

When some people take on the task of reading and interpreting the Bible, they expect it to be "easy-peasy lemon squeezy." In approaching it this way, they are (like my son) almost guaranteed not to do the job correctly and to walk away with an erroneous understanding of what it actually says. So we suggest that, rather than thinking of the Bible as a lemon to be squeezed, it is better to think of it more like an onion. Yes, an onion.

If you are culturally astute (said tongue in cheek), you might know the movie *Shrek*. The lead character and hero of that movie—an antisocial, snot-green ogre named Shrek—tells his talking donkey friend, "Ogres are like onions. . . . Onions have layers; ogres have layers." In saying this, Shrek wants Donkey to know there is more to him than meets the eye and that to truly understand him, Donkey needs to look past his appearance and see who he is on the inside.

The same is true with the Bible. To accurately grasp what it's saying, we need to invest time and energy into peeling back its layers and examining it properly.

In our experience, whether intentionally or not, many critics of the Bible count on most people having only a shallow understanding of the biblical text. As mentioned in the previous chapter, Bart Ehrman is a prime example of this approach. He relishes Bible contradictions and enjoys talking about problematic passages, but he does so (in our opinion) based on superficial readings of the text. In his lecture "Are the Gospels Historically Reliable?" he repeatedly exclaims, "Just read the text!" as if a casual analysis will justify what he's saying.[1] He also argues that he believes trying to harmonize passages is "complicated" and disingenuous. But is it? Isn't this what any competent, fair-minded historian or detective does with conflicting eyewitness reports? In fact, we find it surprising that Ehrman showcases certain supposed contradictions that can be easily resolved by applying basic interpretive principles.

Some other critics like Richard Dawkins and Sam Harris—despite presenting themselves as authorities on the Bible—have almost no formal training or education in the discipline of biblical studies or the science of interpretation (hermeneutics) and little to no training in theology or ancient Near Eastern literature, as evidenced by the countless misleading statements and false assumptions they make about the Bible. Yet because of their credentials and achievements in other fields of study, some people accept their surface readings of the Bible unreservedly. Ironically, Sam Harris once posted a meme that said in part, "Pretending to know things one doesn't know is a betrayal of science."[2] Indeed!

To make sure we are not betrayed by cursory interpretations, untrained critics, and pseudo-experts, over the next several chapters we will learn how to look at Scripture, one oniony layer at a time.

Everyone and Their Brother

After reading the above introduction, you might be thinking, *But wait—I thought the Bible was for everyone.* It is! Along with the doctrines of inspiration, inerrancy, and sufficiency, the clarity ("perspicuity," in technical terms) of Scripture is one of the foundational tenets of Protestant Christianity. It means the message of the Bible is unambiguous, is understandable, and does not require clergy or biblical scholars to make sense of it. Reformers like Martin Luther, John Calvin, and their precursors, such as John Wycliffe and William Tyndale, held strongly to this doctrine in defiance of their Roman Catholic counterparts. The Catholic leaders believed the Scriptures were too difficult and obscure for common people to understand and therefore too dangerous to put into their hands.[3] If you own a Bible translated in a language you can read and hold to the idea that it is for everyone, you owe a debt of gratitude to these men. These reformers were convinced that kings and peasants alike could understand and apply the message of the Scriptures to their lives.[4] Fueled by this belief, they worked tirelessly and suffered persecution to the point of prison and martyrdom to fulfill their vision of a biblically literate church, where both clergy and laity directly benefit from the words of God.[5]

Besides this, the Bible itself claims to be written for all. Here are just a few examples:[6]

> This command I am giving you today is not too difficult for you, and it is not beyond your reach. It is not kept in heaven, so distant that you must ask, "Who will go up to heaven and bring it down so we can hear it and obey?" It is not kept beyond the sea, so far away that you must ask, "Who will cross the sea to bring it to us so we can hear it and obey?" No, *the message is very close at hand; it is on your lips and in your heart so that you can obey it.*
>
> DEUTERONOMY 30:11-14, NLT

> The teaching of your word gives light,
> *so even the simple can understand.*
>
> PSALM 119:130, NLT

> I am writing to God's church in Corinth, to you who have been called by God to be his own holy people. He made you holy by means of Christ Jesus, just as he did *for all people everywhere* who call on the name of our Lord Jesus Christ, their Lord and ours.
>
> 1 CORINTHIANS 1:2, NLT

> You have been taught the holy Scriptures *from childhood*, and they have given you the wisdom to receive the salvation that comes by trusting in Christ Jesus. All Scripture is inspired by God and is *useful to teach us what is true and to make us realize what is wrong in our lives.* It corrects us when we are wrong and teaches us to do what is right.
>
> 2 TIMOTHY 3:15-16, NLT

Notice how the Bible repeatedly addresses everyday people, such as parents, who are instructed to teach their children the words of God. It is described as a light *for all*, making the simple wise. It is good news to be believed and received by the world.

The doctrine of Scripture's clarity means that the Bible is open for *all* to read, study, ponder, and apply. It means that what can be known about God's nature, character, and will, especially as it pertains to salvation history, is accessible to the common person and does not require any special gifting or prophetic insight. This should encourage us that no matter how difficult we might find it to relate to the Bible, if we keep approaching it in good faith and with due diligence, our efforts will not be wasted.[7]

That's Not What I Said

By now, you might be asking, *If the Bible is so clear, why did you say that the Bible is like an onion and not a lemon? And why is it so many people—even smart people—have misunderstood it?* These are great questions, but before we can answer them, we need to better understand what the doctrine of Scripture's clarity is *not* saying.

First, it is not saying that every passage or verse in the Bible is equally clear. Rather, the doctrine applies specifically to the "big picture" of Scripture, the central message of salvation history.[8] To deny this caveat would be to deny Scripture itself. Even the apostle Peter cautions his readers about how hard it can be to grasp some of what Paul writes in his letters: "Some of his comments are hard to understand, and those who are ignorant and unstable have twisted his letters to mean something quite different, just as they do with other parts of Scripture" (2 Peter 3:15-16, NLT).

Second, it is not saying that a person hearing or reading the Bible does not need to study or interpret it. Certainly, no one should expect that the "biblical meaning will be delivered up by some mystical process of hermeneutical osmosis." Rather, it is the opposite! The doctrine of Scripture's clarity, by acknowledging everyone's ability to comprehend the Bible, encourages people to actively pursue the truth and work to discover what the text actually says. The necessity of diligent study does not contradict the Bible's clarity. As theologian Kevin Vanhoozer argues, it validates it: "The idea that the Bible is clear . . . makes the work of interpretation even more important. The clarity of Scripture means that understanding is possible, not that it is easy."[9]

Third, it is not asserting that there is no need or place for experts such as translators, teachers, or theologians. That Protestant Christianity has produced so many, both past and present, is evidence the doctrine was never construed that way. The *Westminster Confession of Faith* (1646) explains it well:

> All things in Scripture are not alike plain in themselves, nor alike clear unto all: yet those things which are necessary to be known, believed, and observed for salvation are so clearly propounded, and opened in some place of Scripture or other, that not only the learned, but

> the unlearned, in a due use of the ordinary means, may attain unto a sufficient understanding of them.[10]

Or, as Charles Hodge writes, "It is not denied that the Scriptures contain many things hard to be understood; that they require diligent study; that all men need the guidance of the Holy Spirit in order to right knowledge and true faith. But it is maintained that in all things necessary to salvation they are sufficiently plain to be understood even by the unlearned."[11]

The Obvious Question

> Truly, you are a God who hides himself.
>
> ISAIAH 45:15

Of course, the question remains: Why *aren't* all Scriptures "plain in themselves" and "clear unto all"? Why should any portion be difficult to interpret? If the Bible is truly God's revelation to his people and God wants us to follow it, why didn't he make it as simple as possible to understand? To answer this question, we would have to enter the mind of God. But let's look at a few reasons why we believe every chapter and verse of the Bible is not equally plain and simple.

First, while the words of Scripture were clear to their original audiences, they are now so distant from us that they have become obscure. The more time that passes and the less we have in common with the ancient world, the more difficult it becomes to fully understand what the Bible is saying. This is because God has chosen to reveal himself in history. Much like the incarnation, in which God entered history at a particular time and place and became one of us, fully immersing himself into our creaturely existence, he has also "incarnated" himself through the sacred writings of his people—using their native language and culture. All this means that today we need translators and guides to help us navigate our journey into the biblical text.[12] You could rightfully say that every time we open our Bibles, it is like we are traveling back in time to a foreign land. Perhaps this is why God chose to disclose himself, for the most part, to one group of people instead of many.

Second, the Bible is often hard to understand and obscure because of our own sinfulness.[13] While the immense differences in time and culture play an important role, we should not underestimate the negative impact our own biases and prejudices have on understanding the Bible. Generally speaking, human beings can be quite unreceptive to things we find disagreeable. It is worth considering that Jesus, when confronting the audience of his day about their misinterpretations of the Bible, never once faulted the Scriptures for being confusing or hard to understand. Instead, he consistently held his audience accountable, using phrases such as "You have heard it said . . . but I say to you . . . ," "Haven't you read in the Scriptures?" and "You are wrong, because you know neither the Scriptures, nor the power of God."[14] On multiple occasions, Jesus also rebuked those holding skewed interpretations and applications of Scripture, especially when they were being used to justify sinful attitudes.[15] Likewise, we must be careful when we approach the Bible that we are not letting our own sinful attitudes and desires obscure what it says.

Third, and most significantly, we believe the Bible is not plain and simple in its entirety because it has God as its ultimate author. Because of his divine nature, God and his ways sometimes are elusive and inscrutable. So it's natural that some parts of his revelation would be more challenging to understand than others.[16] In other words, the reason why the Bible is puzzling in some places is because God is mysterious and intends it to be that way. To have it any other way would diminish his glory and majesty, which are essential qualities of his divine nature. As pastor and writer R. A. Torrey notes, "Whatever man has produced, man can exhaust; but no man, no generation of men, not all the tens of thousands of men together that have devoted their best abilities and the best years of their lives to the study of this book, have been able to exhaust this book."[17]

Dietrich Bonhoeffer, a German theologian, made the following thought-provoking statement: "A god who could be proved by us would be an idol." In other words, a deity that can be *empirically* proven or demonstrated loses a central part of its divine essence and becomes nothing more than an idol—a mere object of human construction and understanding. Bonhoeffer's statement leans forcefully on the idea that God will always remain elusive at some level because an essential aspect of God's divine nature is that he is beyond description and transcendent.[18] This makes some people feel like God is distant or absent. However, it also forever lures those who genuinely want to explore God and deepen their knowledge and love for him.[19] There is always more to learn about God. It is for this reason that the Bible, as much as it is simple and clear, is also vast and immeasurable.

Jesus Reveals and Conceals

This elusiveness of God was also embodied by Jesus, who often communicated through parables and riddles. Scholars have offered several reasons why Jesus chose to speak this way, but there is no need to speculate. Jesus directly answers this question:

> To those who listen to my teaching, more understanding will be given, and they will have an abundance of knowledge. But for those who are not listening, even what little understanding they have will be taken away from them. That is why I use these parables,
>
> For they look, but they don't really see.
> They hear, but they don't really listen or understand. . . .
>
> But blessed are your eyes, because they see; and your ears, because they hear. I tell you the truth, many prophets and righteous people longed to see what you see, but they didn't see it. And they longed to hear what you hear, but they didn't hear it.
>
> MATTHEW 13:12-13, 16-17, NLT

His answer, in a nutshell, is twofold: to *reveal* and *conceal.*[20] For those who are not truly his followers, the parables, as well as many other challenging parts of Scripture, will be difficult to understand and even more difficult to apply.[21] But for those who are receptive to God's Word, who have hearts made of "good soil," his Word will provide an opportunity to grow deeper in the knowledge of God and his Kingdom.[22]

In his letter to the Ephesians, the apostle Paul says he is praying that God will give them "spiritual wisdom and insight so that [they] might grow in [their] knowledge of God" (Ephesians 1:17, NLT). We share in this prayer for everyone reading this book who truly wants to better understand the Bible so they can grow closer to God. We believe the Holy Spirit will illuminate the deep things God has revealed in his Word for you if you "hold it fast in an honest and good heart" (Luke 8:15) and in faith humbly ask him to assist you. We pray you will be able to discern "the wonderful things God has freely given us" in his Word (1 Corinthians 2:12, NLT).

Hidden in Plain Sight

King Solomon once observed, "It is God's privilege to conceal things and the king's privilege to discover them" (Proverbs 25:2, NLT). At one time, only kings had the privilege—time, education, and resources—to study God and his mysterious ways in depth.[23] This wasn't because the Scriptures were too difficult to understand, or because those in authority thought they were too dangerous to put in the hands of the people. It was because there were so few copies of the Scriptures in existence that only political and religious leaders had access to them. However, about a thousand years later, when the gospel began to spread across the Roman Empire, this was no longer the case. The Scriptures were now readily available for the people of God to use in their places of worship. We know this because when the good news of Jesus reached the synagogue in Berea, "the people . . . searched the Scriptures day after day to see if Paul and Silas were teaching the truth" (Acts 17:11, NLT). Today accessibility is no longer an issue for most people, especially in nations where religious freedom is protected. This now means that the honor and privilege of discovering things God has concealed is no longer limited to kings but belongs to all people.

So then, taking into consideration both the clarity of Scripture and the elusiveness of God, we can agree that the goal of interpreting the Bible accurately is a noble undertaking, as well as a never-ending labor of love. It is an adventure in its own right, and one that promises great reward. For Christians, reading and studying the Bible should be a way of life, for truly it is a "lamp to guide [our] feet and a light for [our] path" (Psalm 119:105, NLT), able to make us wise and "equip [us] to do every good work" (2 Timothy 3:17, NLT).

Whether you are a Bible enthusiast, skeptic, or somewhere in between, if you ever struggle with understanding the Bible, don't despair. There are things you can learn and do that will make the process less formidable. Let's now move on to some helpful techniques for interpreting the Bible—fully convinced of our ability and need to do so.

CHAPTER 7

The Case of Mistaken Interpretation

False Assumption #3: The Bible Is Simple, Part 2

Seekers of truth, as distinct from alleged possessors of truth, will employ "double vision"—they will give others the benefit of the doubt, they will inhabit imaginatively the world of others, and they will endeavor to view events in question from the perspective of others, not just their own.

MIROSLAV VOLF

While I (Shawn) do not read much fiction these days, detective stories have always fascinated me, and none more so than those featuring Sir Arthur Conan Doyle's mastermind detective, Sherlock Holmes. What sets his character apart from any ordinary detective is his uncanny powers of observation and investigation. Though only a fictional character, Sherlock Holmes has been credited as "a pioneer in forensic science."[1] The techniques and skills Conan Doyle ascribes to Holmes predate by decades the forensics that would later be adopted by real police detectives (for example, the use of fingerprints, footprints, typewriters, and animal behaviors to solve cases). Throughout his numerous adventures, Sherlock Holmes makes comments, usually to Dr. Watson, about his approach to solving whatever mystery is before them. In preparation for this book, I reread many of the adventures of Sherlock Holmes, and I couldn't help but notice how many of his methods and techniques help illustrate those common to biblical interpretation.[2]

Art and Science

Just as the primary goal of forensics is to solve a mystery related to a crime, the primary goal of biblical interpretation is to accurately uncover what the Bible and its various authors are trying to communicate to their respective audiences. On several occasions, we have referred to the discipline of interpretation as a science, and it is. But it is not *only* a science—it is also an art. It is a science because there are well-defined rules that govern how to perform the task to obtain consistently accurate results. It is an art because it is not enough to know the rules and principles. We must also know when and how to apply them. Since the Bible is a collection of books spanning more than a millennium, filled with many literary forms, written by various authors, and edited by numerous scribes, this task is not simple. It requires us to be extra observant, to look for the right clues, and to ask the right questions. So, what are some of these rules, and how do we apply them?

First, when we approach a biblical passage, we must lay aside our agendas and hobbyhorses. Failure to do this will inevitably result in our misreading, twisting, or even contradicting the meaning of a biblical text. Whether we are a defender or a detractor of the Bible, no one is beyond this trap. Sherlock Holmes would warn us "it is a capital mistake to theorize before one has data. Insensibly one begins to twist facts to suit theories, instead of theories to suit facts."[3] If we find we have done this, our pride will keep us from acknowledging our mistake and changing course. We must not be so committed to an interpretation that we are not willing to reconsider it when we gain new insight.

For those of us who believe the Bible is inerrant, we must remember our interpretations are not.[4] Principled interpreters remain humble and are willing to go where the evidence leads them. They must be willing to say, along with Mr. Holmes, "I confess that I have been as blind as a mole, but it is better to learn wisdom late than never to learn it at all."[5]

Second, after we have laid aside our biases and prejudices (as much as possible), we should read the text and look for clues that will help us better understand it. We do this by asking basic interrogative questions, such as . . .

- Who wrote this passage? Who is speaking in the passage? Who is the passage written to?
- What happens in the passage? What question does this specific text answer?
- Where was it written? Where do the events in the passage take place?
- When was it written? When do the events in the passage take place?
- Why did the author write this? How does the author want readers to respond?

It is important while we are asking and answering these questions that we do not breeze past what might seem like minor details. Careful observation of the text is mandatory if we are to discover its "clear" and "obvious" meaning, if only because we do not know what information will be critical to our interpretation. Mr. Holmes would say, "How much an observant man might learn by an accurate and systematic examination of all that came in his way."[6]

Third, as a detective searches for motive by investigating everyone and everything involved in the case, it is vital we consider the literary context of a passage—where it is found in the text (what precedes and follows it) and its literary form (genre). Locating a passage will help clarify its purpose and illuminate its significance. It is important that we realize "every Bible verse fits within a larger story."[7] And whenever we read a verse, we also want to read the surrounding paragraphs and chapters and consider the genre not only of the verse we are studying but of the entire book. Identifying the genre of the verse and book is helpful in making sense of a passage, as it directly informs what our expectations about the passage should be and what additional questions we need to ask. Below are some of the most frequent genres found throughout Scripture and the questions that help us understand them:

- *Narrative:* What happened, and why did it happen?
- *Law:* What is our responsibility to God and the community?
- *Poetry:* What feelings does this passage express, and how are they fulfilled in God?
- *Wisdom:* What observations about life does this passage make? What godly advice does it give?
- *Prophecy:* What does this passage reveal about God's heart (motives, plans, decisions)?
- *Gospel:* What does this passage teach about Jesus, and why is this good news?
- *Parable:* What spiritual truth is this passage illustrating?
- *Letter:* What specific occasion caused the author to write this passage?

- *Homily:* How does this passage help me grow and mature in my faith?
- *Apocalyptic:* What cosmic mysteries does the passage reveal? What hope does it provide for God's persecuted people? What encouragement does it give them to endure hardships and trials?

It cannot be stressed enough just how important this third rule is to the process of interpretation.[8] We have counseled many people who have become disillusioned with God and grown to distrust the Bible because they have failed to account for the genre and context of a passage. For example, a mother whose son abandoned his Christian faith came to me (Shawn) after she had prayed for her son for years with no positive results. She opened her Bible and read to me, "Train up a child in the way he should go; even when he is old he will not depart from it" (Proverbs 22:6). As she read the verse, she wept. She told me, "I believed in this promise with all my heart. And I lived it with every ounce of my strength. Yet my son has walked away from the faith and wants nothing to do with me. When will God make good on his promise?" I was heartbroken for her. I knew her son and the way he was treating her. She deserved better! After we discussed a few things about her son and how she was feeling at the moment, I had the unenviable job of explaining to her how she had misunderstood what that proverb meant. I explained that a proverb is an easy-to-remember saying that states a general truth or gives a piece of advice for godly living. Then I said, "That proverb you are holding on to as promise is not a promise at all—it is an observation. It describes the way things normally happen. It is not a guarantee." She asked a couple of questions about my answer and cried a little more. I prayed and offered to contact her son for her. Sadly, to this day, he has not returned to the Lord and still refuses to talk with his mother. This example shows us how important it is to determine the genre of a passage before interpreting it. Failure to do so will inevitably lead to mistaking what it says. We will discuss how other genres affect the meaning of biblical passages throughout the remainder of the book.

Fourth, as a detective might look for fingerprints, weapons, and other clues, a Bible interpreter must keep an eye out for literary devices, such as hyperbole, contrast, and metaphors. Hyperbole—purposeful exaggeration not meant to be taken literally—is commonly found in the use of superlatives and the word "all." Contrast is a literary technique where two subjects—persons, places, things, or ideas—are juxtaposed in the text to highlight their differences. Contrast typically helps direct our attention to a major point of the passage. A metaphor is a creative way to describe something by referring to something else with similar characteristics. In some way, every parable is an extended metaphor. When we come across any of these literary devices, we must slow down, pay attention, and ask questions.

Fifth, a good Bible interpreter must also keep an eye out for emphasis (how much space is given to a story or topic), repetition (which words or concepts keep popping up), and movement in the flow of the text (some common movements within a text include from general to specific, lesser to greater, question to answer, and cause to effect).[9] All these seemingly minor details help emphasize the point of the passage. Sherlock Holmes would advise us to "never trust . . . general impressions . . . but concentrate yourself upon details."[10] We must also take special note of word choice and grammar, and ask ourselves,

- What key phrases or terms are in this passage, and what do they mean in context?

- How are these phrases and terms used elsewhere in Scripture?
- Is this passage written in past, present, or future tense?
- What pronouns are used, and do they change in the course of the text?

Sixth, we must consider the supernatural. For those of us who believe that the Bible has God as its ultimate author and editor, the realm of the supernatural is not just a distinct possibility but a certain reality. Therefore, we are open to the idea that a passage can have a deeper meaning beyond what the human authors intended. We see this most prominently in the case of prophecy.[11] However, we also think interpreting a passage this way requires extra care and discernment. There needs to be careful analysis and supporting evidence that confirms this kind of subjective interpretation.[12] That said, we profoundly believe that in order to interpret the Bible correctly, we must allow for this possibility. True forensic scientists never limit their options. In light of Sherlock Holmes's most famous quote—"When you have eliminated the impossible, whatever remains, *however improbable*, must be the truth"[13]—we hope you will keep an open mind on this matter as you interpret the biblical text.

Seventh, it is vital we seek help when and where we need it. Because God chose to reveal himself in history using specific human languages—Hebrew, Aramaic, and Greek—which the majority of the world today does not speak, we encourage you to seek help in understanding the possible range of meaning that words might have. Where can you find this help? Bible interpreters should have several Bible dictionaries, handbooks, commentaries, and translations to assist them in understanding the passage. There is an abundance of these resources available to you via the internet. There is one caveat to this rule, though: We think you should study the passage on your own before turning to the voice of experts. As we mentioned in chapter 3, experts are helpful but need to be chosen wisely. You will be amazed how many times pseudo-experts or experts with an agenda make mistakes and overlook important clues. You will almost certainly miss these unseen clues if you rely too much on secondary sources. That is because secondary sources, while necessary and useful, have a way of swaying our analyses, for better or worse. Perhaps this is why the great detective believed "there is nothing like first-hand evidence."[14]

Eighth, by the time we reach this rule, we should have a good feel for what the passage is saying and what it is not saying. But this is also where everything can go wrong. It is imperative to ask the key question we asked in the very first chapter: *How does this text fit in with the overarching theme of salvation history?* The reason this question is so foundational is because we cannot hope to understand what the Bible is saying without first understanding what it says about who God is, who we are in relationship to him, what he has done for us, and what he will do for us one day. In asking this question, we are leaving room for Scripture to interpret Scripture, knowing that "no prophecy in Scripture ever came from the prophet's own understanding. . . . Those prophets were moved by the Holy Spirit, and they spoke from God" (2 Peter 1:20-21, NLT). It is in this sense that Jesus could say the Bible is ultimately about himself.[15] This final question grounds every interpretation, making sure we do not arrive at a conclusion that does not fit the heart of God revealed in the grand narrative of the Bible.

Dashing Babies Against Rocks?

The above rules should help us interpret various passages correctly. By way of example, let's take Psalm 137:9, one of the most controversial passages in the Psalms, and see if we can make proper sense of it. Here is my (Shawn's) translation: "Blessed is the one who takes your little ones and dashes them against the rock!"

Many skeptics, based on this verse and others like it, have accused God of being a moral monster. They have explicitly pointed to this psalm as an example of the horrific violence sanctioned in the Bible. For example, Dan Barker, an evangelical minister turned atheist, once argued during a debate, "In Psalm 137:9, [God] told us that we should be happy to take the innocent babies and dash them against the stones. That's—even if that God did exist, I might not necessarily want to worship such a monster. I might ask him to confess his sins to me. What a guy—what if I were to treat my kids like this?"[16]

Brian McLaren and others have used this verse to accuse the Scriptures of communicating contradictory positions on the treatment of enemies. They point out that whereas Jesus teaches people to love their enemies (as in the Sermon on the Mount), this psalm teaches them to "dash their infants against a rock." McLaren uses this verse elsewhere to demonstrate how Christians are inconsistent in their application of the Bible and "throw out anything that doesn't appeal to them."[17]

At first glance, the words of the psalm do strike a harsh tone, especially to our modern ears, and read like something out of a horror book, or worse, a book about the Holocaust.[18] But are we understanding this Scripture correctly? Could there be more to this verse than initially meets the eye? "There is nothing more deceptive than an obvious fact," Mr. Holmes would say.[19] Therefore, using the limited skills we have learned in this chapter, let's take a closer look at Psalm 137:9.

First, we must lay aside our biases and agenda to the best of our abilities. We must take extra care our predispositions and prejudices do not get in the way of our interpretation. For a Christian, that means avoiding the temptation to defend the Bible's words by twisting them to fit our idea of what we think they should say and instead seeking to understand the message the author intends to convey and how that message fits into the grand story of God's people. When we do this, the Scriptures will stand on their own merits.

Next, we need to ask some key questions about the psalm. Who wrote it? Who is it written to? Why was it written? To answer those questions, let's look at the full psalm:

A Lament of the Exiles in Babylon

1 Beside the rivers of Babylon, we sat and wept
as we thought of Jerusalem.
2 We put away our harps,
hanging them on the branches of poplar trees.
3 For our captors demanded a song from us.
Our tormentors insisted on a joyful hymn:
"Sing us one of those songs of Jerusalem!"
4 But how can we sing the songs of the LORD
while in a pagan land?

5 If I forget you, O Jerusalem,
let my right hand forget how to play the harp.
6 May my tongue stick to the roof of my mouth
if I fail to remember you,
if I don't make Jerusalem my greatest joy.

7 O LORD, remember what the Edomites did
on the day the armies of Babylon captured Jerusalem.
"Destroy it!" they yelled.
"Level it to the ground!"
8 O Babylon, you will be destroyed.
Happy is the one who pays you back
for what you have done to us.
9 Happy is the one who takes your babies
and smashes them against the rocks!

PSALM 137, NLT

Since there is no author given, the exact identity of the author will have to remain a mystery. However, in the first verses of the psalm, the psalmist is identified as being among the captives deported to Babylon (verses 1-3).[20] This means the events described in the psalm take place shortly after Jerusalem was conquered, the Temple was destroyed, and many people—including trained musicians and poets like the psalmist—were dragged across the desert to be slaves.[21] The psalm situates itself outside the borders of Israel, in the realm of the neo-Babylonian Empire, near its once-famed canals, dams, and dikes (verse 1).[22] It is written to others suffering in exile (verses 1-6), to the Lord (verse 7), and to their enemies (verses 8-9). It was written to express the feelings associated with captivity and is a response to the psalmist's captors, who demand the psalmist and his companions sing "one of those songs of Jerusalem." How difficult this must have been for the psalmist and his Jewish brothers and sisters. They have lost everything—their freedom (verses 1-3), homes (verses 4-7), and children (verses 8-9)—and now are being mocked and goaded into singing a song about all they have lost. How do we know they have lost their children? A careful reading of the text shows that verses 8 and 9 are in direct parallel. "Happy is the one who *pays you back for what you have done to us*" in verse 8 is further explained in verse 9: "Happy is the one who *takes your babies and smashes them against the rocks!*" (emphasis added). In short, the psalmist is saying, "May you have done to you what you have done to us."

Being a psalm, the genre of the text is poetry, but not just any kind of poetry. It is a Jewish exile slave song. Since it's a slave song, we expect the psalm to be full of poignant hyperbole and dreams of home and emancipation, and this is what we find in verses 5 and 6.

Notice the dramatic and exaggerated language. The psalmist sings, "If I forget you, O Jerusalem, let my right hand forget how to play the harp" (as if forgetting either were remotely possible) and "if I don't make Jerusalem my greatest joy" (this is not intended to be literal, but the superlative is used for emphasis—to convey the psalmist's deepest sincerity). The psalm expresses feelings of swelling sorrow and homesickness, as emphasized by the repeated mention of Jerusalem (five times), which eventually leads to anger and a cry for justice as the psalmist considers the cruelty of his captors. Notice the movement in the psalm. There is increasing passion, moving from sorrow and pathos (verses 1-3) to anger and defiance (verses 4-6) to retribution and imprecation (verses 7-9). Indeed, "every line of [the psalm] is alive with pain" and with each line the "intensity grows" until it reaches its "appalling climax."[23]

The very last words of the psalm record an unrehearsed emotional outburst. What is of peculiar interest is that these words are encased in a common Israelite beatitude formula. It is because of this that many modern-day readers wrongly assume that this passage is prescriptive.[24] But this interpretation does not fit the context. With a little research, we find the phrase "dashing [your] little ones" elsewhere in Scripture.[25] In every passage where the phrase is used, it tells the horrors of warfare—a brand of warfare employed exclusively by pagans and *not* by the people of God.

All this amounts to the conclusion that the controversial verse should be taken with a great deal of poetic license. The psalmist is longing for the day when God will justly repay the Babylonians for their cruelty and brutality. Indeed, he is resting in Jeremiah's prophecy of Babylon's ultimate destruction (verse 8).[26] The fact that when the Persians did finally conquer Babylon, they did so without raising a sword[27] and did not treat its citizens the way the Babylonians had treated Judah, confirms that verse 9 was never intended to be either prophetic or prescriptive. These words, then, while giving fodder to modern critics and skeptics, were meant to strengthen those in exile, evoke pity and sympathy from the Lord, and call out the Babylonians for their awful deeds. When you read the full psalm and arrive at verse 9, don't you feel the pain the psalmist and his fellow Jews are in? They cannot sing songs of joy—they have lost everything they love! The only thing in their hearts and on their minds is an overwhelming desire for retributive justice, which has been promised to them by the prophet Jeremiah.

So we must not read these words in isolation. To understand them, we must enter into the world of the violently oppressed. If your freedom was taken from you by a violent oppressor, you were forced into a labor camp, and your children were slaughtered cruelly in front of you by having their heads dashed against a rock, how would you respond? You would cry for justice and would not be wrong to do so, for "there is nothing vengeful about the expectation of a punishment equivalent to the injury."[28] What Psalm 137 and others like it teach us, then, is to take these desires for justice and leave them at the Lord's feet. In the end, we think the psalmist would agree with the apostle Paul: "Never take revenge. Leave that to the righteous anger of God. For the Scriptures say, 'I will take revenge; I will pay them back,' says the LORD" (Romans 12:19, NLT). For the Old Testament, like the New Testament, although less explicitly, also teaches us to love our enemies.[29]

So we should avoid two extremes in interpreting Psalm 137:9. First, we should avoid the temptation to lessen the gravity of its severe words. In these harsh words are the pain, suffering, and hurt the psalmist has felt after being exiled from his home and watching his children being slaughtered in a gruesome way by the Babylonians. To lessen his witness is to cheapen it. That his words seem at variance with other portions of Scripture that call us to love our enemies is indeed problematic but not unresolvable. The other extreme is to read too much into his words. Poetry aims to be immoderate and melodramatic. It does this by the use of unrestrained, extravagant words and by the use of memorable figures of speech. Slave poetry specifically focuses on justice, deliverance, and freedom. In this case, the psalmist is not truly eliciting people (or even God) to massacre children like the pagans. He is simply asking God, in a passionate way, to be true to his word and exact justice upon those who have treated him and his people cruelly.[30] This request, of course, fits nicely into salvation history, for it ultimately finds its resolve either at the cross, where Jesus Christ pays for those sins of the past, or in the final consummation, when he will judge the world.[31]

Putting in the Effort

Every year when election days roll around in California, along with our ballots we receive our political party's endorsements. Not surprisingly, many people cast their votes according to the party line. They do this because they trust the party they belong to, and rather than doing the hard work of figuring things out for themselves, they would rather rely on this quick-and-easy method. Following the party line *does* save time, but people also sacrifice their own growth as informed voters and open themselves to casting a vote for something they may later regret.

In the same way, few people make the effort to figure out what the Bible actually says for themselves but instead rely on others to do the work for them. If you want your faith in the Bible to grow, studying it using the tried-and-true methods we've explored in this chapter is a must. We understand that this process might seem overwhelming at first, but just like riding a bike, the more you practice, the easier it will be, until it becomes so easy that you barely think about it. Sherlock Holmes once said, "The world is full of obvious things which nobody by any chance ever observes."[32] We hope that with the skills you have learned in this chapter, you will begin not just to see but also to *observe* every passage in the Bible. Like Psalm 137:9, some passages will seem excessive and bizarre at first, but don't let them intimidate you. "As a rule . . . the more bizarre a thing is the less mysterious it proves to be."[33]

Yes, Sherlock Holmes said that too.

CHAPTER 8

A Fish out of Water

False Assumption #4: The Bible Is Written to Me

Most of my important lessons about life have come from recognizing how others from a different culture view things.

EDGAR H. SCHEIN

When I attended seminary, I (Shawn) was given a wonderful opportunity to visit Israel. This life-changing experience impacted me on multiple levels. Bible passages for which I had little to no geographical context now came alive. What would have taken a year of schooling was accomplished in a month. Beyond the physical landscape and archaeological visits, the cross-cultural experience also left an indelible mark on me. During one of our lunch breaks, when we visited the Jewish Quarter in Jerusalem's Old City, I found a local pizza shop. Longing for a taste of home, I made my way into the quaint restaurant. The place must have had a good reputation, because there was a line. When it was my turn, I ordered a slice of pepperoni pizza. The man behind the counter looked at me with shock and disgust, as did the other patrons. He shook his head, saying, "No, no, no. No meat." I couldn't believe it, but I shrugged and ordered a slice of cheese pizza with whatever topping he recommended. He served me a perfectly baked pizza with green olives on top, which was absolutely delicious. When I returned to my group, I shared what had happened, and one of my professors explained that places that want to be recognized as kosher cannot mix meat and cheese. And while there is no state law in Israel saying pizzerias cannot serve meat and cheese together, this custom, rooted in Torah, pervades the entire land. I knew about Jewish dietary laws, but this was my first time living under their influence.

Later I found that this custom was not applied in the same manner everywhere. For example, when our group visited McDonald's for lunch, I tested the water and asked whether I could order a cheeseburger. Expecting a flat-out no, I was shocked when the worker informed me they could make me one, but I couldn't eat it inside the building. You can imagine my growing confusion.

And this led to one more related moment near the end of our time in Israel. When we went out to eat at a restaurant by the Sea of Galilee, the host intentionally seated our group at the back of the restaurant in an isolated section. I did not take offense, though, as I hoped this would mean meat and cheese would be on the menu. But when I asked our server about it, he told me that to keep the kitchen kosher, there would be no dairy products available. Perplexed, I asked the server why we were seated in the isolated section. He hesitated, but then softly whispered, "No offense, but Americans are loud."

I promptly shut my mouth, glanced around the restaurant, and took in the entire scene. Every other table in the adjoining section was very quiet compared to us. They communicated with one another in such a way as not to stand out or draw attention to themselves. We were the exact opposite. We were obnoxiously loud. Suddenly, I was mortified. Of course, we were just enjoying each other's company at the end of a month studying together in the Holy Land. Even so, let it be said, Americans speak, laugh, and even breathe loudly! And then it hit me like a foreign freight train: We were doing this as outsiders and visitors.

Culture Shock

Much like my fish-out-of-water experience traveling in Israel, the Bible itself is like a foreign land, and reading it can be quite the cross-cultural experience. Every time we open a book of the Bible, we leave the familiarity of our daily lives and enter a strange new world—a world in which most of us do not speak the language or know the customs and conventions, or the tradition and history behind them. We do not recognize the lay of the land, its many landmarks, or their significance. We are not aware of what words have deeper meanings, what behaviors are expected, or which ones are considered rude and impolite. We are unfamiliar with deep-rooted tribal histories, unofficial borders, important highways and byways, and the politics of the day. We are not even sure what the expected weather is throughout the seasons of the year. As you can imagine, if we don't find out about these things, we will read into the passage our own context and almost certainly draw misguided conclusions. Hopefully this drives us not to despair but to gain a bigger perspective by studying the historical and cultural background of every text we read, especially those we find disturbing or problematic for one reason or another.

Because reading the Bible is like visiting a foreign land, we should expect a decent amount of culture shock when we immerse ourselves in it. Culture shock is "the feeling of disorientation experienced by someone when they are suddenly subjected to an unfamiliar culture and way of life."[1] There are several reasons for this. First, our ignorance of the everyday language and expressions, common social cues, and established customs of the world of the Bible disorients us. Imagine a man from Bible times visiting our culture and hearing someone say, "There is more than one way to skin a cat" or overhearing one sports fan say to another, "The Cowboys destroyed the Chiefs." Second, we have difficulty relating to the Bible because it is so distant, both geographically and historically. For example, most of us in modern Western culture do not have farms, go to a temple, or have leaders who have multiple wives. We do not sacrifice animals, have servants living with us, or wash each other's feet. As we saw earlier, the Bible is written *for* everyone, but it is not written *to* everyone. To put it bluntly, we do not share much in common with those who lived across the oceans thousands of years ago. Third, as we learn more about the history and culture of the Bible, we will eventually reach information overload. There is only so much we can take in before we get overwhelmed and can no longer synthesize the information we are learning.

The negative effects of culture shock have been well documented.[2] Scholars agree that after we have engaged with a foreign culture for a short period of time and the novelty has worn off, most of us will experience uncertainty and frustration. It is no different when we enter the foreign land of Scripture and encounter those passages that surprise and confuse us and are hard to make sense of from our present-day perspective. These difficult and baffling texts, which are beyond our natural range of understanding, slowly mount up.[3] Soon, we no longer view them as a curiosity but as uninviting and even offensive. Of course, most of this reaction derives from our limited, outsider perspective.[4]

It is important while experiencing this form of culture shock that we realize we are not alone. In fact, if we want to truly grasp what the Bible is saying, we must read and study it *in community* and listen to an array of voices (male and female, rich and poor, young and old, clergy and parishioner, liberal and traditional, local and global, and skeptic and believer).[5] Where do we hear these voices? In sermons, Bible studies, books (like this one), films, and so on. These voices inform our limited perspectives and often set right our misapprehensions about a passage.[6] From what we have observed, failure to do this will inevitably result in increased disenchantment and unwarranted hostility toward the Bible, or in increased narrowness of perspective.

If we invest our time and energy into exploring the biblical world in community, over time we will feel more comfortable and at home in the biblical setting. We will pick up key vocabulary (even if we never truly learn the language), basic customs, common social cues, and the allusions that imperceptibly infuse almost every conversation and event. Once we arrive at this level of familiarity, we can confidently share our interpretations with others, help those who have become disillusioned, and challenge ourselves to understand the history and culture of God's people even more.

It is at this time that a believer might also experience a kind of *reverse* culture shock, where they become highly critical of their own culture and other people's lack of perspective. They might be tempted to idealize the Bible's culture and think people today should adopt the same customs and social conventions that the Israelites and early church did. This is a hazard we must guard against. For example, just because believers in Paul's day washed one another's feet and greeted one another with "holy kisses" does not mean believers today are required to do so. (We will look into this specific topic in the next chapter.) It is important when experiencing reverse culture shock that we do not stop listening to and learning from the culture around us. While knowledge of our own culture does not help us interpret the Bible, it does help us better communicate biblical truth to those around us and properly apply its message.

Another Time

Throughout this book we've talked about encountering God through the Bible. For many today this means approaching the text as if it is some kind of medium or channel by which human beings communicate with God directly. In this reader-centric approach, what God says in the Bible requires no literary or historical context. It only matters "what it says to me." We reject this individualistic approach, not because we think God *can't* speak to us in this way but because we think God hasn't *chosen* to speak to us this way.[7] We reject it because we have seen repeatedly how this approach has led to divisions, cults, and the rationalization of horrible and unbiblical interpretations. To clarify, we believe God can and does speak personally to individuals and communities. But the Bible—sacred revelation given by God and recognized by the community of faith—is the standard by which all personal encounters should be measured.

We believe that to interpret a passage from the Bible correctly, not only is it critical to consider its literary context, but we must also take into account its historical context. In other words, what is recorded in the Bible—its laws, stories, poetry, and letters—belongs to another time and place that is vastly different from ours. Because of this, a basic familiarity with this history is essential to interpreting it correctly.[8]

The historical context of any given passage differs from book to book (sometimes from passage to passage) and includes cultural, geographical, and political factors of the author and the text.[9] So when we approach a passage in the Bible, in addition to the questions from the previous chapter, we must also answer these questions:

- What historical and cultural events are described or alluded to in the text?
- How are these events portrayed in the text?
- What was happening in the world at the time of these events?
- Based on this information, how would the original intended audience have understood what the author is communicating in the text?[10]

We are fortunate that answering questions like these is no longer difficult. We have resources at our fingertips to assist us in every key field of study. Most scholars agree that "our ability to understand the historical setting of Scripture is at an all-time high."[11] Still, while every portion of Scripture has its own historical peculiarity and deserves its own specific attention, there are a few overarching concepts that have been brought to greater light in recent scholarship that are worth mentioning before we move on.

First, an essential quality of the cultures of the Bible was their sense of *group identity*. Whereas those of us who belong to democratic Western cultures are inclined to define and evaluate ourselves by our degree of individuality, independence, and personal discovery (the "you do you, and I'll do me" mentality), those who belonged to the cultures of the Bible were inclined to define themselves by whatever group or collective they belonged to.

Second, this reality meant that the highest honor was passing down and enforcing the values and ideals of their identity group (family, community, tribe, or nation). The greatest shame was failing to exhibit their group's ideals and values. Shame—the loss of honor—also resulted in a loss of identity. In an honor-shame culture the idea of self-esteem would be viewed as an oxymoron, for "the only esteem one has is bestowed not by the self but by the group." In this honor-shame environment, peer pressure would not be perceived as a negative force or something to resist but a vital aspect of society—restraining and empowering those under its influence for the survival and preservation of the group.[12] Viewing honor and shame as a form of currency, though not a precise metaphor, can help us understand it. Using this metaphor, then, we should keep in mind that every social interaction is a transaction that either increases honor or diminishes it, for both the individual and the group.

Finally, whereas Western culture prioritizes individuality over community, tasks over people, and time over events, the reverse is true for the cultures represented in the Bible. They prioritize community over individuality, people over tasks, and events over time.[13] Keeping these priorities results in greater honor, and failure to keep them results in greater shame. It is vital we keep this overarching dynamic in mind when we read Scripture.[14]

Overdoing It

We hope you have come to agree with us just how essential it is for us to familiarize ourselves with the ancient world in which the texts of the Bible were produced before attempting to interpret them. That said, let's not forget that interpreting the Bible is not just a science but an art. It is easy to misapply what we have learned, especially if we are inexperienced. Specifically, once we have studied and grown familiar with the historical and cultural setting of a passage, we need to avoid the trap of overstating its relevance. Let me explain.

Because of our limited knowledge and the cultural gap that lies between our world and the biblical world, all historical understandings of the past are approximations.[15] For example, it is universally accepted that messianic hope was at a fever pitch at the time of Christ and that the Jews were yearning for the Messiah to come and restore the (physical) kingdom of Israel.[16] We know that Judas Iscariot was a Jew and can safely assume he was looking for the kingdom to come as well. But is *this* (as is often suggested by scholars and filmmakers) what motivated Judas to betray Jesus? Perhaps. But perhaps not.

The problem is that nowhere does any biblical text suggest this as Judas's motivation. The only things we are told in Scripture about Judas are that he betrayed Jesus for "thirty pieces of silver," that he was a thief, that he did not care about the poor, and that at some point Satan entered his heart.[17] Judas, therefore, is not portrayed as struggling with messianic disillusionment, but with greed. In fact, the Bible tells us Jesus chose him as a disciple despite knowing he was "a devil" (John 6:70-71). It is important in situations like this to match the influence we grant historical data to how certain we are of its sway on the text. And since we have no direct or indirect statements asserting that Judas was motivated by messianic disillusionment, we must be extra careful not to assume this, as it could skew our interpretation of significant passages and unintentionally create a sympathetic, pitiable person.[18] For much of our young adult lives, this is precisely how we felt about Judas. In the back of our minds, we always wondered if Judas got a fair shake.

As you can see, it's easy to overstate a historical insight and create our own meaning. When we do this, we force an idea onto a passage that, while rooted in history, might add something to our interpretation that should bear little or no weight whatsoever. Hopefully, it is easy to see how this can lead to misleading interpretations and hazardous applications and how important it is not to add to the text something that is not intended.[19] As C. S. Lewis once wrote, "Almost anything can be read into any book if you are determined enough."[20] It is our responsibility to make sure, as much as it is possible, that we are only reading into the text what the author either assumes we know or has artfully invited us to read into the text.

Stone Him with Stones

Since properly understanding the historical context can help us discover the true meaning of a passage, let's see if it helps us understand another difficult passage from the Old Testament. In Deuteronomy, there is a challenging section that has often been used by critics and skeptics as an example of why not to believe in the Bible. The passage reads like this:

> [18] If a man has a stubborn and rebellious son who will not obey the voice of his father or the voice of his mother, and, though they discipline him, will not listen to them,
> [19] then his father and his mother shall take hold of him and bring him out to the elders of his city at the gate of the place where he lives, [20] and they shall say to the elders of his city, "This our son is stubborn and rebellious; he will not obey our voice; he is a glutton and a drunkard."
> [21] Then all the men of the city shall stone him to death with stones. So you shall purge the evil from your midst, and all Israel shall hear, and fear.
>
> DEUTERONOMY 21:18-21

At initial reading, this passage seems unnecessarily cruel and harsh to our modern ears. Is God really saying "stubborn and rebellious" children should be stoned to death? From reading the text, the obvious answer seems to be yes, but what should be equally obvious is that it is probably not that simple. When a verse seems over-the-top like this, we should immediately ask ourselves, *What am I missing here?* Before diving into the historical-cultural context of this passage, though, let's examine it from a literary perspective using the guidelines we touched on in the last chapter.

First, we begin by trying to set aside our biases and agendas. Christians must resist the urge to explain away the severity of a passage and must instead let the passage speak for itself. Skeptics must set aside the predispositions that God is, as Richard Dawkins calls him, "a capriciously malevolent bully" and the people of ancient times were barbaric.[21] Neither perspective is accurate nor helpful in understanding the passage.

The author of this passage is traditionally held to be Moses. The date he wrote it, if we accept the biblical witness, is after the exodus from Egypt, sometime just before the Israelites entered the Promised Land of Canaan. The genre is law, and the purpose of this law was to help Israel, a fledgling nation, gain its footing. In the last chapter, we learned that one of the keys to unlocking a law passage is to ask, What is our responsibility before God and the community? In this case, what is the responsibility of Israelite parents if they have a stubborn and rebellious child? As we read over the text, several more questions jump out as well:

- What negative outcome is this law trying to prevent?
- What does it mean to be "stubborn and rebellious" (verses 18 and 20)? Is this phrase used elsewhere in the Bible?

- Why are gluttons and drunkards singled out as opposed to others (see verse 20)?
- Finally, when and how was this law applied?

By answering these questions, we should be able to make sense of this law and see if there is something in it for us today.

So, what is the responsibility of parents to the community if they have a "stubborn and rebellious" child? To bring that child before the community to stone them (see verses 20-21). But! Before they do this, they must first be sure their child's behavior qualifies as rebellious and stubborn. To qualify, the child must be utterly unresponsive, both to instructions and to discipline (see verses 18, 20). In fact, the words "stubborn and rebellious" form a literary device called a *hendiadys* (sort of like "nice and cozy"), which refers specifically to ongoing, continual, remorseless sin, which is not just against the parents but against the community and God himself.[22] To qualify, the sin must also be *egregious*, along the lines of parental abuse. This is clear when other laws of similar consequences are cross-referenced. For example, "Whoever strikes [beats, injures, or kills] his father or his mother shall be put to death. . . . Whoever curses [abuses] his father or his mother shall be put to death" (Exodus 21:15, 17).

"A glutton and a drunkard" (another *hendiadys*) refers to a prodigal, or, as one source states, "a voluptuous profligate."[23] It refers to "those who squander" their very existence, whether their own bodies or their inheritance. This behavior, obviously, would be extremely detrimental to the family, community, and nation's future, especially if the family wealth and land ended up in the hands of enemies. The designation of "a glutton and a drunkard" also suggests that this law was never intended to apply to little children but only to adult children, who are in a unique position to put the family inheritance and future generations at risk.[24]

When we consider that this law was given to a new nation about to possess its own land, and when we look at the laws that precede and follow it, it becomes clear that the purpose of this law was to protect Israel from squandering its national inheritance *from the Lord*, which by pure volume of text indicates this was of utmost importance to God and the people of Israel.[25] This law unmistakably puts the responsibility of safeguarding the inheritance from one generation to the next squarely on the shoulders of individual families.[26] Similar laws are found throughout the ancient world, showing this was a common way to secure a nation's sovereignty and protect a family's honor.[27]

Despite the gravity of the offense, putting someone to death was still a last resort. Think about it. The child's father and mother had to *both* be in agreement that their child was a hopeless cause and putting the entire community at risk. What father or mother would do this? Only those who actually feared losing everything. But even that was not enough. If both parents ever did agree to this, they were next required to drag their child before the elders of the city (verse 19).[28] This requirement not only suggests that the parents had to give their consent but that the city elders needed to give *their* consent as well (verse 20). Finally, if found worthy of death, the actual execution was to be performed by the community (verse 21). That means a sufficient number of people from the community would also have to be in agreement for the execution to take place. It is no wonder that there is no historical evidence this law was ever enforced.[29]

So why would Moses prescribe such a harsh punishment for a stubborn and rebellious child? He was establishing the importance of the family unit and wanted children to take honoring their parents—and their community responsibilities—seriously. Why? Because this would directly determine whether Israel would prosper as a nation. But if this law was never brought to bear (and likely was never meant to be), why record it as sacred text? We suggest that the law, as most laws are, was intended to be preventative. It was aimed specifically at young Israelites to discourage them from squandering their family's inheritance (which was a real and serious possibility, as with Jacob and Esau in Genesis 27–28).

From a salvation-history perspective, this law demonstrates that stubborn rebellion against God (our heavenly Father) deserves death as well. And God wants us to understand this so we understand how compassionate he has been toward us, especially in Christ, who died in our place.[30] In fact, after now reading and interpreting this passage in its proper cultural context, we encourage you to take a few moments to read the parable of the prodigal son (found in Luke 15:11-32) and see how much more meaningful it is. You should be able to relate to all the characters in Jesus' story in a way you likely could not before you took a closer look at this law.

Cultural Sensitivity

Scripture teaches that "a word fitly spoken is like apples of gold in a setting of silver" (Proverbs 25:11). That is, to say the right word to the right person at the right time is a wonderful and beautiful thing. Of course, this also implies that the same word, given at the wrong time to the wrong person, will be despised and rejected.[31] Many people despise and reject Scripture because when they read it, they do not realize it was intended for another time and place. Regardless of our background, we all come to the Bible with assumptions that get in the way of its intended message. Through sincere self-reflection, study, and dedication, let's be more culturally sensitive readers when we read the Bible. Let's never forget that while the Bible was written *for* us, it was not written *to* us.[32] We believe that if you follow this mantra, you will discover that the Bible is not the book you thought it was but something fuller and richer, bursting at the seams with a compelling history and culture all its own.

CHAPTER 9

Doing the Right Thing

False Assumption #5: The Bible Is a Rule Book

Rules are not necessarily sacred; principles are.

FRANKLIN D. ROOSEVELT

In fourth grade, I (Shawn) had an abusive teacher. Mr. Papi (not his real name) could be overly kind at times, allowing us to set up forts in class, choose what music we listened to when we were taking tests, and eat lunch with him in the air-conditioned classroom when it was hot outside. But he had a dark side. When he was not in a gracious mood, if any of us broke even a minor rule, he would draw a circle on the chalkboard. He called it the "circle of shame," and he would force the rule breaker to put their nose in it while he continued to teach.

One day, a classmate asked to use the restroom but did not follow the proper procedure. He was told to put his nose in the "circle of shame." A few minutes later, his nose still planted on the chalkboard, he peed his pants in front of the whole class. Tears rolling down his face, the distressed boy fearfully looked at Mr. Papi, who berated him for not telling him it was an emergency. He then sent him to the office to call his parents to get a change of clothes.

A few weeks later, just before summer break, another classmate broke one of Mr. Papi's inane rules. However, unlike all those who preceded him, my friend refused to put his nose in the "circle of shame." Mr. Papi was livid. He marched angrily over to the boy's seat and dragged him from his desk to the front of the room to force him to accept his punishment. Unfortunately, in the process of compelling him to comply, Mr. Papi slammed him into the chalkboard, smashing his back hard into the metal ledge at the bottom of the board. We did not see Mr. Papi for the remainder of the school year, and by the start of the next year, we were told he was no longer employed at the school.

To this day, when I tell these stories, I cringe. Although I never had to put my nose in the "circle of shame," I dreaded the possibility. Looking back, I'm well aware I broke many of Mr. Papi's rules. I was just lucky I never caught him in one of his less tolerant moods. I also know that what Mr. Papi was doing was wrong, but back then my rule-following instincts dissuaded me from saying anything.

Sadly, many people think of God the same way I think about Mr. Papi. A Christian psychologist might suggest people see God this way because they have been either neglected or abused by various authority figures in their lives. And while this might ring true for some, we suggest they might also see God like this because this is what they have been inadvertently taught about him. This is because the Bible has not been understood as a means of growing closer to God but as a rule book or instruction manual to be followed. And when anyone approaches the Scriptures like this, they will unsurprisingly begin to think of God the way Richard Dawkins describes him:

> The God of the Old Testament is arguably the most unpleasant character in all fiction: jealous and proud of it; a petty, unjust, unforgiving control-freak; a vindictive, bloodthirsty ethnic cleanser; a misogynistic, homophobic, racist, infanticidal, genocidal, filicidal, pestilential, megalomaniacal, sadomasochistic, capriciously malevolent bully.[1]

In other words, he is like Mr. Papi, only far worse. But the Bible is not a rule book, and God is not "a petty, unjust, unforgiving control-freak," despite how he is often unintentionally presented to us to by those who teach and preach about him. When we treat the Bible like a rule book, we will inevitably *universalize*, *spiritualize*, and *moralize* its message.[2] These recurring interpretive pitfalls are the ones, from our experience, that most readers of the Bible—not just skeptics like Mr. Dawkins—fall into time and again.

Common Mistakes

To *universalize* a text is to take something exceptional or unusual and assume it applies to every person, place, or time. For example, we might presume the miracles Jesus and his apostles performed are for us today, or we might think the laws and promises given to ancient Israel apply directly to us as well. When we do this, we will unavoidably fall into the trap of cherry-picking which passages to follow. This reminds us of something Bart Ehrman wrote about determining which Bible verses are authentic and which ones to toss aside:

> Some people may think that it is a dangerous attitude to take toward the Bible, to pick and choose what you want to accept and throw everything else out. My view is that everyone already picks and chooses what they want to accept in the Bible. The most egregious instances of this can be found among people who claim not to be picking and choosing. I have a young friend whose evangelical parents were upset because she wanted to get a tattoo, since the Bible, after all, condemns tattoos. In the same book, Leviticus, the Bible also condemns wearing clothing made of two different kinds of fabric and eating pork. . . . Why insist on the biblical teaching about tattoos but not about dress shirts, pork chops, and stoning?[3]

Ehrman's response raises a valid point about how many Christians are selective in which rules they follow. This is the problem we encounter when we universalize Scriptures without first contextualizing them. (We will discuss how to do this later in the chapter.) Fortunately, now aware of this interpretive error, we can more readily avoid it. That said, this does not mean the law is irrelevant. The commands and laws given throughout the Bible all reveal something about God and have their proper place.

To *spiritualize* a text is to take a straightforward passage and read into it a deeper spiritual or hidden meaning. When we spiritualize a text, we rob Scripture of its authority as we favor the personalized "spiritual message" or "allegory" over the plain meaning of the passage.[4] As a case in point, a favorite passage people like to inappropriately spiritualize is the story of when Jesus calmed a violent storm, as told in Matthew 8:23-27. When we hear this story, we typically, almost instinctively, identify with the disciples on the boat and identify the storm with the hardships and chaos of life. The problem with this interpretation is not necessarily that we end up believing something false. Rather, it completely misses the point of the story. The story is about Jesus and his power over the forces of nature. The disciples' lack of faith was not a failure to trust God in their circumstances. It was a failure to understand who Jesus is. By now, after the miracles they had witnessed, they should have come to realize that Jesus was more than an average human being or messenger of God. This is reflected in their final question: "What *sort of man* is this, that even winds and sea obey him?" (Matthew 8:27, emphasis added). This is the subject of the passage and the question we should be asking and answering when we read it.

Spiritualizing a text is attractive to anyone who reads and teaches the Bible. It requires less effort to interpret and apply. But cutting corners in life is never a good idea, and it is an even worse idea when interpreting and applying Scripture. It can lead to many wrong ideas about how God operates and relates to us in this world. There are no promises God will calm the storms in our lives if we trust him. Think about it. If we are the disciples and the storm is the chaos of our lives, what does it represent that Jesus was "in the stern, asleep on the cushion" (Mark 4:38)? So why did the Gospel writers include this story? To reveal what they came to know: that Jesus, who was completely human—as demonstrated by his being asleep in the boat—has power, not just over sickness and illness, but over all nature. Therefore, he must be the prophesied Messiah, the Son of God! And given that he performs this miracle by his own power, he must be not only human but divine.[5]

Finally, to *moralize* a text is to derive principles for living from passages that do not call for it and without understanding their context first. Moralizing a text insists on asking, "What is the moral of the story?" when there is none. Of all the errors common to interpreting the Bible, this is the most pervasive and, in our opinion, the most dangerous. Why? Because moralizing a passage reinforces some pretty horrific conclusions. Perhaps this is why the apostle Paul warns, "The letter [of the law] kills, but the Spirit gives life" (2 Corinthians 3:6).

For example, how many of us remember the Sunday school story of when a couple of she-bears tore up a group of little boys for teasing the prophet Elisha for being bald? How terrifying, right? If you were especially unlucky, like us, you might have had the scene depicted with flannelgraphs or in your Sunday school handout. We remember thinking, *What a far cry this is from Jesus, who said, "Father, forgive them" when he was mocked and ridiculed as he hung on the cross!* The "moral" of the story was hammered home: Do not poke fun at other people, especially your balding elders or church leaders, or you, too, might end up as bear food!

Regrettably, the above interpretation is how most people have learned the passage. It is how we learned it too. So, many skeptics point to this verse as another reason to doubt the authority and trustworthiness of the Bible. Most commentaries are not very helpful in getting to the bottom of this strange passage either. So, let's see if we can come to a better understanding—one that avoids moralizing it. Making sure we are not allowing biases to sway our interpretation—such as the way we were taught the passage when we were children—let's briefly dive into this exceedingly misunderstood passage.

Suffer the Little Children?

> 23He [Elisha] went up from there to Bethel, and while he
> was going up on the way, some small boys came out of
> the city and jeered at him, saying, "Go up, you baldhead!

> Go up, you baldhead!" [24]And he turned around, and when he saw them, he cursed them in the name of the LORD. And two she-bears came out of the woods and tore forty-two of the boys. [25]From there he went on to Mount Carmel, and from there he returned to Samaria.
>
> 2 KINGS 2:23-25

When Elisha travels to Bethel, he is confronted by a group of what most English translations call some variation of "little children" or "small boys." It might come as a surprise that the Hebrew expression translated "little children" (*na'arim qatanim*) has a wide range of meanings.[6] The noun *na'ar* can refer to a baby, a young man, or a young servant, such as an armor-bearer, king's official, priest, construction worker, or warrior.[7] It most commonly refers to a young man between twelve and thirty years old.[8] The word emphasizes youthfulness and greenness, not so much a specific age group. The adjective *qatan* is used to describe something or someone that is small or young, but it, too, has a wide range of meanings. It is frequently used to describe young men and women of marriageable or working age.[9] When combined, the two words elsewhere describe someone young and inexperienced (a novice) for whatever role they're in, such as Hadad the Edomite and Solomon, who were both around twenty years old when they took the throne.[10] In light of this, it is probably best to understand Elisha's mockers not as small boys or little children but as novices.

But novices at what? Seeing as they hail from Bethel, the capital of the northern kingdom of Israel and a stronghold of Baal worship, these novices were likely attendants to the priests and prophets of Baal.[11] That there are forty-two of them suggests they might have been acting like a street gang on this day and that the prophet's life was in danger.[12] Notice how this interpretation, which is rooted in history and avoids moralizing the text, makes better sense of the passage and fits the topic of the chapter: the passing of the prophetic mantle from Elijah to Elisha.

But why is Elisha bald and why did these young upstarts make fun of him for being bald? It is likely not because he suffered from alopecia, but because he had shaved his head in mourning of his mentor Elijah's recent departure.[13] Shaving the head bald was a common custom to mark that one was in mourning.[14] So when the young novices of the Bethel shrine yell, "Go up, you baldhead" (verse 23), they are mocking Elisha's grief and intimidating him to go away just as his master did. These false prophets are taunting Elisha and challenging God's new prophet, claiming Bethel as their own.[15] Elisha steps up to the challenge, and God wins the day again. It is not by chance that Elisha moves on to Mount Carmel after this episode (verse 25), the place where Elijah also had a great victory over Baal and his servants.[16]

So when we follow basic principles of interpretation, we see this brief story is but another episode in the war between the God of the Bible (Yahweh) and the Canaanite god Baal. It recalls the first two commandments, which are there to keep us from becoming deceived by false gods and trapped in idolatry. Only when we moralize this narrative does it turn into a horrible story of God slaughtering little children because they made fun of a bald person.

Context, Context, Context

The phrases *he was caught stealing*, *he was thrown out*, and *we were robbed* mean something different when said at a bank instead of a ballpark. This illustrates the importance of contextualizing our words, especially the words of the Bible.[17] So the final task of interpreting a Bible passage is to *contextualize* it to properly apply and communicate it for today.[18] This is a necessary final step, and, much as painters or poets expect their admirers to interpret and contextualize their work, the Bible expects and invites us to use it in the same way.[19] But properly applying the Scriptures, as we've already seen, is no simple task. Theologian Jennine Brown points out,

> Contextualizing the message of Scripture for our own settings is not simply an add-on. . . . It is integrally related to a careful study of the biblical text in its own context so that we might hear it rightly in ours. Contextualization is about taking the message of Scripture so seriously that it shapes and directs our whole selves—our being, our thinking, and our doing.[20]

Until this point, we have stressed that we cannot determine what a passage means to us until we figure out what it meant when it was written. We have stressed that "to apply a passage accurately, we must define the situation into which the revelation was originally given." Once this task is completed, and all necessary work has been done to interpret a passage accurately, we can finally ask the million-dollar question: What does it mean for *us*?[21]

To answer this question, we must first determine what we in the modern world do and do not share in common with the original readers. The more analogous a situation, the more the message will resonate with us. Second, we must keep in mind that while almost every law or command has some transcendent moral component to it, this is not necessarily true for other literary forms.[22] Even so, all Scripture, by its very nature, is transhistorical; that is, no matter the historical or geographical distance of a passage, if it is properly contextualized, we should be able to apply it to whatever time and place we reside in now. This is what we mean when we say the Bible was written *for us*.[23]

But, again, be mindful that the Bible was not primarily written to give us a collection of rules to live by so we can live "good lives." It was written to reveal God and his plan of salvation throughout history. *This is its primary purpose.* And it does this through different authors, literary forms, and historical settings. Every strange law, odd story, poignant poem, and passionate prophecy ultimately fits into this grand narrative. "Scripture's true purpose transcends the mundane and draws us into the mystery of God's person, God's love, and God's promises."[24] Lastly, in order to answer our million-dollar question, we must locate the timeless principles in a given passage so we can contextualize them. We will now discuss how to do this.

The Art of Contextualization

The art of contextualization is rooted in the process of taking what is concrete in one culture, distilling it into abstract principles, and then condensing it into our contemporary culture. Familiarity with Hayakawa's "Abstraction Ladder" can help in this process.[25] Here it is in visual form:

Wealth

Asset

Farm Asset

Livestock

Cow

Bessie the Cow

Notice that the higher we are on the ladder, the more abstract the subject is. The more abstract it is, the more universally understood it is. The lower we are on the ladder, the more concrete the subject is. The more concrete it is, the more contextualized it is. As we move up the ladder, we move from what is *concrete* to what is *abstract*, what is *tangible* to what is *intangible*, and what is *locally understood* to what is *universally understood*. This is because concrete things naturally belong to their own historical setting, but abstract things belong to any setting.

The New Testament provides several examples of how to contextualize using the above concept. For instance, the apostle Paul takes a very specific law from the Old Testament (found in Deuteronomy 25:4) and applies it to the Christian life:

> The law of Moses says, "You must not muzzle an ox to keep it from eating as it treads out the grain." Was God thinking only about oxen when he said this? Wasn't he actually speaking to us? Yes, it was written for us, so that the one who plows and the one who threshes the grain might both expect a share of the harvest.
>
> 1 CORINTHIANS 9:9-10, NLT

> Elders who do their work well should be respected and paid well, especially those who work hard at both preaching and teaching. For the Scripture says, "You must not muzzle an ox to keep it from eating as it treads out the grain." And in another place, "Those who work deserve their pay!"
>
> 1 TIMOTHY 5:17-18, NLT

Notice how Paul climbs up and down the ladder of abstraction in his interpretation.[26] Here is a breakdown of his process of interpretation:

- Do not muzzle an ox while it treads out grain. (Concrete)
  - Do not starve a farm animal that is working to feed you. (Less concrete)
    - *Do not fail to provide for a worker who provides for your sustenance.* (Abstract)
  - Do not fail to take care of a church worker who ministers to you. (Less concrete)
- Do not fail to pay the pastor at your church who preaches the Word of God to you. (Concrete)

Now let's do this for ourselves, looking at another, similar law:

> When you build a new house, you shall make a parapet for your roof, that you may not bring the guilt of blood upon your house, if anyone should fall from it.
>
> DEUTERONOMY 22:8

First, the original context of this law should be established. Historically speaking, the Israelites were about to enter the Promised Land, where they would need to build new houses. Unlike our typical homes today, the roof then was often used as an additional room.[27] It would take extra money and time to add walls around the roof, so it would have been tempting to cut a few corners and not build these walls, despite the possible danger of someone falling. Now, let's contextualize it:[28]

- When you build a new house, you shall make a parapet for your roof, so people don't fall. (Concrete)

- When you build, build safe structures, regardless of the cost, so people don't get hurt. (Less concrete)
  - *When you build something, make the safety of others a priority.* (Abstract)

In the above interpretation, we intentionally left off the application portion of the contextualization process. How would you complete it if you were starting your own restaurant or home childcare business? What if you were adding a new room to your house or building a patio? Or what if you were purchasing a new building for your church? Finally, what does the fact that God wants us to make safety a priority say about his character?

The above technique can be used across the board when interpreting laws, customs, and traditions. It gives us an artful and accessible way to take ancient rules from the Bible and rightly place them in our contemporary context. It can help us make practical sense out of seemingly strange and bizarre texts, such as food laws and peculiar cultural customs that are no longer observed (such as wearing two kinds of fabrics, getting tattoos for the dead, and washing the feet of your guests).

One word of caution: When using this method, we must make sure we do not get lost in the process. To help make sure we stay on course, we must end the contextualization process by asking ourselves the following questions:

- Has the spirit of the law, custom, or tradition been maintained?
- Would the author go along with our contextualization?
- Does it complement the rest of Scripture, or does it subvert it?
- Does it fit what we know about God and his character from other biblical passages?

Using all we have learned so far about interpreting a text, let's interpret a passage that has often been used to support the idea that Christians pick and choose what commands they follow in the Bible.

To Kiss or Not to Kiss—That Is the Question

> Finally, brothers, rejoice. Aim for restoration, comfort one another, agree with one another, live in peace; and the God of love and peace will be with you. Greet one another with a holy kiss. All the saints greet you.
>
> The grace of the Lord Jesus Christ and the love of God and the fellowship of the Holy Spirit be with you all.
>
> 2 CORINTHIANS 13:11-14

At the end of four of his letters, Paul instructs the church to "greet one another with a holy kiss" (Romans 16:16; 1 Corinthians 16:20; 2 Corinthians 13:12; 1 Thessalonians 5:26). Peter, at the end of his first letter, directs his readers to do the same, only he dubs it "the kiss of love" (1 Peter 5:14). Since this command is clearly stated in multiple places and modeled elsewhere,[29] one might ask whether we should be doing this in our churches today. And if we choose not to follow this command, isn't this a clear example of picking and choosing which verses to follow and which verses not to follow? And if we are not going to follow the command, what relevance does this passage have for us today? Using the tools we've learned, let's see if we can answer these questions in a meaningful way.

A kiss in the ancient world was a common expression within families and in other social contexts. It conveyed more than just affection, though. It also communicated loyalty and respect (especially to someone of higher status). It was not the passionate caress that we think of today; it was not given on the mouth but on the cheek, forehead, hand, and even the feet.[30] But to interpret it as merely a common custom would be to underestimate its significance. Publicly, it was often used to seal a contract or treaty, as a way of congratulating the victor at the games, or as a means of paying homage to the emperor or a dignitary. Kisses also played a significant role in religion, often associated with entrance into a pagan cult and signifying the close relationship between a mentor and an initiate.[31] Beyond this, as a form of *public* greeting, it was likely limited to a rural setting. Dio Chrysostom, a first-century Greek historian, writes about an embarrassing situation in which a farmer greeted an old friend he came across in the city with a kiss, only to be laughed at by those nearby. Chrysostom notes, "Then I understood that in the cities people do not kiss one another."[32]

Of significance is that Paul exhorts his readers from *Corinth*, a bustling metropolis, to greet one another with a *holy* kiss.[33] Some groups today (for example, Orthodox churches) believe this suggests that the kiss was a Christian ritual and an important part of church worship.[34] Paul's use of the word "holy" then would have been used to distinguish it from the *unholy* kiss associated with pagan cult practices. But is this what Paul had in mind when he encouraged church members to "*greet* one another with a holy kiss"? Surely, Paul's use of "holy" distinguishes it from any common kiss. Still, we do not need to assume a liturgical or religious act to explain his meaning, which is not suggested by the text at all. It can be difficult to differentiate between religious and cultural aspects in Scripture. But Paul places this instruction exclusively at the *end* of his letters, which is typically reserved for personal greetings. And based on how it is modeled in the Gospels and the book of Acts, it is clear that Paul's purpose is not to push a liturgical act of worship. Rather, he wishes to commend familial loyalty and unity among Christians through this symbolic act.[35]

For Paul and the early church, a "holy kiss" was a way of symbolically communicating a spiritual or theological truth—that all Christians are members of one family. This interpretation is supported by the fact that Paul calls them "brothers,"[36] speaks of unity (verse 11), and refers to them as saints (literally, "*holy* ones," verse 13).[37] That Paul calls them "brothers and sisters" and insists they greet one another with a "holy kiss" in the same breath is not insignificant, for "the tightest unit of loyalty and affection" in the ancient Mediterranean world was that of siblings.[38] Whereas the marriage bond is considered the most sacred bond today, in the days of the early church it was the sibling bond.[39] When Paul wrote to the Corinthians, he was aware that they were immature in their faith, easily dividing over various issues.[40] So Paul's entire closing remarks are all about promoting unity. This answers the question, What specific occasion caused Paul to write this passage? Even in his final benediction is a rare direct appeal to the Trinity. Usually, if at all, Paul mentions only God the Father and the Lord Jesus, but this time he also includes a prayer that the Corinthians might experience the "fellowship of the Holy Spirit" (verse 14). It is in this context that Paul tells them to "greet one another with a holy kiss." The "holy kiss"—as opposed to the common social kiss—is a physical, intimate expression of Christian unity and liberty that breaks down barriers between sex, race, and social class, for the kiss was to be exchanged by "all the saints" (2 Corinthians 1:1).[41] Considering that Corinth was a diverse and cosmopolitan city, this fact alone is astounding and fits nicely into the story of salvation history, in which God's redeeming love is for all those made in his image.[42]

In Thessalonica, where the threat of persecution was constant, the exhortation to "greet *all* the brothers and sisters with a holy kiss" would have also served the purpose of strengthening the bond of the church that was under constant pressure to abandon their faith and turn on each other.[43] The audience probably remembered Christ's poignant words as well: "Judas, would you betray the Son of Man with a kiss?" (Luke 22:47-48). The irony here is powerful. Judas was taking a symbol of familial loyalty and love and using it to betray Jesus. This vile act is not lost on Jesus. The word "holy," then, also serves as a contrast to Judas's infamous *unholy* kiss of betrayal.[44]

Having established the literary and historical context first, we can now apply the ladder of abstraction to properly contextualize the passage for us today. When the apostle Paul instructs early Christians to "greet one another with a holy kiss," he is encouraging them to act like a close-knit family. The "holy" kiss itself was a concrete expression of this loyal love and familial unity toward one another. So while the instruction to kiss one another is not a moral requirement, the principles of love, loyalty, and respect are. And these are things all Christians should practice. This answers the question, What is a Christian's covenant responsibility before God and the community? And while some will insist that only a kiss fulfills Paul's command here, this would be treating the Bible like a rule book and missing the point of the passage. The kiss itself is not what is important. What is important is what it symbolizes. In fact, a kiss might convey something altogether different today, especially where esteemed members of various churches have abused their positions of trust.

We (living in Southern California) ask ourselves, *What symbolic act might express warm, familial love without too much risk of being misunderstood or exploited?* Some have suggested replacing the kiss with a hug or handshake. We have attended some local churches that include a time in their worship service to do just this. But even in this we must be cautious. If Paul were alive today, would he really call Christians to greet one another with "holy" hugs or handshakes, especially considering the recent moral failures of those in positions of authority, even within the church?

While greeting others with a kiss was common to first-century rural families, it was something city dwellers laughed at, not cringed at or questioned the propriety of. Perhaps due to the currently increased sensitivity to sexual exploitation, nothing in our culture today can adequately reflect the "holy kiss" of the ancient world. But certainly a church wishing to show its bond of love can still greet and treat one another "like family" by making an intentional effort to converse and interact respectfully with *all* members, not only those who fit their preferred identity circles. Of course, to fulfill the spirit of Paul's command to "greet one another with a holy kiss," the church must interact not in words only but in actions and deeds as well. For example, opening a door for someone or giving up a seat could very much communicate the same thing as a holy kiss and be less likely to be misunderstood. And what should it communicate? All who put their faith in Jesus Christ are our family, regardless of their race, sex, or social class.

One Rule to Rule Them All

As you have probably figured out, while the Bible is not a rule book, it still has a lot to say about doing the right thing.[45] Fortunately, when it comes to the ethical teachings in the Bible, Jesus revealed to us the highest rung of every ladder of abstraction. He taught us that the entire law and all the demands of the prophets boil down to two commandments:

> "You must love the LORD your God with all your heart, all your soul, and all your mind." This is the first and greatest commandment. A second is equally important: "Love your neighbor as yourself." The entire law and all the demands of the prophets are based on these two commandments.
>
> MATTHEW 22:37-40, NLT

So whenever we interpret a passage of Scripture, no matter its genre or literary context, if there is an ethical teaching to be found, we can quickly get to the bottom of it by asking, How specifically does this passage teach the original audience to love God and their neighbor? Once we answer that question, we will find it much easier to contextualize the passage for us today.

So That We Might Have Hope

Mahatma Gandhi is reported to have said, "You Christians look after a document containing enough dynamite to blow all civilization to pieces, turn the world upside down, and bring peace to a battle-torn planet. But you treat it as though it is nothing more than a piece of literature."[46] Or, as we've seen in this chapter, as nothing more than a rule book for life. While it is true that the Hebrew Scriptures have over six hundred laws and the New Testament has over a thousand commands, if we treat the Bible as if it is only a rule book, not only will we miss the point of most passages, but we will drive ourselves and others to the conclusion that

God is, recalling the words of Richard Dawkins, "a petty, unjust, unforgiving control-freak." That said, if we avoid the pitfalls of *universalizing*, *spiritualizing*, and *moralizing* the Bible, it is possible to contextualize its ancient revelation for our modern lives in such a way that does not distort its true, intended message. For we believe that "whatever was written in former days was written for our instruction, that through endurance and through the encouragement of the Scriptures we might have hope" (Romans 15:4). And, in the end, "every word of God proves true" (Proverbs 30:5).

CHAPTER 10

Behind the Times

False Assumption #6: The Bible Is a History Book

History is not the past, but a map of the past drawn from a particular point of view to be useful to the modern traveler.

HENRY GLASSIE

A little over twenty years ago, the Middle East Media Research Institute (MEMRI) released a bulletin announcing that Dr. Nabil Hilmi, dean of the law school of Egypt's Zagazig University, and a group of Egyptian expatriates, were of the mindset to bring a lawsuit against "all the Jews of the world." The contents of the bulletin were an excerpt of an interview with Hilmi in which he claimed that the Jews stole "gold, jewelry, cooking utensils, silver ornaments, clothing, and more" and fled Egypt "in the middle of the night with all this wealth, which today is priceless." Based on the description found in the book of Exodus, which records the gold and other articles used to furnish the Tabernacle, Hilmi estimated that around three hundred tons of gold were plundered.[1]

As expected, the majority of the non-Islamic world found this imaginative case amusing and treated the potential lawsuit as little more than a symbolic stunt. Many critics, even in Islamic circles, warned Hilmi that his case was a legal catch-22, for "by presenting the Bible as evidence in a lawsuit, Hilmi [was] legitimizing the use of the Bible as a history book and [was] thus actually promoting Israel's claim to the Holy Land."[2] One Islamic expert cautioned that "such a lawsuit paves the way to acceptance of the Zionist claims" and "the Bible [as] an historic document." Another criticized the lawsuit as lacking all sense and said that filing the lawsuit would "grant actual contemporary legitimacy to the text of the Bible, which gives Israel the right to adhere to plundering the entire land of historic Palestine."[3] Perhaps because of these admonitions, Dr. Nabil Hilmi's complaint against the Jewish people, despite drawing significant media attention, never culminated in any court procedures or judgments.

What is of interest to us in the above story is not the case itself but how the Bible is viewed by those involved. Hilmi clearly regards the Bible as a historical document and wants to use it to substantiate the crimes he believes happened against his country thousands of years ago. His fellow Islamists worry that in doing so, he would be "legitimizing the use of the Bible as a history book," which, in their minds, would have the undesired outcome of "promoting Israel's claim to the Holy Land." Their dilemma helps raise an important question for us, not about who owns the land but about whether the Bible is a history book.

History in the Making

A historical document is a writing that has historical value. This typically refers to an original document, a primary source, that contains or provides important historical information about a person, place, or event. Historical documents allow researchers to get as close as possible to what happened during an event or time period.

When compared with other historical documents of antiquity, the Bible is as informative and accurate as any of them, if not more so. While it is beyond the scope of this book to offer a defense of the historicity of the Bible, let's consider a few renowned experts who through meticulous research have come to this conclusion. Even though the Bible is a religious book—or more specifically, a collection of sacred writings—it has been deemed by most scholars a trustworthy and reliable guide in what it records about people, places, and events.

First, consider the late professor Robert D. Wilson of Princeton. He was a highly esteemed linguist who held several doctorates and mastered forty-five languages and dialects, reading with ease from ancient manuscripts, especially those of the Near East.[4] He provided exhaustive research and an irrefutable defense of the veracity and integrity of the Hebrew Scriptures based on lingual evidence. It is not possible here to examine his work in detail, but he shows there is more than reasonable grounds "for concluding that the text of the Old Testament which we have is substantially correct, and that, in its true and obvious meaning, it has [the] right to be considered a part of the 'infallible rule of faith and practice' that we have in the Holy Scriptures."[5]

Next, we turn to Sir William Ramsay, a leading archaeologist and New Testament scholar. In his day, he was the recognized authority on the history of Asia Minor.[6] He attests to the historicity of the Bible, and particularly to Luke's ability as a historian. He boldly asserts that "Luke's history is unsurpassed in respect of its trustworthiness,"[7] and adds this praise for the biblical author:

> Luke is a historian of the first rank; not merely are his statements of fact trustworthy; he is possessed of the true historic sense; he fixes his mind on the idea and plan that rules in the evolution of history; and proportions the scale of his treatment to the importance of each incident. He seizes the important and critical events and shows their true nature at greater length, while he touches lightly or omits entirely much that was valueless for his purpose. In short, this author should be placed along with the very greatest of historians.[8]

Taking into consideration that he began as a full-fledged skeptic, Ramsay's witness is persuasive, especially since he claims it was his study and research as an archaeologist that led him to this conclusion.[9] He credits his conversion to the book of Acts, asserting that it can withstand the most intense examination and that "it was written with such judgment, skill, art, and perception of truth as to be a model of historical statement."[10]

Another expert to consider is Nelson Glueck, recognized as one of the world's foremost biblical archaeologists. His record of archaeological achievements is unparalleled. During his years of research, he discovered and excavated over 1,500 archaeological sites, including King Solomon's mines, and he served as president of Hebrew Union College from 1947 until his death in 1971.[11] This is what he writes about the Bible:

> As a matter of fact, however, it may be stated categorically that no archaeological discovery has ever controverted a Biblical reference. Scores of archaeological findings have been made which confirm in clear outline or in exact detail historical statements in the Bible. And, by the same

> token, proper evaluation of Biblical descriptions has often led to amazing discoveries. They form tesserae in the vast mosaic of the Bible's almost incredibly correct historical memory.[12]

Finally, in addition to the above men, the Smithsonian, a group of museums and research centers noted for their strong naturalistic worldview, has this to say about the Bible:

> Much of the Bible, in particular the historical books of the Old Testament, are as accurate historical documents as any that we have from antiquity and are in fact more accurate than many of the Egyptian, Mesopotamian, or Greek histories. These Biblical records can be and are used as are other ancient documents in archeological work. For the most part, historical events described took place and the peoples cited really existed.[13]

The above testimonies to the Bible's historicity do not in and of themselves prove everything in it is true, but they put to rest the suggestions that the Bible is a collection of legends and is full of geographical and historical mistakes.[14] It also should silence the notion that trusting in the Bible is akin to believing in stories about fairies or modern-day folkloric fictions such as Santa Claus, the Easter Bunny, or the tooth fairy.[15]

Ancient History?

The Bible's reputation for accuracy has led many people to treat it like an ancient history book. However, while the Bible is historical and does contain verifiably accurate history, it should not be thought of in this manner—at least not in an academic or formal sense.[16] Modern history books, ideally, are the product of scientific discovery, systematically seeking to precisely communicate human actions from the past and interpret whatever evidence there is with the goal of better understanding humankind.[17] This requires exactitude in naming involved persons, dates, and geographical locations. History books are an effort to open a window into the past, especially as it relates to *human beings* and how we have progressed or regressed through the passage of time. Ideally, they are produced with a desire to understand and explain the past as objectively as possible.[18] History books are typically laid out in chronological order and reflect on historical causes and effects. Despite being historically reliable, the Bible does not meet these criteria, disqualifying it as a history book. Let us explain.

While the Bible has a lot to say about human behavior and the natural world, we rightly do not think of it as a psychology or natural science book. Why not? Because it does not comprehensively cover those subjects or explore them in a scientific or systematic way. Likewise, we should not think of the Bible as a history book, as history is not its primary concern. As Glueck explains, "[The Bible] is above all concerned with true religion and only secondarily with illustrative records. Even if the latter had suffered through faulty transmission or embellishments, the purity and primacy of the Bible's innermost message would not thereby be diminished."[19]

In fact, without secondary sources, it is impossible to put together a complete history of Israel or the early church.[20] This is because the biblical authors are "highly selective" in the matters they choose to report on and write about.[21] As a general rule, they are not concerned about transmitting *precise* historic information when it is irrelevant to their purpose. It is essential that when we interpret the Bible, we bear all this in mind. Even *The Chicago Statement on Biblical Inerrancy* acknowledges that biblical narratives are often nonchronological and imprecise.[22] As Carl F. H. Henry, who signed and first published the original statement, explicitly states, "The Bible is not a textbook on science or on history."[23]

To approach a biblical text as one would a history book is a recipe for interpretive disaster. The problem with assuming the Bible is a history book is that it distracts from its essential message and character, causing an interpreter to miss the mark of what it is saying. When the authors of the Bible report history, they do so not for the sake of later historical discovery but to contextualize the passage and reveal the God of history.[24] This is why when someone approaches the Bible as a history book, it inevitably results in false conclusions that there are blatant contradictions or mistakes in it. So when we study the Bible, especially historical narrative portions, we must be careful not to approach it as a history book but instead as a religious text that contains history.

Making Progress: Intertextuality

Approaching the Bible as a religious text means we can cautiously open our interpretive gate just a little wider. Until this point in the book, we have focused mostly on the *history* part of "salvation history," interpreting Scripture almost exclusively through its historical and literary context. Now, we want to focus more on the *salvation* part, which has its own method of interpretation. This method has been common to the community of faith for thousands of years and is what Jewish and Christian scholars refer to as the *intertextual method.* This method is firmly rooted in the idea that the Bible is one grand story. As history progresses, God slowly reveals more and more about himself. It is a means of understanding earlier texts of the Bible in the light of later revelations.[25] The strength of this method is that it takes seriously both the unity and prophetic nature of the Bible—that as more biblical material was gathered, new revelation was built upon old revelation. The *intertextual method* leans heavily on the idea that the kaleidoscope of texts that comprise the Bible form one cohesive whole and have one "big idea" tying them all together.

Think of this interpretive method like enjoying a well-written mystery for the second time. Once you know the end of the story, the next time you read it, you experience it in a completely different (and more accurate) way. Events, conversations, actions, and behaviors are all reinterpreted and better understood.[26] In other words, the final revelation informs all previous revelations. Small things that once seemed petty or trivial (for example, Deuteronomy 21:22-23: "anyone who is hung [on a tree] is cursed" [NLT]) take on unmistakable importance. When we approach the Bible this way—something it invites us to do—we will recognize everywhere clues such as allusions, patterns, and foreshadowing that we missed the first time we read it.

As for God's motives for revealing himself in a progressive manner, we refer back to chapter 6, where we discussed the clarity of Scripture and the elusiveness of God. In addition to this, let's be mindful that the sacred Scriptures have come to us through manifold genres, including mystery and riddle, which is often overlooked by biblical scholarship.[27] Perhaps this is because they are usually found tucked away within other genres. Anytime the text does not disclose the essential details about a revelation, it leaves a mystery for us to ponder. The greatest of those mysteries in the Hebrew Scriptures surrounds the person and work of the future "son of David," the Messiah. When Jesus finally reveals himself as the Messiah and executes his plan to save the world on the stage of history, suddenly everything else in the Scriptures takes on new meaning and makes greater sense—from the seed that would crush the head of the serpent, to the animal sacrifices, to the virgin birth, to the founding of the church on the day of Pentecost.

Taking Jesus Seriously

For the record, we hold the intertextual approach as both true and sound not because it is self-evident but because, like the apostles and the authors of the New Testament, we take seriously Jesus' insistence that the (Hebrew) Scriptures ultimately speak about him and anticipate his history-changing work of redemption.[28] For example, in his Sermon on the Mount, Jesus taught his disciples and the listening crowd, "Do not think that I have come to abolish the Law or the Prophets; I have not come to abolish them but to fulfill them. For truly, I say to you, until heaven and earth pass away, not an iota, not a dot, will pass from the Law until all is accomplished" (Matthew 5:17-18). Jesus also said to the Jewish religious leaders of his day, "You search the Scriptures because you think that in them you have eternal life; and it is they that bear witness about me. . . . For if you believed Moses, you would believe me; for he wrote of me" (John 5:39, 46).

According to Luke, on the day Jesus rose from the dead, he encouraged two disciples on the road to Emmaus, "O foolish ones, and slow of heart to believe all that the prophets have spoken! Was it not necessary that the Christ should suffer these things and enter into his glory?" Then "beginning with Moses and all the Prophets, he interpreted to them in all the Scriptures the things concerning himself" (Luke 24:25-27). Later that day, Jesus taught his followers,

> "These are my words that I spoke to you while I was still with you, that everything written about me in the Law of Moses and the Prophets and the Psalms must be fulfilled." Then he opened their minds to understand the Scriptures, and said to them, "Thus it is written, that the Christ should suffer and on the third day rise from the dead, and that repentance for the forgiveness of sins should be proclaimed in his name to all nations, beginning from Jerusalem."
>
> LUKE 24:44-47

Jesus forces us to reconsider our purely humanistic interpretations and reshape them according to the revelation that he is the hope of Israel and the Savior of the world. Since the Bible is the history of salvation and has Christ as its driving force and everything revolves around him, this should profoundly affect the way we interpret it.[29] J. C. Ryle describes it this way:

> Let it be a settled principle in our minds in reading the Bible that Christ is the central sun of the whole book. So long as we keep Him in view, we shall never greatly err in our search for spiritual knowledge. Once losing sight of Christ, we shall find the whole Bible dark and full of difficulty. The key to Bible knowledge is Jesus Christ.[30]

So after we have understood a passage in its historical and literary context and determined its place in salvation history, we can and should properly ask the following questions:

- How does this text help clarify other texts written elsewhere?
- How does this passage anticipate or point to Jesus and his mission?

- Does the passage directly speak about Jesus Christ? If not, does it foreshadow his life or work?
- Is it part of a pattern or type? If yes, where does the pattern or type reach its climax?

David's Census

Before concluding this chapter, let's glance at two parallel passages that help demonstrate the lessons we have hopefully learned in this chapter:

2 Samuel 24:1	1 Chronicles 21:1
Again the anger of the LORD was kindled against Israel, and he incited David against them, saying, "Go, number Israel and Judah."	Then Satan stood against Israel and incited David to number Israel.

If we were to approach the texts above as if they were snippets from two different history books, we might jump to the conclusion that they give contradictory accounts of why David performed his imprudent census of Israel and Judah. The author of 2 Samuel identifies *Yahweh* (the Lord) as the instigator, while the chronicler identifies *Satan* as the impetus for David's census.[31] Many skeptics have noted the blatant contradiction in these two records. But is this how we should interpret these passages? Do we simply dismiss one verse as a mistake and move on?

When both chapters detailing David's census are read side by side (2 Samuel 24 and 1 Chronicles 21), many other discrepancies stand out as well. For example, the census numbers and the price David paid to Araunah/Ornan to purchase the future site of the Temple do not line up with each other. This adds further weight to the contention that one of the texts is in error.[32] However, when we make a genuine effort not to read them as a history book, we quickly realize that neither author is concerned about precise totals.[33] Rounded numbers, different accounting methods, and varying specifics for the most part resolve these minor issues and have no bearing on the meaning of the text.[34]

So let's ask again: Who incited David to take a census? Was it the Lord (Yahweh) or Satan? To answer these questions, we must first figure out *when* each book was written, *why* it was written, and *what* the author and his readers knew about the relationship between God, Satan, and humankind. The books of Samuel were written to warn and inspire future rulers of Israel. The Chronicles were written several hundred years later as supplements to the books of Samuel and to bring hope to the postexilic nation of Israel, specifically by connecting them to their glorious past. At the time the books of Samuel were written, there was very little knowledge about Satan and the role he plays in the affairs of humankind. The chronicler, on the other hand, had access to two important sources in his day: the book of Job and the prophecies of Zechariah. In these two occurrences the name "Satan" is preceded by an article, intimating that it was originally a title (which when translated means "the adversary").[35] However, in 1 Chronicles 21:1, there is no definite article, suggesting that over time what was once a title had developed into a personal name.[36]

Putting this all together, the chronicler likely took the theological insight gained through the book of Job and applied it to the account he found in 2 Samuel.[37] For in Job's account, "there is a mysterious sense" in which God uses Satan without Job's knowledge to accomplish his will.[38] Of course, the revelation of Satan as the archenemy of the people of God continues to develop until it is fully realized in the New Testament. In the New Testament, he tempts Jesus in the wilderness, binds people with crippling ailments, fills the heart of Judas, sifts Peter, hinders the spread of the gospel, and sends one of his messengers to be a thorn in the side of Paul. Finally, he makes his monstrous appearance in the book of Revelation, where no longer working behind the scenes, he actively seeks to devour and destroy God's people.[39] Amazingly, in every one of these instances, God in his wisdom uses Satan to accomplish his will.

Returning to our initial passage, we notice that there is no mention of why the Lord is so angry with and, therefore, against *Israel* that he would permit Satan to incite David to take a census that leads to the death of many Israelites.[40] There is also no obvious reason given as to why David's census displeased the Lord so much. This is left to our interpretive imagination. That said, there is strong *secondary* evidence found in Josephus and other rabbinic sources that the plague on Israel was a direct result of David's failure to collect the half shekel offering from Israel as required by the law of Moses when he took the census. The law reads like this: "When you take the census of the people of Israel, then each shall give a ransom for his life to the LORD when you number them, that there be no plague among them when you number them. Each one who is numbered in the census shall give this: half a shekel . . . as an offering to the LORD" (Exodus 30:11-13).

This intertextual interpretation also has the explanatory power of making sense of the strong disciplinary actions ascribed to the Lord.[41]

A Sacred Map

At the beginning of this chapter we asked whether the Bible is a history book. We came to the conclusion that while the Bible is historical, it is not a formal history book. To treat it that way is to ignore its essential and revelatory character and raise the possibility of misleading interpretations, as in the above case. It is a record of sacred history by which the mysteries of God are disclosed over time—the biggest of those being the mystery of Christ.[42] So then, the Bible is not only historical, it is prophetic. As such, it is also an epic work of literary art![43] As we discovered, this is precisely what makes the Bible unique in terms of the history it records.[44] It is a treasure map of the past, and Christ is the X that marks the spot. As Charles Spurgeon once observed,

> Don't you know young man that from every town, and every village, and every little hamlet in England, wherever it may be, there is a road to London? . . . And so from every text in Scripture, there is a road to the metropolis of the Scriptures, that is Christ. And my dear brother, your business in when you get to a text, is to say, "Now what is the road to Christ?" . . . I have never yet found a text that had not got a road to Christ in it, and if I ever do find one that has not a road to Christ in it, I will make one; I will go over hedge and ditch but I would get at my Master.[45]

The more we learn to read the Bible not as a history book but as sacred history, the more we will find that "the word of God is living and active, sharper than any two-edged sword, piercing to the division of soul and of spirit" (Hebrews 4:12) and helping us "grow in the grace and knowledge of our Lord and Savior Jesus Christ" (2 Peter 3:18). For as we read Scripture, we come to understand God better in the process—and as we come to understand God better, we become better equipped to read Scripture.[46]

CHAPTER 11

It's Not Rocket Science

False Assumption #7: The Bible Is a Science Book

Science can purify religion from error and superstition; religion can purify science from idolatry and false absolutes.

POPE JOHN PAUL II

Aaron graduated summa cum laude from a liberal arts college with a passion for biology, chemistry, and medicine. When he came to college, he was certain he would remain a young earth creationist. He expected that his atheistic professors would try to convince him away from this view with lies about the natural world. But after years of study, he not only grew to admire his professors, but he also came to believe that the universe was very, very old. And to his great surprise he became convinced that evolution was true.

Given his commitment to a young earth interpretation of Genesis, he found himself in a faith crisis that caused him to question everything he believed about God, Jesus, and the Bible:

> I felt as if my whole world had come crashing down. There was now a dichotomy that was present in my life

> that didn't seem possible to merge. On one side, there was my faith, where I believed that God created the world, Jesus died and rose from the dead, and the Holy Spirit empowered me to serve him. On the other, there was the science that I had devoted my life to learning and seeking to understand; the biology, chemistry, physics, anatomy, and physiology that had demonstrated realities I couldn't escape. I now viewed evolution as the most likely explanation for how life developed, but this didn't fit with my worldview. It couldn't fit my worldview. I had to choose. It had to be one or the other. It was science . . . or it was God. How could I possibly make that choice? . . . I was distraught. I was tormented. I felt as if I was losing myself.[1]

Aaron's story has a happy ending. Unlike many who have a similar experience, Aaron managed to retain his faith. But it wasn't easy. To do so he had to reconsider a deeply held assumption about the Bible and how it relates to science. He had to rethink what it means for the Bible to speak truthfully when it speaks about the natural world. But for every story like Aaron's there are many more that end in the loss of faith resulting from an inability to reconcile what they believe the Bible teaches and the claims of science.

Deconversion and Science

Every study we are aware of indicates that a large and increasing percentage of Americans identify as nones. If the current trend continues, by 2070 there will be more nones in the United States than Christians. So where did all the nones come from?

The majority renounced their identity as Christians and adopted a nonreligious identity in its place.[2] And while there are a number of reasons why people deconvert, many cite conflicts between science and the Bible as the chief reason they left.

In 2011 and 2018, the Barna Group conducted two major studies of the faith of millennials and Gen Z. In 2011, they discovered that 29 percent of millennials who grew up in the church but ultimately left it said that "churches are out of step" with science. A further 25 percent said that "Christianity is antiscience," and 23 percent said they were "turned off by the creation-versus-evolution debate."[3] In 2018, Barna surveyed teenagers who still attended church. They discovered that 49 percent of teenagers thought "the church seems to reject much of what science tells us about the world."[4]

Clearly there is a perception among young people who are leaving the faith that the church and science are incompatible. The question is, why do they think this? We suspect it is the result of a powerful combination of two mistaken assumptions. First, that science is the ultimate criterion of truth. Second, that for the Bible to be true, it ought to reflect the findings of modern science. In this chapter we will challenge both of these assumptions.

Scientifically Speaking

Although the purpose of this book is to address mistaken assumptions about the Bible that lead to doubt, it is important to briefly identify some of the mistaken assumptions about the nature of science. These ideas, when combined with mistaken assumptions about the Bible, prove to be detrimental to faith. While we are not science skeptics—quite the contrary—it is important to point out that science isn't always what many think it is—the ultimate, objective criterion of truth that stands in judgment of all other truth claims. That assumption rests on at least three further assumptions, all of which are mistaken.[5]

ASSUMPTION 1: SCIENCE EMPIRICALLY PROVES ITS CONCLUSIONS

Science is often assumed to be objective because it is based on what can be proved, not metaphysical speculation. And by proved, it is meant that empirical observations alone can be used to separate fact from fiction. But this isn't quite correct. All observations of empirical facts are founded on metaphysical assumptions. For example, even the most empirically demonstrable theory in cosmology, the Big Bang, is beholden to metaphysical speculation. As theoretical astrophysicist and professor of astronomy Geoffrey Burbidge notes, "Big bang cosmology is probably as widely believed as has been any theory of the universe in the history of Western civilization. It rests, however, on many untested, and in some cases untestable, assumptions. Indeed, big bang cosmology has become a bandwagon of thought that reflects faith as much as objective truth."[6]

In pointing out that Big Bang cosmology rests on assumptions, we are not intending to cast doubt on it. Rather, we are simply saying what many are unaware of, which is that no scientific observation can occur without presupposing ideas that are philosophical in nature. And when it comes to many accepted scientific theories, there are a range of models that can explain observations. When that happens, it is not empirical observations that determine which one will win the day. It is philosophical criteria that are used to choose the "best" model.[7]

ASSUMPTION 2: SCIENCE HAS A UNIQUE METHOD

On a popular subreddit thread debating religion and science, a commenter to a post expresses the second assumption well: "The scientific method is the best tool we have for explaining how the universe actually works. It takes nothing on faith, and protects the disciplined scientist from fallacious thinking."[8] Yet contrary to this belief, there is no clear-cut scientific method but rather a cluster of practices employed in various contexts that can loosely be called scientific methodologies. Sometimes scientists employ what the poster referred to as "the scientific method"—the process of identifying a problem, suggesting a possible hypothesis, designing an experiment, analyzing the data, and drawing a conclusion. But that is only one way scientists go about their work. Another is the creative process of educated guesswork known as adduction. By an act of imagination, scientists adduce a conceptual pattern that models the phenomenon in question. In doing so, often theological or philosophical ideas are used as the guiding pattern, not observation. More methodologies could be cited, but we trust this will suffice to make our point: Scientists rely on a number of methods for their investigations, which are open to the same critique as those in other domains.

ASSUMPTION 3: SCIENCE IS FALSIFIABLE

It is sometimes claimed that what sets science apart as the ultimate criterion for truth is that it can be falsified. To falsify means to show something to be wrong. It is thought that since scientific theories can be disproved by empirical evidence, that sets them apart from philosophical or theological claims. But it isn't so easy to identify whether a theory has been falsified. All theories have a number of supporting theories and auxiliary assumptions that are at work during experiments. This makes it difficult to know which one has been falsified when the experiment fails. Depending on how committed a scientist is to their theory, almost no evidence against it will falsify it. There will always be a way to explain why the core of the theory has not been falsified but merely the auxiliary theories that are not essential.

Science has provided us with an array of technological advances that have made our lives better. From antibiotics to cell phones, science has allowed us to harness and control aspects of the world for our benefit. But science has its limitations. It isn't as objective as it is often assumed. It rests on untestable metaphysical assumptions; uses multiple methods, all of which have subjective elements; and can't always be shown to be false by contradictory evidence. So what's our point? Simply this: Science is one means of discovering the truth, but it should not be thought of as the ultimate, objective criterion of truth that all other truth claims must align with. Sometimes science gets it wrong. In fact, the history of science is littered with discarded theories that at one point were considered accurate descriptions of reality. We ought to remember that when it appears the claims of the Bible don't align with the claims of science. But there is at least one more important thing to remember when encountering what seems to be a scientific error in the Bible.

The Bible: Science Book?

A common view that many Christians and skeptics assume when approaching the Bible is what is known as concordism. Concordism is the view that the teaching of the Bible and the findings of science should harmonize. The assumption goes like this:

- Science makes objective truth claims.
- The Bible makes objective truth claims.
- Therefore, the findings of science and the teachings of the Bible should harmonize.

It doesn't take long for anyone with even a rudimentary knowledge of contemporary science and the Bible to feel the tension between what the Bible *appears* to teach and the claims of science. Are humans the special creation of God, as the Bible says, or the end result of an unguided evolutionary process, as most scientists affirm? Is the universe only six to ten thousand years old, as a straightforward reading of the Bible seems to imply, or is it billions of years old, as modern cosmology indicates? Given the elevated status science has in our culture as the ultimate criterion of truth, the assumption about the need for science and the Bible to harmonize leads to the following conclusion:

- The claims of science and the Bible do not harmonize.
- Either science or the Bible is wrong.
- Science is not wrong; therefore, the Bible is.
- Therefore, the Bible cannot be the Word of God.

One way to avoid the above conclusion is to question the assumptions that lead to it. Specifically, the assumption that the Bible and science need to harmonize. Instead of beginning with an impulse to harmonize, we suggest that a more faithful approach is to determine how the original author and audience would have understood the text, regardless of whether their understanding aligns with modern science. Rather than trying to force the Bible and science to harmonize, we ought to try to understand the Bible as it would have been understood by those to whom it was written.

To do so requires that we bracket our knowledge of modern science and put ourselves in the shoes of the ancient Hebrews. Only then will we be able to evaluate how it relates to current scientific theories.[9] In short, rather than trying to show that the Bible aligns with current science, which in some cases is impossible to do, a better approach is to understand the Bible on its own terms. But what if, after our examination, it can't be harmonized with science?

Whose Truth?

As stated previously, we believe the Bible speaks truthfully about whatever it affirms. We also believe that to speak truthfully means a claim must correspond with reality. Together, these assumptions mean we believe that if or when the Bible makes what are called "scientific claims," those claims reflect reality accurately. However, it is vital to point out that just because the Bible speaks about the natural world does not always mean it is affirming, teaching, or making "scientific claims." Many times the Bible simply takes for granted the scientifically inaccurate assumptions of the culture from which it was written in order to communicate a theological truth. This is an example of what we mentioned in chapter 5, God accommodating his message to those with whom he was communicating. For example, it seems the ancient Israelites assumed—as did all their ancient neighbors—that the world was a flat disk supported by pillars with a solid dome overhead that kept back the waters above. Beyond this dome was the throne of God.[10] Clearly, that view doesn't reflect reality. But God allowed this preexisting misconception about the universe to remain unchallenged because correcting it was not essential for the truth he wanted to communicate.[11] In doing so God was not affirming or teaching truths of cosmology any more than he was teaching truths of botany when he inspired Isaiah to write, "The trees of the field shall clap their hands" (Isaiah 55:12). Or astronomy when Jesus referred to the "sun ris[ing] on the evil and on the good" (Matthew 5:45). And if the Bible is not affirming or teaching cosmology when it employs ancient cosmological assumptions to teach theological truths, then it cannot be accused of contradicting science. We should be careful, then, when drawing scientific conclusions about areas such as physiology, meteorology, astronomy, cosmic geography, genetics, or geology from the Bible.[12] Because although the Bible speaks about the natural world, it does so from within the cultural assumptions of the original audience, not according to modern science.

When you stop and think about it, what else could God do *but* communicate in the language and assumptions of the time? Your initial response might be "Well, he could have corrected their false assumptions about the physical world by providing them with beliefs that harmonized with science." But that poses two problems. One, if God did that, it is hard to see how any of it would have made sense to the original audience. They lacked even the most basic categories to think about the world in the way modern, post-Enlightenment thinkers do. And remember, it was written to *them*, not us. Had God chosen to speak in a way that harmonized with our understanding of science, doing so would have undermined his purpose in communicating theological truths to them. Two, given that science is always changing—sometimes incrementally and sometimes seemingly all at once, as entire paradigms are suddenly replaced—how could God possibly communicate in a way that harmonizes with the claims of science in the eighteenth century, the twenty-first century, and the twenty-fifth century, since they are, and presumably will be, so different? For instance, in 1687 Isaac Newton in his groundbreaking work *Mathematica*

Principia argued for a static, steady-state, infinite universe. Today, few if any scientists believe that. Instead, the majority hold to some version of Big Bang cosmology. So which scientific theory should God have communicated to the Israelites? If he told them the universe was infinite and static, he would have harmonized with the science of Newton's day but would have been completely out of step with the science of ours. And if God chose to communicate to the Israelites in a way that harmonized with Big Bang cosmology, that will likely not harmonize with the reigning cosmological theory in the future. This one example should suffice to demonstrate why it is misguided to ask why God didn't communicate in a way that aligns with science. Science is always changing.

And while we may wish he had taken a different approach, God seems to have few qualms about employing the mistaken assumptions about the nature of the physical world rather than correcting them. He does so regularly throughout the Bible. As John Walton points out,

> In the ancient world people believed that the seat of intelligence, emotion and personhood was in the internal organs, particularly the heart, but also the liver, kidneys and intestines. . . . In the ancient world this was not metaphor, but physiology. Yet we must notice that when God wanted to talk to the Israelites about their intellect, emotions and will, he did not revise their ideas of physiology and feel compelled to reveal the function of the brain. Instead, he adopted the language of the culture to communicate in terms they understood.[13]

In fact, we are unaware of any verse in the Bible where God revealed a scientific fact beyond the cultural assumptions of those to whom it was originally written. As far as we can tell, there aren't any passages that provide a perspective on the natural world that was uncommon to the assumptions of the original audience.[14] Consequently, because the Bible is written to ancient Israelites, not modern Americans, we shouldn't expect it will reflect current science.

In the Beginning . . . ?

When it comes to the relationship between science and the Bible, there is no more debated text than Genesis 1 and 2. Countless readers of the Bible have stumbled over the incompatibility of a literal reading of the creation account and the claims of contemporary science. But as we have argued above, unless Genesis 1 and 2 are making claims about physical science, there isn't a contradiction between how Genesis speaks about creation and what current science claims about the origin of the universe. Which raises the question: Is Genesis making a scientific claim about the origin of the universe? We don't think so. That's because when we ask the most important interpretive question—what did it mean to the original audience?—it seems to us the purpose of the passage was not to teach *how* the universe was created. Rather, it was to use the cosmological assumptions of the ancient Israelites to communicate *theological* truths about God, humanity, and the role humans are to play as image bearers. Why do we say this?

To answer that question, we need to take a brief look at the original context of Genesis. The immediate backdrop of Genesis is the exodus from Egypt. But before the Israelites were slaves in Egypt, they were nomads in the land of Canaan. And before that, God called Abraham out of Mesopotamia. When we look at the creation accounts of those three nations, what we discover is they share similar cosmological assumptions about the nature of reality. But it's not just those three nations who have similar cosmological assumptions. It's the Israelites as well. Many scholars have noted the similarity between the creation accounts of the Egyptians, Mesopotamians, Canaanites, and Israelites. Miller and Soden note,

> Many of the details of Genesis 1 clearly correlate with ancient Near Eastern perceptions, especially the Egyptian viewpoint: the initial conditions from which God creates, his means of creating by his word, the presence of light before the luminaries (days 1 and 4), the separation of the light from the darkness, the separation of the waters above the expanse from the waters below, the order of the events, the making of man in the image of God, and God resting.[15]

We should not be surprised at these similarities given that the Israelites and the Egyptians were neighbors both geographically and culturally. Consequently, they shared a basic understanding of the nature of reality. And yet, for all the similarities between the creation accounts of the Egyptians, Mesopotamians, and Canaanites, when compared to the Genesis account, there are important theological differences that God wanted the Israelites to know. As Miller and Soden note, "Genesis does not merely elevate God over other gods; it presents God as transcendent and unique in *all* creation and as the *sole* claimant to deity. . . . While all other gods were aspects of creation, Israel's God alone was outside of creation and in complete control of all creation. Genesis 1 proclaims that God alone is Creator, the Sovereign of everything." Genesis makes similar theological distinctions from Egyptian cosmological accounts concerning the nature of humans and the cosmos as well. For example, in Genesis, all humans are intermediaries between God and creation, not just the pharaoh ruling on behalf of God. And even more theological distinctives could be added.[16]

Although God, through Moses, does not choose to correct the scientifically inaccurate assumptions about how the universe was created, he does correct the wrong theology of those accounts. But his instruction does not depend on accurate scientific claims about the material world.[17] In other words, in the Genesis account, God corrected the Israelites' spiritual worldview, not their physical picture of the world.[18] And if Moses wasn't challenging the ancient Israelites' assumptions of the physical world but instead used those assumptions to communicate correct theology, then there isn't *in principle* a contradiction between science and the creation account in the book of Genesis.[19]

Interpreting "Scientific" Verses

In chapter 7, we discussed the importance of identifying the genre when interpreting a text and provided a list of frequently found genres in the Bible and the key questions associated with each one. One of the genres purposely not included on that list was "textbook." A textbook is a more formal and detailed book designed for people engaged in deep study of a subject. And while there is some evidence that textbooks existed in ancient civilizations such as Egypt, India, China, Rome, and Greece, this genre was virtually nonexistent to the authors of the Bible.[20] So whenever the Bible makes observations about the natural world, we must be careful we are not treating it like a science textbook (or worse, a scientific journal). The Bible makes *no* scientific claims, at least in the modern sense. We should not turn to the Bible to learn about scientific theories, such as the Big Bang, general relativity, or genetics. We should also be cautious about integrating modern scientific ideas with biblical doctrines.[21] Of course, that does not mean the Scriptures do not have a lot to say about things that concern science, such as the origin of the cosmos, human life, and the environment.[22] In light of this, we want to present a few guidelines and examples of how to interpret Scripture that includes observations about the natural world without making the error of treating it like a science book, which can and will lead to misinterpretations, misunderstandings, and misapplication of the biblical text.

First, obviously the Bible is not written in scientific language. Instead of using scientific language, the Bible uses *phenomenological language*—that is, "the language of appearance."[23] For example, the Bible's authors speak of the sun setting, the moon pouring out its light, and the morning star rising. None of these are scientific claims. The Bible's authors are simply using the language of appearance, much like we do today.

Second, and equally obvious, the Bible has no intention of teaching astronomy, biology, chemistry, mathematics, physics, or their respective branches. As with history, it does not comprehensively cover any of these subjects or explore them in a systematic way. For example, in the first chapter of the book of Genesis, the Bible categorizes various plants and animals, but it does so simply by referring to them each "according to its kind" (Genesis 1:11-12, 21, 24-25). While it is understandable how some might interpret this as a form of taxonomy, the purpose of the text is not to provide a scientific categorization and classification of various species, or the order of some evolutionary process. Rather, the point of the passage is to reveal the one true God who created everything and that the climax of his creation was human life, made in his image.

Drawing conclusions from the Bible in this regard will inevitably lead to missing metaphoric language and clear cases of hyperbole. For example, let's consider when Jesus identifies the mustard seed as the "smallest of all the seeds on earth" (Mark 4:31). As you may already know, the mustard seed is *not* "the smallest of all the seeds on earth." Nettlesome verses like this usually don't destroy faith in the Scriptures, but they have a way of adding up over time, chipping away at it if we do not work to interpret them correctly. While many scholars offer apologetical answers to this particular statement by Jesus, we suggest the problem is more fundamental. It is once again a problem of interpretation. We need to ask ourselves, was Jesus making a scientific claim, or was he using everyday language to drive home a point? The answer seems clear. For when Jesus spoke these words, he was *not* teaching botany. He was teaching about the Kingdom of God through the use of a parable. As such, he used hyperbole and contrast to make his point—both literary devices common to parables. So then, his description of a mustard seed as "the smallest of all the seeds of the earth" is no different than someone saying they just saw "the biggest spider in the world." He was teaching his disciples that just as the tiny mustard seed grows into a large tree, big enough for birds to make their nests and find shade in it, so it will be for the Kingdom of God. Though small at the moment, it, too, will grow to the point where many outsiders will find shelter and sustenance in it.

The point is, the Bible usually does not conflict with science because it makes few (if any) scientific claims. In this regard, Christians would do well to heed Augustine's exhortation:

> Now, it is a disgraceful and dangerous thing for an infidel
> to hear a Christian, presumably giving the meaning
> of Holy Scripture, talking nonsense on these topics

> [about nature]. . . . If they find a Christian mistaken in a field which they themselves know well and hear him maintaining his foolish opinions about "our books," how are they going to believe those books in matters concerning the resurrection of the dead, the hope of eternal life, and the kingdom of heaven, when they think their pages are full of falsehoods on facts which they themselves have learnt from experience and the light of reason?[24]

Third, while the Bible does make observations about nature, it does so in a nonscientific way. It is said of Solomon that "he spoke of trees . . . also of beasts, and of birds, and of reptiles, and of fish" (1 Kings 4:33). And while this might sound scientifically driven, he did this not to educate his audience about the natural world, but in order to write "proverbs" and sing "songs" (verse 32). In other words, when Solomon spoke of the natural world, it was not to make scientific claims but to give voice to the wisdom of nature and sing praises to God about his wonderful creation and how it reveals his character.[25] For example, in the book of Proverbs, Solomon turns our attention to the ant and observes the following:

> Go to the ant, O sluggard;
>   consider her ways, and be wise.
> Without having any chief,
>   officer, or ruler,
> she prepares her bread in summer
>   and gathers her food in harvest.
> How long will you lie there, O sluggard?
>   When will you arise from your sleep?

A little sleep, a little slumber,
  a little folding of the hands to rest,
and poverty will come upon you like a robber,
  and want like an armed man.

PROVERBS 6:6-11

In this passage, the humble ant is held up as a noble model of hard work in spite of having no ruler over her to spur her on. Even though modern scientific study has discovered that an ant colony has a hierarchy, it is irrelevant. And one may wish to offer a scientific rebuttal that a colony can continue for a short time without a queen and even work effectively without one, and that perhaps this is what Solomon was referring to, but this only serves to distract from the point of the wisdom being shared.[26] Solomon's advice is aimed at the typical lazy person—they should learn from the ant's example to work diligently and save for a rainy day. For failure to do so will predictably lead to poverty and ruin.

The Bible: Down to a Science?

Many well-intentioned people wrongly assume that the Bible is a science book and have used it improperly to draw scientific conclusions. This approach has often put modern science at odds with the Bible, bringing disrepute upon the Scriptures, even to the point that some have left the faith because they believed it to be unscientific. This is unfortunate, because, as we have learned, science and the Bible have two very different, independent sets of goals. Science endeavors to understand and explain the natural world and how it works. The Bible, on the other hand, aims to reveal God and his plan to redeem humankind. This is not to say that the Bible and science never overlap or always see eye to eye.

For example, when science crosses over into theology, such as theorizing about the origins and ultimate purpose of the universe and life, or the complexity of the mind and soul, we can intelligently push back because the Bible rightly has much to say about those things.[27]

So despite what you might have heard, the Bible is not anti-science. Actually, the opposite is true. It encourages us to study the cosmos and everything in it, for "great are the works of the LORD, studied by all who delight in them" (Psalm 111:2). Indeed, the Bible would have us routinely "stop and consider the wondrous works of God" (Job 37:14), because "in wisdom [he] made them all" (Psalm 104:24).

CHAPTER 12

Truth, Justice, and a Better Tomorrow

False Assumption #8: The Bible Is a Social Justice Book

When the Bible talks about justice and injustice, it doesn't start giving us a litany of the perpetrators. It gives us a litany of the victims, the wounded ones—the widows, the orphans, and the aliens.

NICHOLAS WOLTERSTORFF

Back in the early 1990s, two of my good friends and I (Shawn) decided to go on a cross-country road trip for almost six weeks. We quit our jobs, pooled our money, shaved our heads (to make it easier to care for while traveling), and bought the minimum camping gear needed to survive. We plotted a course that wove through our country's most scenic national parks and famous landmarks. We hopped into a smooth-riding gray Oldsmobile and were off. During our adventures, we hiked Angels Landing, felt the stillness of the Badlands, and stared in awe at Niagara Falls. We visited the viewing floor of the Sears Tower (the tallest building in the world at the time), descended into the deep darkness of the Carlsbad Caverns, and waded into the saline waters of the Great Salt Lake. We peered over the edge of the Grand Canyon, drove through the heart of the Midwest and its endless farmlands, and ate elk meat at a resort in Estes Park, sitting in the shadow of the Colorado Rockies' peaks. We did all this and more.

But the memory that left the deepest imprint on us is when we visited Gary, Indiana. We were on our way from Cleveland to an acquaintance's house near Chicago and had not planned to stop until we arrived there. But we were exhausted, and the sun was setting, so we decided to use some of our remaining funds to hunt down a motel and get a good night's rest. We were not sure where we should stop, but the name "Gary" kept popping up on the highway signs, so we figured that was our best chance to find a room and crash for the night. We had no idea of the demographics of Gary at the time, and we knew little of its history or role in the race riots of 1968—when the National Guard was "called in to help quell the disorders."[1] We pulled off the highway, and there we were—three naive, young, white males with shaved heads, one of us wearing army camouflage and boots, driving through the primarily Black city. All eyes were on us as we slowly rolled through the neighborhood.

We arrived at a T intersection, unnerved and debating whether we should still look for a place to stay or find our way back to the highway. We noticed straight across from us an elderly Black woman sitting on her porch. She made eye contact with us. Then, with an expression I would describe as grandmotherly compassion, she simply pointed to her left. We followed her wordless directions, which led us straight back to the highway.

I tell this story as a confession. While some may defend our apprehension as reasonable, others may point out how our attitudes and beliefs, though perhaps excusable, were nonetheless rooted in racial stereotypes and irrational fears. Regardless of whether our feelings were appropriate, what was indefensible was our historical, cultural, and geographical obliviousness. How was it that the three of us knew almost nothing about the race riots of 1968 or the role that Gary played in them? Why was it we felt so out of place in this city?

All three of us had grown up in affluent Orange County, the home of John Wayne and surfing. We lived a few minutes from the beach in what we called "the OC Bubble." We avoided nearby cities like Los Angeles and Compton unless we were attending a sporting event or concert, or flying into or out of LAX. The topics of social justice and inequality were admittedly not a priority to our community or to us personally. While overt racism and other forms of bigotry were neither tolerated nor espoused, they also were not studied or explored at any great length. Even our local churches barely discussed the issue, except to point out that Jesus died for *all* people, regardless of their nationality or background. I am grateful that my parents did not pass down prejudices, but they also did little to teach me about the recent injustices our country had endured. In fact, I remember when President Reagan signed a bill making Martin Luther King Jr. Day a federal holiday. It was truly the first time I had heard about him.

Fortunately, the Bible is neither ignorant nor unaware that bigotry and oppression exist. It does not ignore them. Indeed, it has a lot to say about them and how we should respond.

Biblical Justice

One of the major themes in the Bible is God's great concern for the disadvantaged and downtrodden, especially for the widow, the fatherless, the foreigner, and the poor.[2] The Bible teaches that God "executes justice for the fatherless and the widow, and loves the sojourner, giving him food and clothing" (Deuteronomy 10:18).

It requires God's people to do the same.[3] King Lemuel's mother taught her son to stay sober so he would not "pervert the rights of all the afflicted" (Proverbs 31:4-5). She emboldens her son (and all of us), "Open your mouth for the mute, for the rights of all who are destitute. Open your mouth, judge righteously, defend the rights of the poor and needy" (Proverbs 31:8-9).[4]

The Bible exhorts Israel that they should be compassionate to foreigners, because they of all people knew what it felt like to be outsiders, for they once "were sojourners in the land of Egypt" (Deuteronomy 10:19). God specifically wanted outsiders to feel welcomed to the religious festivals kept by Israel for his honor.[5] Israel is instructed to "do no injustice in court" (Leviticus 19:15) and to "treat the stranger who sojourns with you as the native among you, and you shall love him as yourself." Why? "For you were [once] strangers in the land of Egypt" and "I am the LORD your God" (Leviticus 19:34). Specifically, the Lord warns Israel to make certain they do not harbor hate and ill feelings against those nations and people groups that once treated them poorly: "Do not detest the Edomites or the Egyptians, because the Edomites are your relatives and you lived as foreigners among the Egyptians" (Deuteronomy 23:7, NLT).

When it comes to worship and religious practice, the Bible teaches that there should not be separate sets of rules for different groups of people. Rather, "you and the sojourner shall be alike before the LORD. One law and one rule shall be for you and for the stranger who sojourns with you" (Numbers 15:15-16).

Jesus, as witnessed in the Gospels, also singled out and exhibited special concern for all these groups. For example, he pointed out widows' great faith and condemned those who took advantage of them, and Jesus' followers carried on the practice of honoring widows and orphans.[6] Jesus also showed great compassion and love for foreigners, especially demonstrated in healing a centurion's servant and the Syrophoenician woman's daughter and feeding thousands in the region of the Decapolis.[7] Of course, when he died to make atonement for sins, he did so not just for Israel but for the whole world.[8] His early followers carried on this practice of highlighting and embracing foreigners, though it often took persecution and added prompting by the resurrected Jesus and the Holy Spirit to accomplish this task.[9] And it was Paul's mission to bring the gospel to Gentiles.[10] Of great importance is the vision of the end times found in the book of Revelation, where all tribes, languages, peoples, and nations are seen among heaven's citizenry and where the gospel is proclaimed to all "those who dwell on earth" (Revelation 14:6) and God is revealed to be the "King of the nations" (Revelation 15:3-4).[11]

Biblical Justice vs. Social Justice

As we have seen, the Bible and its prophets and apostles consistently and repeatedly speak up for the plight of the afflicted, especially widows, orphans, foreigners, and the poor. In doing this, they are speaking up for everyone who is powerless and oppressed, especially those who are likely to be dehumanized and marginalized and have no voice and no one to speak up for them.

It is also instructive that God personally identifies with the oppressed and afflicted. After Cain murders his brother, God tells him, "The voice of your brother's blood is crying to me from the ground" (Genesis 4:10). And God tells Moses, "I have surely seen the affliction of my people who are in Egypt and have heard their cry because of their taskmasters. I know their sufferings, and I have come down to deliver them out of the hand of the Egyptians" (Exodus 3:7-8). Jesus confronts one of the chief persecutors of his fledging church with these haunting words: "Saul, Saul, why are you persecuting *me*?" (Acts 9:4, emphasis added). Jesus reveals himself here as the ultimate victim, sympathizing with *all* victims of injustice, but especially those who are his followers.[12] Let us never forget:

> The ultimate victim of crime and violence is not the aggrieved person whose rights have been infringed upon, nor is it society in general whose laws have been scorned at the expense of social unity and public order. . . . We see crime for what it is: an offense against God, the Creator of life. It is a repudiation of His honor, a violation of the dignity of the Sovereign of the universe, a rejection of transcendent divine law, a thumbing of one's nose at God's revealed will.[13]

At its most ideal, social justice is concerned about equal rights, equal opportunity, and equal treatment—all things the Bible recognizes and supports. So it is understandable when people are shocked to find out that the Bible does not take on various social justice issues to the degree or in the manner they would expect. The problem is not with the idea of social justice but with how it is often taught and applied today. Social justice by definition longs for a "better tomorrow." The problem is there isn't much agreement on what that "better tomorrow" should look like.[14] Perhaps this is why conservative economist Friedrich A. Hayek believed social justice is a "mirage," because there is no consensus on what the end goal looks like.[15] The by-product of this shaky identification of a "better tomorrow" is an ever-changing, nebulous morality that shifts with the winds of culture. This is why the prophets were constantly imagining and preaching about the world to come—so we would know how and where to ground our expectations, especially as we interpret the words of Scripture.[16]

Modern Christians are often unaware that the term *social justice* was coined by a Jesuit priest named Luigi Taparelli in the 1840s and based on the teachings of Thomas Aquinas. Taparelli's ideas are expressed in the Catholic catechism: "Society ensures social justice when it provides the conditions that allow associations or individuals to obtain what is their due."[17]

The problem with this definition, though, is that there is a large area of disagreement about what somebody is due (especially if the Bible is removed from the equation) and about how society should provide those proper conditions. Even Nicholas Wolterstorff, a hero to the Christian social justice movement, readily confesses, "Social justice movements are hardly ever genteel. Almost always they are laced through with conflict, hostility, and resistance."[18] How come? Because their aims are usually to overthrow and replace. They endeavor not to reconcile Jews and Gentiles, Blacks and whites, men and women, masters and slaves, but to turn the tables, to procure payback and temporal liberation as a means of retribution and earthly penance. This flies in the face of the biblical message and should not and cannot be read into the biblical text if we are expecting to properly interpret it.[19]

Standing in the Gap

By pointing out the difference between biblical justice and what is often described as social justice today, we are not saying the Bible teaches pacifism. In the words of Martin Luther King Jr., "To accept an unjust system is to cooperate with that system, and thereby to become a participant in its evil."[20] What the Bible teaches is that God wants his people "to stand in the gap":

> I looked for someone who might rebuild the wall
> of righteousness that guards the land. I searched for
> someone to stand in the gap in the wall so I wouldn't
> have to destroy the land, but I found no one.
>
> EZEKIEL 22:30, NLT

Elsewhere, it teaches the importance of not sitting idly by:

> Rescue those who are unjustly sentenced to die;
>   save them as they stagger to their death.
> Don't excuse yourself by saying, "Look, we didn't know."
>   For God understands all hearts, and he sees you.
> He who guards your soul knows you knew.
>   He will repay all people as their actions deserve.
>
> PROVERBS 24:11-12, NLT

Based on passages like these, we believe that the Bible, when considered in its entirety, offers a nuanced view on justice, urging non-retaliation sometimes and confrontation other times. For example, Jesus teaches humility and sacrificial love over personal revenge, but also fiercely defends the vulnerable and oppressed.[21] Paul encourages obedience to the governing authorities and overcoming evil with good rather than hatred or violence, while elsewhere Peter and John underscore the importance of obeying God over corrupt human authorities.[22] The Bible, in some cases, clearly permits self-defense, and in other cases urges us to turn the other cheek.[23] Ultimately, true justice is rooted in the gospel, promoting grace and transformation rather than mere cultural activism. This is why the Bible calls for God's people to stand up for righteousness, extend mercy, and trust God, accepting that many wrongs will not be righted until the day God judges the world. For as Solomon notes in his penultimate proverb, "Many seek the face of a ruler, but it is from the LORD that a man gets justice" (Proverbs 29:26).

Clearing the Mechanism

I (Shawn) am a baseball fan. Growing up I bought baseball cards at the local corner store and devotedly watched the Dodgers with my father, who would tell me about Jackie Robinson, Sandy Koufax, and his favorite baseball player, Frank Howard. But nothing could surpass the feeling of actually playing the game. My favorite position was pitcher. One of the most impactful things I learned from one of my pitching coaches was a technique now referred to as "clearing the mechanism." To "clear the mechanism" is to remove *all* distractions and fully commit to each pitch so you can perform it to the best of your ability. In the same way, when it comes to interpreting a passage of the Bible, we must learn to "clear the mechanism." In other words, we need to make sure our own culture and personal hang-ups are not distracting us from interpreting the passage correctly.

Conversations on racism, political correctness, and social justice are so deeply embedded in our present culture, they have infiltrated our way of thinking without us being fully aware of it. This tends to distract Bible students and scholars, producing skewed interpretations of the biblical text. The two biggest ways it has impacted biblical interpretation are either to cause us to ignore ethnic language in the Bible or to cause us to insert our own modern cultural sensitivities and expectations into the meaning of the text.[24] Failure to clear the mechanism results in us overlooking crucial historical and cultural clues as to what is going on in a passage and to read offenses into the text that do not actually exist. It is essential we do not ignore statements about ethnicity or nationality. They are important clues to understanding a text, as the following examples will demonstrate. It is also important we do not read into a passage our modern-day hang-ups and cultural sensitivities. They are red herrings, false clues that will lead us astray.

The Case of the Cushite Woman

> Miriam and Aaron spoke against Moses because of the Cushite woman whom he had married, for he had married a Cushite woman.
>
> NUMBERS 12:1

Racism against Black people and other minorities is a relatively recent phenomenon and did not develop, at least as we think of it today, until long after the Bible was recorded and canonized.[25] Hate, jealousy, and violence, however, have been around since Cain murdered his brother Abel.[26] This has not stopped Bible interpreters—both liberal and conservative—from interpreting Miriam and Aaron's complaint against Moses as a racial issue.[27] They suggest that Miriam and Aaron disapproved of Moses' marriage because the Cushites, who were from Nubia (roughly modern-day Ethiopia), were dark-skinned. Some go as far as to say this implies Moses married a slave and that Miriam and Aaron's problem was with "the indignity of a such a union."[28] These Bible interpreters believe this despite evidence that while the Egyptians enslaved the Cushites, they also enslaved other people groups as well (including Israelites). Indeed, they took slaves from all those they defeated in battle, for this was the standard practice of nearly all nations at the time.

This interpretation also flies in the face of ancient interpretations of the passage that imagine Moses married a princess. For example, Josephus writes,

> Tharbis was the daughter of the king of the Ethiopians [i.e., Cushites]: she happened to see Moses as he led the army near the walls, and fought with great courage; and admiring the subtility of his undertakings . . . she fell deeply in love with him; and upon the prevalency of that passion, sent to him the most faithful of all her servants to discourse with him about their marriage. He thereupon accepted the offer . . . [and] gave thanks to God, and consummated his marriage.[29]

Josephus's account is not supported by either the biblical text or historical discovery. But it does highlight how authors from different times project onto the text realities familiar to them.[30] Josephus imagined a prosperous Ethiopian (Cushite) kingdom, which at least fits the time of Moses and the exodus, while modern scholars imagine slaves and racial prejudices based on skin color, which do not. As for the biblical witness, Cushites are not associated with slavery but are described as powerful hunters and warriors, savvy traders, and possessors of a great kingdom.[31]

Miriam and Aaron's complaint, then, is that Moses had taken a non-Israelite wife, not that she was dark-skinned or a slave. In fact, in ancient Israel, Cushites were viewed in a positive light and referred to as a people who are "tall and smooth" (Isaiah 18:2, 7).[32] So when God punishes Miriam after her complaint, he solidifies God's love for the foreigner and that Moses did not sin in marrying her. This is significant, for later, when we read the biblical injunctions against marrying foreigners, we know they are not referring to interracial or intercultural marriages but to interfaith marriages.[33]

Women and Children First

> [26]Now the woman was a Gentile, a Syrophoenician by
> birth. And she begged him to cast the demon out of
> her daughter. [27]And he said to her, "Let the children be
> fed first, for it is not right to take the children's bread
> and throw it to the dogs." [28]But she answered him, "Yes,
> Lord; yet even the dogs under the table eat the children's
> crumbs." [29]And he said to her, "For this statement you
> may go your way; the demon has left your daughter."
> [30]And she went home and found the child lying in bed
> and the demon gone.
>
> MARK 7:26-30

This passage appears during a time when Jesus attempts to withdraw to have alone time (verse 24), and a Gentile woman interrupts him and begs for him to have mercy on her little daughter who is oppressed by a demon (verses 25-26). It is notable that Mark emphasizes through repetition that she is truly not Jewish. She is *Syrian*, *Phoenician*, and *Greek* ("Gentile" in verse 26 literally means "Greek"). She represents three groups of people the Jews shared a peculiar disdain for. This disdain was rooted in each of these groups having shown great hostility and malice toward the Jews in recent history.[34] It is somewhat surprising, then, that this woman comes to Jesus at all, even if it is to beg for healing for her demon-oppressed daughter. She has no social leverage in this situation. Jesus could very well ignore her and send her on her way, without anyone blinking an eye or any loss of honor. She is a foreign woman, a distrusted one at that, and she is interrupting Jesus' attempt to rest. For Jesus to engage her is to put his own honor and standing at risk, considering her ethnic background.[35]

That said, there are three more surprises in this encounter. First, it is surprising how Jesus responds to her: "Let the children be fed first, for it is not right to take the children's bread and throw it to the dogs" (verse 27).[36] It is surprising, not just because of our modern sensibilities, but because it does not fit the character of Jesus we see portrayed elsewhere in the Gospels. Jesus is presented elsewhere as being accommodating to everyone who calls upon him.[37] His answer here seems curt, if not bigoted, considering the historical animosity between "her people" and "his people." With only a cursory read of the encounter, one might say Jesus is revealing himself to be a Jewish nationalist.

This is a popular view among some lay scholars who suggest that Jesus was only human and was acting like a product of his time, and what makes Jesus great was that he overcame his bigotry.[38] Admittedly, his answer does seem unnecessarily harsh at first glance, as he seemingly embodies how many commentators suppose an average Jewish male of his day might respond: Gentiles are like dogs.[39] They are scavengers, unclean, and outside the covenant community, lacking honor. But a brief study of the use of the insult "dog" in the Bible reveals that it was not reserved exclusively for Gentiles. It was used to refer to *anyone* with no honor.[40] This would fit the context well here, as the way she—a foreign woman—approaches Jesus lacks all dignity common to her culture. That Jesus does not use the expected word for "dog" (which refers to a wild or untamed dog) but refers to her as a "house dog" is hardly enough to overcome the *perceived* sting of the rebuff.

The problem with the above interpretation is that it reads a lot of our own modern offenses and struggles with bigotry and racism into the encounter. It also leads to the conclusion that Jesus is a bigot. This conclusion is so out of character, it should immediately cause us to ask, *What are we missing? Why would Mark (and Matthew) include a story like this about Jesus?* Some scholars, emphasizing Jesus' humanity, suggest the story was included to show how Jesus' attitudes about foreigners changed over time and how it took a foreign woman to bring it about. But this is projecting our own cultural sins and hang-ups onto Jesus and into the encounter. Bearing in mind the overwhelming biblical witness to Jesus' godly love and compassion for foreigners, women, and children, this interpretation falls short. Jesus came to seek and save the lost, which the apostolic witness says he did without sin and without prejudice.[41] So we return to the basic interrogative questions, and the key question related to the genre: *What does this passage teach me about Jesus, and why is this good news?* But before we can answer that question, we must first "clear the mechanism."

Before unpacking what Jesus said, let's note that by answering the way he did—with a question—he gives the woman a chance to reply, which she does. And herein lies the second surprise of the encounter: her humble response. "Yes, Lord; yet even the dogs under the table eat the children's crumbs" (verse 28). She is neither offended nor discouraged by his remarks. This indicates that *we* should not be offended or discouraged either. She understands that what he has said is not an insult but a metaphor about priorities. And while this metaphor is not one we would use today, it was not a problem for Jesus or for her. She does not read too far into the metaphor, and neither should we.

Rather, by agreeing with the heart and logic of Jesus' analogy, she embraces her role as a beggar, outside the promises of Israel, in need of grace. This grace, she admits, she does not deserve. She acknowledges the truth of what Jesus told her—*children*, in fact, *should* come first. By using the word *first*, Jesus implies that the Gentiles will be blessed in the future but not right now. Right now he has been called to do his work among the Jews. This priority is appropriate, considering the burden they have shouldered and the role they have fulfilled. What role is that? They were entrusted with the Word of God.[42] This priority is a pattern Jesus' apostles would follow later in their evangelism.[43] But the woman is not asking for Jesus to change his plans or start some revolutionary work among her people right now. She just wants a crumb! She did not come to him looking for salvation and justice for her people. She came to him in hopes he could help her child!

Now, with his disciples and others around him, here comes the third and greatest surprise of this encounter: Jesus concedes her point, agrees to her request, and heals her daughter (verses 29-30). In Matthew's version, Jesus emphasizes her "great . . . faith" (Matthew 15:28), but here in Mark, which relied on Peter's eyewitness, Jesus praises her for her clever and humble riposte.[44] In their joust of words, Jesus allows her to win the day. We say "allow" because Jesus is presented elsewhere as having such a way with words that he wins every verbal contest. Because he concedes this moment, and chooses to bear the shame that comes along with it, an invisible but notable transfer of honor ensues, and all his disciples (male and female), especially Peter, are there to witness it. They learn to look at her—and in the future, every woman and foreigner—in a new light. If they are to be like Jesus, they, too, will need to bear their cross and the social shame that comes with it and be willing to lose worldly honor so that others might find restoration and reconciliation in God.[45]

Through this encounter, we learn that Jesus is not worried or concerned about his earthly honor. He is preparing the disciples for the coming messianic Kingdom, and it is different from the kingdoms of the world (including earthly Israel). Jesus' healing of the Syrophoenician woman's daughter suggests that the Kingdom of God will soon dawn upon the Gentiles. This is confirmed by what follows: Jesus performs more miracles in the borderlands of the Decapolis—dropping more "crumbs" to the Gentiles before he eventually dies on the cross and rises again. In this act, Jesus brings not crumbs but the great feast of salvation and reconciliation to the whole world, irrespective of race, ethnicity, nationality, sex, social status, or age.[46] In this encounter we learn that the time was shortly coming when Jesus would share the blessings and promises of Israel with the Gentiles and they would take their place at the table as children of God.

Justly and Fairly

> Masters, treat your bondservants justly and fairly, knowing that you also have a Master in heaven.
>
> COLOSSIANS 4:1

In chapter 1, we interpreted a couple of passages that at first glance seemed to be condoning slavery. After we delved into them, we came to realize they weren't. To get to the heart of the passages, we asked one key question: *How does this text fit in with the overarching theme of salvation history?* The answer to this question was straightforward: Paul wanted *Christian* slaves to obey their masters for the same reason Jesus wants his followers to "not resist an evil person" and to turn the other cheek and to go the extra mile (Matthew 5:39-42, NLT). He wants them to be salt and light in this fallen world. It is about winning over enemies with goodness and love.[47]

Now we can come to a better and fuller interpretation and

finally answer the question, Why does Paul tell masters to be "just and fair to your slaves" (Colossians 4:1, NLT) instead of simply commanding them to set them free?

First, we should not imagine that the slavery of the Roman Empire was like the slavery of the antebellum South, rooted in human trafficking and racism. At the time of Jesus and the apostles, "slavery was not a matter of race but of circumstance and social standing."[48] Some slaves became slaves as a result of war, kidnapping, or judicial sentence, but others entered slavery voluntarily as a means of escaping poverty and indebtedness. In these cases, to free a slave would put them in a worse position, for they would no longer be protected or provided for. This is why when a slave was freed, they would often continue to work for their master, who would become their patron. In other words, being freed often left a person in a worse position because not all free persons were better off than slaves. Some starved or returned to their masters, especially during times of hardship, such as illness or injury. In addition to this, being a slave also gave a person a substitute family, if they had none, providing them with an opportunity to improve their social and financial position.[49] There were slaves who owned their own businesses, managed large sums of money, and "practiced highly skilled professions." Slaves in the Roman Empire were legally bound by contract to serve their masters for seven years, at which time they were freed and given their wage in one lump sum (the master was legally required to save the slave's wages until they were released).[50] To shorten this process would have been devastating.

Another reason Paul did not advocate for masters to set their slaves free but instead to treat them "justly and fairly" was because of how it would affect the witness of the Christian community. Directing masters to emancipate all their slaves could be interpreted by the Roman Empire as a seditious act. This would have been fatal to the fledging church, which had little or no political clout and was already being viewed suspiciously by Rome.[51] Instead, Paul—unlike Aristotle, who held that "there can be no injustice" toward slaves[52]—exhorts masters to treat their slaves in the same respectful way their slaves are to treat them and to "stop your threatening, knowing that he who is both their Master and yours is in heaven, and that there is no partiality with him" (Ephesians 6:9). This teaching advances the golden rule as taught by Jesus, for masters are to treat their servants not only as they want to be treated but as if they are both under the constant, watchful eye of Christ. Here Paul plants the seeds of reconciliation and restoration.[53] Almost two thousand years later, this would be wonderfully captured in the magnificent Christmas hymn "O Holy Night":

Truly He taught us to love one another;
His law is love and His gospel is peace.
Chains shall He break, for the slave is our brother,
And in His name all oppression shall cease.[54]

Whether or not we personally agree with the approach Scripture lays out, it is clear that the biblical writers never endorsed or accepted slavery. Instead, they worked to undermine it by redefining the relationship between slave and master. It is also clear they did not preach social justice as we think about it today, and we must be careful not to read that into the biblical text. It is worth noting that history teaches us their approach worked. Despite its revival during the Middle Ages, slavery dimmed slowly because of the light of Christianity, which held strongly to the idea that we are all brothers and sisters in Adam and, more significantly, in Christ.[55] This legacy of proclaiming "liberty to the captives" and setting the oppressed free (Luke 4:18) is supremely exemplified in the lives and works of William Wilberforce, John Newton, and the entire abolitionist movement.

A Book of Reconciliation

One of the most oft-repeated criticisms we have faced in our conversations with those who struggle with the Bible is that it tolerates and condones slavery and other social evils. This conclusion is rooted in the assumption that the Bible is a social justice book. While the prophets and apostles brought hope to the oppressed, they did so through the message of the gospel (yes, the gospel is in the Old Testament too!). Their primary message was one of reconciliation, to reveal God's desires and actions to redeem or restore lost souls and break down the dividing wall that separates humankind from each other.[56]

To be clear, the Bible has a lot to say about social justice issues, but it does not seek to change the world through revolution but through reconciliation and restoration. And the Bible tells us that the best way to do that is not by getting even or revolting against our enemies but by holding up a mirror to an unjust society and allowing it to see itself. And we do this through preaching, praying, and living out the truth of the gospel, which is "the power of God for salvation to everyone who believes" (Romans 1:16). When we keep this in mind, many passages of Scripture, which seem to fall short of our modern thoughts about social justice, will make better sense. The Bible does not teach us to overthrow institutions and governments through violence but by turning hearts back to God and endearing all people to each other. We can bear this patient approach because we trust that God will one day right every wrong and judge the world justly and fairly.[57]

Final Thoughts

The Bible is a subversive book (for good). Just ask the leaders of dozens of countries where it is outlawed or restricted.[58] But it is *not* a social justice manifesto. To approach it as such is to lose the heart of its message—a message so powerful that it has reshaped the world in wondrous ways. It is a message of restraint, not revenge or violence.[59] It is a message of hope to the oppressed and a warning to their oppressors. It promotes both diversity and unity through love for one another. It acknowledges that we are all sinners (like Adam) and in need of the mercy of God and foresees a day when we all will stand before our Creator. Then there will be no escaping justice, for all of our thoughts, words, and deeds will be exposed and nothing will be hidden from God. On that day, it won't matter if we are Jew or Gentile, male or female, Black or white, rich or poor, slave or free, for "God shows no partiality" (Acts 10:34).[60] On that day, God will not be satisfied until "justice roll[s] down like waters, and righteousness like an ever-flowing stream" (Amos 5:24). The only thing that will matter then is if we have received the forgiveness of sins and our name is written in the Lamb's Book of Life. And for those whose names are found in that Book, truth, justice, and peace will reign. And, as if that would not be enough, we will hear a loud voice from the throne of heaven say,

> Behold, the dwelling place of God is with man. He will dwell with them, and they will be his people, and God himself will be with them as their God. He will wipe away every tear from their eyes, and death shall be no more, neither shall there be mourning, nor crying, nor pain anymore, for the former things have passed away. . . . Behold, I am making all things new.
>
> REVELATION 21:3-5

Conclusion

To the Bible men will return; and why?
Because they cannot do without it.

MATTHEW ARNOLD

We began with the story of Brad, Shawn's cousin who lost his faith by reading the Bible. For Brad, it was a combination of factors, but primarily it was his belief that since the Bible supported slavery, it couldn't possibly be the Word of God. When it comes to faith loss, Brad's not alone in citing problems with the Bible as the reason. In fact, it's fair to say the most popular reason former Christians give for renouncing their faith is that they finally read the Bible for themselves and were shocked at what they discovered. Whether it's that they became convinced it contains contradictions, is scientifically and historically inaccurate, issues immoral commands, or reads like a fairy tale, the Bible for former Christians is anything but the Good Book.

We get it. The Bible being the Good Book is something we took for granted for a long time too. As we gained the ability to think critically, however, we had to face the fact that the Bible isn't quite what we thought it was. Sure, it still had inspiring stories of spiritual heroes, beautiful poetry, and wise sayings. But it also contained a lot of stuff nobody ever told us about. A lot of *troubling* stuff. Enough troubling stuff that we also wondered how the Bible could ever be called the Good Book. Yet over time, we came to realize the problem wasn't with the Bible but with our assumptions about what the Bible is and what it contains.

We've tried to show that if a person who is wrestling with difficult passages in the Bible has a more accurate view of what the Bible is and an appropriate method of reading it, a lot of the problems resolve on their own. We maintain that the lenses modern readers often unknowingly read the Bible through—their assumptions—distort rather than clarify its message. What we need in order to read the Bible well is to become aware of our unhelpful lenses, discard them, and adopt interpretive principles that set us up to better understand its message.

Many criticize Christians today for not knowing their Bibles and for simply accepting what they've been taught without proper study. While this may be true, it's equally true that many critics of the Bible dismiss it without taking the time to properly interpret it. Disagreements over interpretation are inevitable, but that doesn't mean a correct understanding doesn't exist. Our goal in this book has been to help you achieve that understanding. We have tried to both instruct and model how to interpret the Bible well. In each chapter we provided examples of poor interpretation, explained why the interpretation was incorrect, and then did our best to model good interpretation. We did so by tackling some of the Bible's thorniest passages. Our hope was to show that when these passages are understood accurately and interpreted well, the objections raised against them are shown to be the result of faulty assumptions about the Bible and not the Bible itself.

Two of the most common faulty assumptions that individuals bring to the Bible are what kind of book they believe it *is* (or that it *must* be) and what its contents *should* reflect. Concerning the first, readers mistakenly hold one or more of the following assumptions: The Bible is a book written to them, is easy to understand, is a timeless rule book, and *must* be without error to be God's Word. Concerning the second, they believe its contents should reflect a modern scientific view of the world, align with modern standards of historical truth telling, and be consistent with modern moral norms.

When they conclude it doesn't meet their assumptions, readers are left with two choices:

1. Conclude that since the Bible fails to meet their assumptions, it isn't the Word of God.
2. Question the validity of their assumptions.

Too often they choose option one. Why?

We're convinced the reason many people renounce their faith is that their faulty assumptions are so deep, they're unaware they possess them, so questioning them never crosses their mind. And when they do become aware, the assumptions seem so obviously true that questioning them seems unnecessary. Yet that is exactly what we encourage readers to do when they find themselves struggling with the Bible. As we've seen, even though some assumptions about the Bible seem obviously true, they're not. And not questioning our assumptions when they're out of line with the Bible is tragic because often they're invalid criteria in determining whether the Bible is God's Word.

To see this, join us in a thought experiment. Imagine an individual well-versed in current events, who has thoughtful opinions on a range of matters, graduated near the top of their college class, went on to earn a PhD in sociology, and wrote a *New York Times* bestseller. We suspect you will likely agree with us that such a person is worthy of being regarded as intelligent. But what if you find out that in high school they bombed the SAT? Do you still think they're intelligent? It all depends on how you view the SAT. If you assume that to be truly intelligent, a person must score high on the SAT, then no, you won't think they're intelligent—they fell short of your intelligence criterion. But given everything you know about them, what makes more sense: to conclude they aren't intelligent or to question your assumption that a high score on the SAT is required for intelligence? To us it's a no-brainer. We would question our assumption about the SAT.

We hope the same is true when it comes to the assumptions you use to determine whether the Bible is the Word of God. If you assume that for the Bible to be the Word of God, it must meet a certain criterion (such as the eight faulty ones we addressed in this book) and then conclude it doesn't, you also have two choices. You can decide it isn't the Word of God and no longer identify as a follower of Jesus. Or, given everything else you know about the Bible—its impact on art, music, literature, social justice movements, law, and science; its transformative power in the lives of billions of people; and the evidence for its greatest claim, the resurrection of Jesus—you can, as in the thought experiment, question your assumptions about the Bible. We trust that if you choose the second option and question your assumptions, discard them as the lenses you read the Bible through if they're found to be faulty, and apply sound principles of interpretation to your study of the Bible, you'll discover, yes, it really is the Good Book!

Notes

INTRODUCTION

1. "Modeling the Future of Religion in America," Pew Research Center, September 13, 2022, https://www.pewresearch.org/religion/2022/09/13/modeling-the-future-of-religion-in-america/.
2. Ryan Burge, "Can You Ever Really Leave Religion Behind?," Graphs About Religion, January 4, 2024, https://www.graphsaboutreligion.com/p/can-you-ever-really-leave-religion.
3. "Chapter 2: Religious Switching and Intermarriage," Pew Research Center, May 12, 2015, https://www.pewresearch.org/religion/2015/05/12/chapter-2-religious-switching-and-intermarriage/.
4. Pinetops Foundation, *The Great Opportunity: The American Church in 2050* (Pinetops Foundation, 2018), 9.
5. Personal correspondence with author (John).
6. Rodney Wilson, *Killing God: Christian Fundamentalism and the Rise of Atheism* (CreateSpace, 2015), appendix 2.
7. "What on Earth Is the Hebrew Bible?," BibleProject Classroom, video, 33 min., 55 sec., BibleProject, accessed February 13, 2025, https://bibleproject.com/classroom/introduction-to-the-hebrew-bible/sessions/1.
8. Greg Boyd, "The Bible Is NOT the Foundation," *ReKnew* (blog), February 27, 2018, https://reknew.org/2018/02/bible-not-foundation/.
9. See Scot McKnight, *The Blue Parakeet: Rethinking How You Read the Bible* (Zondervan, 2008), 41–54.

CHAPTER 1: NEVER JUDGE A BOOK BY ITS COVER

1. Having each ministered in a church setting for over thirty years, we can tell you the motives for avoiding difficult passages are far less nefarious

than skeptics might presume. For most preachers and teachers, it is a matter of time and priorities. Simply put, problematic passages are some of the most complicated and confusing passages to teach on, requiring additional study time and having little relevance to an average person's life. So these passages are often shelved in favor of passages that are more easily understood.

2. Tremper Longman III, *Confronting Old Testament Controversies: Pressing Questions About Evolution, Sexuality, History, and Violence* (Baker Books, 2019), 4.
3. Adriani Milli Rodrigues, "Scripture," in *Lexham Theological Wordbook*, ed. Douglas Mangum et al., Lexham Bible Reference Series (Lexham Press, 2014).
4. Philip D. Stern, "Loanwords in Biblical Hebrew," Biblical Archaeology Society, October 26, 2020, https://www.biblicalarchaeology.org/daily/loanwords-in-biblical-hebrew.
5. F. F. Bruce, "The Bible," in *The Origin of the Bible*, ed. Philip Wesley Comfort (Tyndale, 2003), 5–12.
6. Chris Bruno, *The Whole Message of the Bible in 16 Words* (Crossway, 2017), 25–31, 43–59.
7. Longman, *Confronting Old Testament Controversies*, 5–6.
8. If you want to know more about this process and why some Christian traditions, such as Catholicism and the Eastern Orthodox Church, recognize additional Old Testament books, we recommend two books on the subject that are informative yet easy to understand: *The Origin of the Bible*, edited by Philip Wesley Comfort, and *A General Introduction to the Bible* by Norman L. Geisler and William E. Nix.
9. See Luke 24:27, 44; John 5:39. See also Acts 17:1-3, 10-13; 2 Timothy 3:15.
10. See John 14:26; 16:12-14; 17:6-8.
11. John E. Goldingay, "The 'Salvation History' Perspective and the 'Wisdom' Perspective Within the Context of Biblical Theology," *Evangelical Quarterly* 51, no. 4 (1979): 196.
12. Eileen Clare Grant, *Understanding the Story of the Bible: An Introduction to Salvation History* (Catholic Truth Society, 2013).
13. For those speeches, see Acts 2:14-36 (Peter); 7:1-60 (Stephen); and 13:16-41; 17:22-34 (Paul). See also Robert W. Yarbrough, "Paul and Salvation History," in *Justification and Variegated Nomism: The Paradoxes of Paul*, ed. D. A. Carson et al., vol. 2 (Baker Academic, 2004), 297.
14. See John 5:39, 46; 8:56. See also Luke 24:27, 44-48.
15. Longman, *Confronting Old Testament Controversies*, 7.
16. Longman, *Confronting Old Testament Controversies*, 4.
17. Martin Luther King Jr., *Strength to Love* (Fortress, 2010), 48.

18. King, *Strength to Love*, 47.
19. See Ephesians 6:7-8; Colossians 3:23-24; 1 Peter 2:18-25.
20. "Can't Judge a Book by Its Cover," The Idioms, accessed June 3, 2024, https://www.theidioms.com/cant-judge-a-book-by-its-cover; Ann H. Gabhart, "Judging a Book by Its Cover," *One Writer's Journal* (blog), Ann H. Gabhart, August 31, 2022, https://www.annhgabhart.com/2022/08/31/judging-a-book-by-its-cover/.
21. George Eliot, *The Mill on the Floss* (Grapevine India, 2022), chap. 3, Kindle, emphasis added.

CHAPTER 2: THE LEGACY OF THE BIBLE

1. Sam Armato, *The Bible and Western Culture* (AuthorHouse, 2012), v–vi.
2. We define the Western world as those countries that share a common European cultural heritage.
3. Vishal Mangalwadi, "How the Bible Created the Soul of Western Civilization: An Interview with Vishal Mangalwadi," interview by Jonathan Petersen, *Bible Gateway Blog*, July 27, 2015, https://www.biblegateway.com/blog/2015/07/how-the-bible-created-the-soul-of-western-civilization-an-interview-with-vishal-mangalwadi/. See also Vishal Mangalwadi, *This Book Changed Everything: The Bible's Amazing Impact on Our World*, vol. 1 (SoughtAfterMedia, 2019).
4. See Matthew 11:19; Luke 7:35.
5. For those interested in this type of research, we recommend Vishal Mangalwadi, *The Book That Made Your World: How the Bible Created the Soul of Western Civilization* (Thomas Nelson, 2012).
6. George A. Lindbeck, "The Church's Mission to Postmodern Culture," in *Postmodern Theology: Christian Faith in a Pluralist World*, ed. Frederic B. Burnham (Harper & Row, 1989), 38.
7. Theodore Parker, *A Discourse of Matters Pertaining to Religion*, ed. Thomas Wentworth Higginson (American Unitarian Association, 1907), 290.
8. *Fall:* that humans sinned and were exiled from paradise (see Genesis 2:4–3:24). We, as human beings, all share in that tragic moment (see Romans 5:12-21). The belief that *all* men and women, despite being made in the image of God, are corrupted and sinful has led to the call for governments to have checks and balances. *Redemption:* that God sent his Son to *save* and *redeem* us and make reconciliation with him and humankind possible (see, for example, Mark 10:45; John 3:16; 2 Corinthians 5:18-21; Ephesians 2:13-22). This was accomplished through the death and resurrection of Jesus. The fact that Jesus died for all, even sinners, proved God loved every nation, tribe, people, and language. This inspired devoted Christians to fearlessly cross both geographical and social boundaries to help those in need. *Consummation:* that one day the Lord will return to judge the world,

both the living and the dead, and usher in a new creation (see, for example, Acts 10:42; 17:30-31; 2 Timothy 4:1; 1 Peter 4:5; Revelation 20:1-15). The belief that Jesus would one day judge Christians and the world produced a strong work ethic. It also encouraged activist Christians like Martin Luther King Jr. to continue their work even when their lives were in danger, even knowing they would not see the results of their labors.

9. For God creating the world, see Genesis 1:1–2:3. For God creating humans in his image, see Genesis 1:27; 5:1; 9:6.
10. See Ephesians 4:24; James 3:9.
11. Thomas F. X. Noble et al., *Western Civilization: The Continuing Experiment* (Houghton Mifflin, 2006), 230.
12. Mangalwadi, *This Book Changed Everything*, 220–248.
13. Dee Dyas and Esther Hughes, *The Bible in Western Culture: The Student's Guide* (Routledge, 2006), 9, 18.
14. "AP 'Napalm Girl' Photo from Vietnam War Turns 40," Associated Press, June 1, 2012, https://www.ap.org/media-center/ap-in-the-news/2012/ap-napalm-girl-photo-from-vietnam-war-turns-40/.
15. Kim Phuc, "The Long Road to Forgiveness," *All Things Considered*, NPR, June 30, 2008, http://www.npr.org/templates/story/story.php?storyId=91964687.
16. "Richard Dawkins: I'm a Cultural Christian," interview by Rachel Johnson, LBC Radio, April 1, 2024, YouTube, https://www.youtube.com/watch?v=COHgEFUFWyg.
17. Friedrich Nietzsche, *Twilight of the Idols, or How to Philosophize with the Hammer*, trans. Richard Polt (Hackett, 1997), 53.
18. Mangalwadi, "How the Bible Created the Soul of Western Civilization," interview by Jonathan Petersen.
19. John Marriott and Shawn Wicks, *Before You Go: Uncovering Hidden Factors in Faith Loss* (Leafwood, 2022), 210.
20. As a disclaimer, this is not a recommendation or an endorsement of the film. The movie is not for the squeamish or faint of heart. And though its themes are profound and worth pondering, it is chock-full of human depravity, blatant brutality, gratuitous violence, and profanity.
21. *The Book of Eli*, directed by Albert Hughes and Allen Hughes (Warner Bros. Pictures, 2010).
22. *Book of Eli*.
23. David Barr Kirtley, host, *The Geek's Guide to the Galaxy*, podcast, season 5, "Episode 164: Gary Whitta," produced by John Joseph Adams, August 21, 2015, https://geeksguideshow.com/2015/08/21/ggg164-gary-whitta/.
24. For the devil misusing Scripture, see Matthew 4:7-10; Luke 4:9-12. For the Pharisees, see Matthew 12:9-14; Mark 7:9-13; 10:2-9. For Peter's statement, see 2 Peter 3:16. For Paul's, see Philippians 1:15-18.

25. It is significant that the early church equated the gospel with the Word of God. For just a few examples, see these passages from the book of Acts: 4:29-31; 10:36; 11:1; 12:24; 13:5-7, 44-49; 15:7, 35-36; 16:6, 32; 17:11, 13; 18:5, 11; 19:10, 20. See also Luke 8:11-12; Romans 10:8, 17; 1 Corinthians 14:36; 15:2; 2 Corinthians 2:17; 4:2; Ephesians 1:13; Philippians 1:12-14; Colossians 1:5; 1 Thessalonians 2:13; 2 Timothy 2:8-9; 4:2; James 1:18, 21; 1 Peter 1:23-25; Revelation 1:9; 20:4.
26. Marriott and Wicks, *Before You Go*, 216.

CHAPTER 3: THE CHURCH'S BOOK

1. We are not saying that just because the LDS Church produced and is intimately acquainted with the Book of Mormon that we should accept their claim that it is a revelation from God. We are saying, rather, that when seeking to understand what the Book of Mormon *teaches*, the views of the LDS Church need to be given consideration and weight.
2. To be clear, we are not saying you shouldn't listen to those who offer critical interpretations of biblical passages. We are saying that before you adopt their critical interpretations, you should listen to interpretations from those within the Christian community qualified to speak with a measure of expertise on the passages in question.
3. We think a good example is when the church changed its teaching on the Earth being the center of the universe because of the advance of science. In this case, the church was in error for believing the Bible taught that the Earth was the center of the universe, when in fact the Bible did not teach that. Therefore, the church's interpretation was wrong, not the Bible.
4. We are not saying that pastors and lay leaders in the church are unqualified to address challenging biblical texts. On the contrary, we think that they are the *first* people Christians should turn to. However, many problems raised about Scripture by those who have encountered atheist apologists, former Christians, or professors of comparative religion at public universities are academic in nature and require an expertise that most pastors and lay leaders do not possess.
5. Brad East, *The Church's Book: Theology of Scripture in Ecclesial Context* (Eerdmans, 2022).
6. Such as Bart Ehrman, Robert Price, James Crossley, Robert Funk, Paula Fredriksen, and Gerd Lüdemann.
7. Hans-Georg Gadamer, *Truth and Method*, rev. ed., trans. Joel Weinsheimer and Donald G. Marshall (Continuum, 2004).
8. Kurt Eichenwald, "The Bible: So Misunderstood It's a Sin," *Newsweek*, December 23, 2014, https://www.newsweek.com/2015/01/02/thats-not-what-bible-says-294018.html.
9. "Reporter Biography: Kurt Eichenwald," *New York Times*, accessed

February 22, 2024, https://archive.nytimes.com/www.nytimes.com/ref/business/EICHENWALD-BIO.html.

10. Eichenwald, "The Bible."
11. Eichenwald, "The Bible." Many skeptics don't follow Eichenwald's line of argument concerning the *copying* of manuscripts. Rather, they maintain that the telephone game describes how the story of Jesus was passed on *orally* before it was written down. This is a much more plausible objection. For a response to this objection, we recommend this article: Michael J. Kruger, "Did the Early Christians Get the Jesus Story Wrong?," The Gospel Coalition, May 2, 2016, https://www.thegospelcoalition.org/reviews/jesus-before-the-gospels/.
12. Bart D. Ehrman, *A Brief Introduction to the New Testament*, 4th ed. (Oxford University Press, 2017), 50; Joe Rogan, host, *The Joe Rogan Experience*, "Episode 1444—Duncan Trussell," March 19, 2020, https://jre.cx/episodes/1444-duncan-trussell-2/.
13. If you would like to read about the reliability of the Old Testament, we recommend Walter C. Kaiser Jr., *The Old Testament Documents: Are They Reliable and Relevant?* (InterVarsity Press, 2001).
14. Eichenwald, "The Bible."
15. Peter J. Gurry, "Myths About Variants: Why Most Variants Are Insignificant and Why Some Can't Be Ignored," in *Myths and Mistakes in New Testament Textual Criticism*, ed. Elijah Hixson and Peter J. Gurry (IVP Academic, 2019), 195.
16. An excellent resource for those who are interested in learning more is Elijah Hixson and Peter J. Gurry, eds., *Myths and Mistakes in New Testament Textual Criticism* (IVP Academic, 2019).
17. Gurry, "Myths About Variants," 210.
18. Bart D. Ehrman, *The New Testament: A Historical Introduction to the Early Christian Writings*, 3rd ed. (Oxford University Press, 2003), 481.
19. F. F. Bruce, *The New Testament Documents: Are They Reliable?*, 6th ed. (Eerdmans and InterVarsity Press, 1981), 14.
20. "Daniel B. Wallace on the New Testament Documents," Apologetics315, July 8, 2012, https://apologetics315.com/2012/07/daniel-b-wallace-on-the-new-testament-documents/. While it is true that we do possess thousands of manuscript copies of the books of the New Testament, it is worth noting that they are of varying quality, size, and temporal proximity to the originals. Some manuscripts are only fragments, while others consist of almost the entire New Testament. Some are quite old—within a hundred years of the originals—while others are from the late Middle Ages. Textual scholars weigh these factors when examining manuscripts.
21. It must be said that while most differences are resolved by textual criticism, some are not. Most of the ones that are not resolved are

minor. However, there are some differences among manuscripts that are significant (for example, Mark 1:1; Mark 16:9-20; Luke 23:34; John 7:53–8:11). These can be disconcerting to learn about for those who assume their copy of the Bible is inerrant. However, it needs to be said that inerrancy does not apply to the copies, only the original manuscripts. Furthermore, no essential Christian belief is undermined by these differences because no doctrine or practice rests on a single passage, but rather the teaching of the entire Bible.

22. Bruce W. Griffin, "The Paleographical Dating of P-46," paper presented at the Society of Biblical Literature annual meeting, New Orleans, November 1966, https://www.biblical-data.org/P-46%20Oct%201997.pdf.
23. We possess only 210 manuscripts for Plato's *Tetralogies*, 109 for Herodotus's *History*, and 251 for Caesar's *Gallic Wars*. See Clay Jones, "The Bibliographical Test Updated," Christian Research Institute, April 12, 2023, https://www.equip.org/articles/the-bibliographical-test-updated/.

CHAPTER 4: ONCE UPON A TIME . . .

1. *Religulous*, directed by Larry Charles (Thousand Words, 2008).
2. InstructionHopeful16, "Yup. I too accepted Christ at age 3," reply to r/Exvangelical, "My mom gave me a 'story' I wrote," Reddit, August 3, 2022, https://www.reddit.com/r/Exvangelical/comments/wfe8ow/my_mom_gave_me_a_story_i_wrote/.
3. Amy Swanson, "Is the Bible a Fairy Tale?," Christianity.com, September 16, 2020, https://www.christianity.com/wiki/bible/is-the-bible-a-fairy-tale.html.
4. Nathan Shane Miller, *The Fine Print of Christianity* (Wipf and Stock, 2010), 84.
5. David Hume, *Enquiries Concerning Human Understanding and Concerning the Principles of Morals*, 3rd ed., ed. P. H. Nidditch (repr., ed. L. A. Selby-Bigge, 1777; Oxford University Press, 1975), 86, 115n.
6. On the claim that Hume believed miracles were impossible, see Robert A. Larmer, "Interpreting Hume on Miracles," *Religious Studies* 45, no. 3 (2009): 325–338, https://www.cambridge.org/core/journals/religious-studies/article/abs/interpreting-hume-on-miracles/95079AFEB694628AAD1716D68B702A3B.
7. Lee Strobel, *The Case for Miracles: A Journalist Investigates Evidence for the Supernatural* (Zondervan, 2018), 54.
8. George Campbell, *A Dissertation on Miracles: Containing an Examination of the Principles Advanced by David Hume, Esq., in an Essay on Miracles [. . .]* (Thomas Tegg, 1824), 31–32.
9. C. S. Lewis, *Miracles: A Preliminary Study* (Macmillan, 1971), 105.

10. In a debate on the *Unbelievable?* podcast with Justin Bass, Bart Ehrman firmly maintains that he does not believe in miracles *because* they are violations of the laws of nature and the laws of nature *cannot* be violated, even by God! It is important to note that Ehrman's view is a philosophical commitment, not one based on evidence. His commitment to the view that the laws of nature cannot be violated determines how he evaluates any evidence for a miracle claim. The result is he dismisses the evidence out of hand because he has already determined miracles cannot, in principle, happen. It is important to see that no amount of evidence for a miracle will ever convince Ehrman because he is not open to evaluating it. Justin Brierley, host, *The Big Conversation*, podcast, season 5, episode 1, "Bart Ehrman vs. Justin Bass: Did Jesus of Nazareth Rise from the Dead?," Premier Unbelievable?, April 6, 2023, https://www.youtube.com/watch?v=LVUQAVQS1-U.
11. This example is modified from Miller, *Fine Print of Christianity*, 84.
12. Miller, *Fine Print of Christianity*, 84. See also Louis Markos, "Do Miracles Break the Laws of Nature?," Explore God, accessed February 26, 2025, https://www.exploregod.com/articles/do-miracles-break-the-laws-of-nature.
13. John Earman, *Hume's Abject Failure: The Argument Against Miracles* (Oxford University Press, 2000), 3.
14. Carl Sagan, *Broca's Brain: Reflections on the Romance of Science* (Random House, 1979), 62.
15. Jonathan McLatchie, "Do Extraordinary Claims Require Extraordinary Evidence? Assessing Carl Sagan's Dictum," Jonathan McLatchie, November 13, 2020, https://jonathanmclatchie.com/do-extraordinary-claims-require-extraordinary-evidence-assessing-carl-sagans-dictum/.
16. Susan Crabtree, "Americans Embrace Religion, Reject Religious Bigotry," RealClear Opinion Research, January 10, 2024, https://www.realclearpolitics.com/real_clear_opinion_research/americans_embrace_religion_reject_religious_bigotry__150295.html.
17. We recognize that *sufficient* is a relative term that introduces a subjective element into evaluating claims. But relative is different from ambiguous. Whereas *sufficient* refers to the *amount* of evidence a person requires to overcome their skepticism, *extraordinary* refers to the *kind* of evidence required. When it comes to sufficiency, each person will require a different amount of evidence to overcome an initial low probability claim. But that's normal. What is not normal is requiring a vague and indefinable special kind of evidence.
18. Charles Taylor, *Modern Social Imaginaries* (Duke University Press, 2003), 23.
19. James K. A. Smith, *You Are What You Love: The Spiritual Power of Habit* (Brazos Press, 2016), 7.

20. Sean McDowell and John Marriott, *Set Adrift: Deconstructing What You Believe Without Sinking Your Faith* (Zondervan Reflective, 2023), 78.
21. Taylor is aware that people still believe in supernatural things, just not the way they once did. Today, as opposed to the past, belief in the supernatural is chosen and contested, not taken for granted.
22. Jeffrey E. Green, "Two Meanings of Disenchantment: Sociological Condition vs. Philosophical Act—Reassessing Max Weber's Thesis of the Disenchantment of the World," *Philosophy and Theology* 17, no. 1/2 (2005): 57, https://www.polisci.upenn.edu/sites/default/files/Green.Disenchantment_1.pdf.
23. It needs to be acknowledged that along with intuition, there were theological reasons for the Roman Catholic Church to affirm the geocentric view. They mistakenly believed the Bible taught the Earth was at the center of the cosmos. The Church no longer believes that the Bible teaches the Earth is the center of the cosmos.
24. Justin Brierley, host, *Unbelievable?*, podcast, "Hugh Ross vs. Peter Atkins: Debating the Origins of the Laws of Nature," Premier Unbelievable?, August 10, 2018, https://www.youtube.com/watch?v=hVCVt-dvVOc; Erik Strandness, "When Atheism Becomes Unfalsifiable. Peter Atkins and the Problem of Evidence," *Unbelievable?* (blog), Patheos, last updated November 6, 2020, https://www.patheos.com/blogs/unbelievable/2020/11/when-atheism-becomes-unfalsifiable-peter-atkins-and-the-problem-of-evidence/.
25. One of the most astounding cases of a verified, documented medical miracle is that of Barbara Cummiskey Snyder, who was healed of multiple sclerosis. This story is recounted in Lee Strobel, *The Case for Miracles: A Journalist Investigates Evidence for the Supernatural* (Zondervan, 2018). The story is also told by her personal physician Thomas Marshall in Scott J. Kolbaba's *Physicians' Untold Stories: Miraculous Experiences Doctors Are Hesitant to Share with Their Patients, or ANYONE!* (CreateSpace, 2016).
26. We recommend the works of N. T. Wright, *The Resurrection of the Son of God* (Fortress Press, 2003); Michael R. Licona, *The Resurrection of Jesus: A New Historiographical Approach* (IVP Academic, 2010); William Lane Craig, *The Son Rises: The Historical Evidence for the Resurrection of Jesus* (Moody, 1981).

CHAPTER 5: TO ERR IS . . . DIVINE?

1. Daniel B. Wallace, "The Gospel According to Bart: A Review Article of *Misquoting Jesus* by Bart Ehrman," *Journal of the Evangelical Theological Society* 49, no. 2 (June 2006): 327, https://etsjets.org/wp-content/uploads/2010/06/files_JETS-PDFs_49_49-2_JETS_49-2_327-349_Wallace.pdf.

2. We do not want to misrepresent Dr. Ehrman by giving the impression that his rejection of inerrancy caused his deconversion. He has publicly stated that although his disillusionment with the Bible started him down the path that led him away from the faith, he attributes his embrace of agnostic atheism to the problem of evil. For more on his deconversion, see his book *God's Problem: How the Bible Fails to Answer Our Most Important Question—Why We Suffer* (HarperOne, 2009).
3. Bart D. Ehrman, *Misquoting Jesus: The Story Behind Who Changed the Bible and Why* (HarperOne, 2005), 11.
4. Timothy Paul Jones, *Misquoting Truth: A Guide to the Fallacies of Bart Ehrman's* Misquoting Jesus (IVP Books, 2007).
5. Norman Geisler and Thomas Howe, *When Critics Ask: A Popular Handbook on Bible Difficulties* (Victor Books, 1992), 181.
6. Zvi Ron, "Dodanim/Rodanim: Three Approaches," *Jewish Bible Quarterly* 34, no. 2 (2006), https://jbqnew.jewishbible.org/assets/Uploads/342/342_Dodanim.pdf.
7. The claim that the Bible is inspired by God is a theological claim and not an empirical one that can be proven or disproven by evidence in the same way that a historical claim can be. The theological argument for the inspiration of the Bible is grounded in the claim that the Gospels are generally reliable accounts of the life of Jesus. As such there is good reason to believe the Gospels accurately reflect the beliefs and teachings of Jesus. And Jesus' view of the Bible (the Old Testament) was that it was the divinely inspired Word of God. The inspiration of the New Testament finds its support in that it is apostolic. The Gospels tell us that Jesus authorized the apostles to be his spokespeople. As such, their writings have Jesus' stamp of approval on them as inspired Scripture. That being said, few Christians arrive at their view of the Bible's inspiration based on such an argument. Instead, most appropriately assume that since they are Christians, they ought to believe what the Bible teaches, and the Bible teaches that it is inspired (see 2 Timothy 3:16; 2 Peter 3:2).
8. There are many reasons to trust that the claims of the Bible are reliable: fulfilled prophecy, the findings of archaeology, corroborating evidence from historical documents outside the Bible, eyewitness testimony, and the willingness of Jesus' first followers to die for the claims they made.
9. C. Michael Patton, "'If the Bible Is Not Inerrant, Then Christianity Is False' . . . and Other Stupid Statements," *Parchment and Pen* (blog), Credo House, accessed March 3, 2025, https://credohouse.org/blog/if-the-bible-is-not-inerrant-then-christianity-is-false-and-other-stupid-statements.
10. While we do not think the Bible must be inerrant to be generally trustworthy, we do think inerrancy is important for doing theology. Without an authoritative text, we are left to decide which parts of the

Bible are true and which aren't. When we stand over the Bible and determine when it speaks truthfully about matters of faith and practice, it becomes tempting to conclude that anything we find objectionable is mistaken and can be rejected. When that happens, we replace the God who stands behind the Bible with a God who reflects our own image.

11. William Lane Craig, host, *Reasonable Faith Podcast*, "What Is Inerrancy?," Reasonable Faith, December 15, 2008, https://www.reasonablefaith.org/media/reasonable-faith-podcast/what-is-inerrancy.
12. "1.5 Deconversion: The Bible (A)," created by Evid3nc3, October 21, 2009, YouTube, 9 min., 53 sec., https://www.youtube.com/watch?v=70SYwkoH_yc&t=292s.
13. Craig Evans, quoted at Rajkumar Richard, "A Beginners Guide to Understand and Answer Dr. Bart Ehrman," Christian Apologetics Alliance, August 18, 2016, https://christianapologeticsalliance.com/2016/08/18/a-beginners-guide-to-understand-and-answer-dr-bart-ehrman/.
14. Craig, *Reasonable Faith Podcast*, "What Is Inerrancy?."
15. Of course, if there is a critical mass of errors in the Bible, that would cause one to wonder if the Bible is generally trustworthy on what it claims about Jesus. In such a scenario, that would make remaining a Christian impossible.
16. Mike Licona, "On Chicago's Muddy Waters," Risen Jesus, June 2, 2014, https://www.risenjesus.com/chicagos-muddy-waters.
17. John H. Walton, *The Lost World of Genesis One: Ancient Cosmology and the Origins Debate* (IVP Academic, 2010), 7.
18. Jackson Wu, "The Doctrine of Scripture and Biblical Contextualization: Inspiration, Authority, Inerrancy, and the Canon," *Themelios* 44, no. 2 (2019), https://www.thegospelcoalition.org/themelios/article/the-doctrine-of-scripture-and-biblical-contextualization/.
19. Craig Blomberg, "An Interview with Craig Blomberg," interview by Justin Taylor, The Gospel Coalition, March 26, 2008, https://www.thegospelcoalition.org/blogs/justin-taylor/interview-with-craig-blomberg/.
20. Kenneth E. Bailey, "Informal Controlled Oral Tradition and the Synoptic Gospels," *Themelios* 20, no. 2 (1995), https://www.thegospelcoalition.org/themelios/article/informal-controlled-oral-tradition-and-the-synoptic-gospels/.
21. This section draws on the work of Darrell L. Bock, "The Words of Jesus in the Gospels: Live, Jive, or Memorex?," in *Jesus Under Fire: Modern Scholarship Reinvents the Historical Jesus*, ed. Michael J. Wilkins and J. P. Moreland (Zondervan, 1995), 74–99.
22. Bailey, "Informal Controlled Oral Tradition."
23. Bock, "Words of Jesus," 78–81, 86.
24. Nevertheless, we do acknowledge that sometimes the differences in

wording can result in differing interpretations of the same event. A robust doctrine of inspiration allows for this.

CHAPTER 6: EASY-PEASY LEMON SQUEEZY

1. Bart Ehrman, "Are the Gospels Historically Reliable? The Problem of Contradictions," moderated by Kurt Jaros, Defenders Media, the Defenders conference, October 2019, posted June 27, 2020, by Bart D. Ehrman, YouTube, https://www.youtube.com/watch?v=AymnA526j9U.
2. Sam Harris, "Meme #8," Sam Harris, May 3, 2017, https://www.samharris.org/blog/meme-8.
3. Bob Sullivan, "Perspicuity of Scripture," *Southern Nebraska Register*, May 29, 2020, https://www.lincolndiocese.org/op-ed/in-laymans-terms/13946.
4. Kristian Brackett, "The Perspicuity of the Scriptures: Presupposition, Principle or Phantasm," *Kairos: Evangelical Journal of Theology* 4, no. 1 (2010): 31–50, https://hrcak.srce.hr/215468.
5. R. C. Sproul, *Knowing Scripture*, rev. ed. (IVP Books, 2009), 39.
6. Italics added in these passages.
7. James Callahan, *The Clarity of Scripture: History, Theology and Contemporary Literary Studies* (InterVarsity Press, 2001), 9.
8. Tremper Longman III, *Confronting Old Testament Controversies: Pressing Questions About Evolution, Sexuality, History, and Violence* (Baker Books, 2019), 10. The big picture of Scripture encompasses creation, fall, redemption, and consummation.
9. Kevin J. Vanhoozer, *Is There a Meaning in This Text? The Bible, the Reader, and the Morality of Literary Knowledge* (Zondervan, 1998), 315, 317.
10. *Westminster Confession of Faith* (1646) 1.7.
11. Charles Hodge, *Systematic Theology*, vol. 1 (Scribner, 1878), 183–184.
12. See, for example, Luke 24:25-27; Acts 8:34-35. See also Romans 12:6-7; Ephesians 4:11-13.
13. Martin Luther, *The Bondage of the Will*, trans. Henry Cole (Baker Book House, 1976), 25–29.
14. Wayne Grudem, *Systematic Theology: An Introduction to Biblical Doctrine* (Zondervan, 2002), 106. For Jesus' statements "You have heard it said . . . but I say . . ." see Matthew 5:21-22, 27-28, 31-34, 38-39, 43-44. For "Haven't you read the Scriptures?" see Matthew 12:3; 19:4; 22:31. For "You are wrong . . ." see Matthew 22:29.
15. See Mark 7:9-13; 10:2-9; 12:9-17.
16. See Romans 11:33-36. See also Deuteronomy 29:29; Job 26:14; Isaiah 45:15; 55:8-9.
17. R. A. Torrey, *The Divine Origin of the Bible: Its Authority and Power Demonstrated, and Difficulties Solved* (Revell, 1899), 38.

18. Dietrich Bonhoeffer, *Ecumenical, Academic, and Pastoral Work: 1931–1932*, ed. Victoria J. Barnett et al., trans. Anne Schmidt-Lange et al., Dietrich Bonhoeffer Works, vol. 11 (Fortress Press, 2012), 260; Tal Gur, "A God Who Let Us Prove His Existence Would Be an Idol," Elevate Society, accessed March 5, 2025, https://elevatesociety.com/a-god-who-let-us/.
19. John Marriott and Shawn Wicks, *Before You Go: Uncovering Hidden Factors in Faith Loss* (Leafwood Publishers, 2022), 209.
20. Craig L. Blomberg, *Matthew*, The New American Commentary, vol. 22 (Broadman Press, 1992), 215.
21. See 1 Corinthians 2:14; 2 Corinthians 2:6-16.
22. See Matthew 13:23; Mark 4:20; Luke 8:15; James 1:21.
23. Duane A. Garrett, *Proverbs, Ecclesiastes, Song of Songs*, The New American Commentary, vol. 14 (B&H, 1993), 205.

CHAPTER 7: THE CASE OF MISTAKEN INTERPRETATION

1. James O'Brien, "Sherlock Holmes: Pioneer in Forensic Science," *Encyclopedia Britannica*, March 31, 2014, https://www.britannica.com/topic/Sherlock-Holmes-Pioneer-in-Forensic-Science-1976713.
2. It was a joy to find others who have noticed the same connection: Trevin Wax, "10 Tips on Solving Mysterious Bible Passages from Sherlock Holmes," The Gospel Coalition, July 2, 2012, accessed June 8, 2024, http://thegospelcoalition.org/blogs/trevinwax/2012/07/02/10-tips-on-solving-mysterious-bible-passages-from-sherlock-holmes/; "How Sherlock Holmes Can Help Us Read Scripture," The River, July 14, 2017, https://theriverupstate.org/how-sherlock-holmes-can-help-us-read-scripture/; Timothy Fox, "Hermeneutics and Sherlock Holmes," Sean McDowell, March 10, 2018, https://seanmcdowell.org/blog/hermeneutics-and-sherlock-holmes.
3. Arthur Conan Doyle, "A Scandal in Bohemia," *The Complete Sherlock Holmes Collection*.
4. Tremper Longman III, *Confronting Old Testament Controversies: Pressing Questions About Evolution, Sexuality, History, and Violence* (Baker Books, 2019), 18.
5. Conan Doyle, "The Man with the Twisted Lip," *Complete Sherlock Holmes Collection*.
6. Conan Doyle, "A Study in Scarlet," *Complete Sherlock Holmes Collection*.
7. Dan Kimball, *How (Not) to Read the Bible: Making Sense of the Anti-Women, Anti-Science, Pro-Violence, Pro-Slavery and Other Crazy-Sounding Parts of Scripture* (Zondervan, 2020), 40.
8. Gordon D. Fee and Douglas Stuart, *How to Read the Bible for All Its Worth*, 3rd ed. (Zondervan, 2003), 28.

9. Howard G. Hendricks and William D. Hendricks, *Living by the Book: The Art and Science of Reading the Bible*, rev. ed. (Moody Publishers, 2007), 147–168.
10. Conan Doyle, "A Case of Identity," *Complete Sherlock Holmes Collection*.
11. Fee and Stuart, *How to Read the Bible*, 31. See 2 Peter 1:20-21. See also 2 Samuel 23:2; Luke 1:70; Acts 1:16; 3:18; 1 Peter 1:11-12.
12. See 1 Thessalonians 5:20-21; 1 John 4:1. See also Jeremiah 29:8; 1 Corinthians 14:29-33. See also R. C. Sproul, *Knowing Scripture*, rev. ed. (IVP Books, 2009), 108–111.
13. Conan Doyle, "The Sign of Four," *Complete Sherlock Holmes Collection*.
14. Conan Doyle, "A Study in Scarlet," *Complete Sherlock Holmes Collection*.
15. See John 5:39, 46; 8:56; compare with Luke 24:27, 44-48.
16. Kyle Butt and Dan Barker, "Butt/Barker Debate: Does the God of the Bible Exist?," University of South Carolina Columbia, February 12, 2009, video, 1 hr., 58 min., 17 sec., Apologetics Press, February 28, 2011, https://apologeticspress.org/video/does-the-god-of-the-bible-exist-video-3639/.
17. Brian D. McLaren, *A New Kind of Christian: A Tale of Two Friends on a Spiritual Journey* (Fortress Press, 2019), 79, 71. For Jesus' teaching on loving enemies, see Matthew 5:44; compare with Luke 6:27-28; Romans 12:20.
18. For example, read the account by SS Stubaf. Haller, chief of police of Bromberg, Poland, in which this method was utilized in the Second World War at Bromberg: "to take the Jewish children by their feet and to break their heads by striking against the wall of the rooms in order to avoid the firing report." Pierre Joffroy, *A Spy for God: The Ordeal of Kurt Gerstein*, trans. Norman Denny (Harcourt Brace Jovanovich, 1971), 292.
19. Conan Doyle, "The Boscombe Valley Mystery," *Complete Sherlock Holmes Collection*.
20. See 2 Kings 20:18; Isaiah 39:7; and Daniel 1:1-4 for historical context.
21. Tremper Longman III, *Psalms: An Introduction and Commentary*, Tyndale Old Testament Commentaries, vol. 15–16 (InterVarsity Press, 2014), 449.
22. John Ahn, "Psalm 137: Complex Communal Laments," *Journal of Biblical Literature* 127, no. 2 (2008): 277.
23. Derek Kidner, *Psalms 73–150: An Introduction and Commentary*, Tyndale Old Testament Commentaries, vol. 16 (InterVarsity Press, 2008), 495.
24. Kyle Butt, "Psalm 137:9—Dashing Babies' Heads Against a Stone," Apologetics Press, May 15, 2016, https://apologeticspress.org/psalm-1379dashing-babies-heads-against-a-stone-913/.
25. See 2 Kings 8:12; Isaiah 13:16; Hosea 10:14; 13:16; Nahum 3:10.
26. Compare Psalm 137:8 with Jeremiah 51:56.
27. Ahn, "Psalm 137," 289.

28. Miroslav Volf, *Free of Charge: Giving and Forgiving in a Culture Stripped of Grace* (Zondervan, 2005), 134.
29. See Exodus 23:4-5; Job 31:29-30; Psalm 7:3-5.
30. For other examples of this type of response in Scripture, see Psalm 94:1-7 and Revelation 6:9-11.
31. For Christ paying for the sins of the past (even Old Testament sins), see Hebrews 10:10-17. For the future judgment of the world, see Ecclesiastes 12:14; Matthew 12:36; Acts 10:42; 17:31; Romans 2:16; 14:10, 12; 1 Corinthians 3:13; 4:5; 2 Peter 2:9; and 1 John 4:17.
32. Arthur Conan Doyle, *The Hound of the Baskervilles* (Signet Classics, 1902), 41.
33. Conan Doyle, "The Red-Headed League," *Complete Sherlock Holmes Collection.*

CHAPTER 8: A FISH OUT OF WATER

1. "Culture Shock Stages: Everything You Need to Know," *Now Health Blog*, January 20, 2020, https://www.now-health.com/en/blog/culture-shock-stages/.
2. Lumen Learning, "2.8: Culture Shock," LibreTexts Social Sciences, accessed March 7, 2025, https://socialsci.libretexts.org/Bookshelves/Anthropology/Cultural_Anthropology/Cultural_Anthropology_(Evans)/02%3A_Culture/2.08%3A_Culture_Shock.
3. Barnabas Piper, *Help My Unbelief: Why Doubt Is Not the Enemy of Faith*, rev. ed. (Good Book, 2020), 17, 148–149. He writes, "I know what Scripture says and I know the arguments, but the questions stack up. Some people think, *God says it, I believe it, that settles it.* But it doesn't settle it. Did God really say it? I don't really believe it. Nothing is settled."
4. Tremper Longman III, *Confronting Old Testament Controversies: Pressing Questions About Evolution, Sexuality, History, and Violence* (Baker Books, 2019), 18.
5. Jeannine K. Brown, *Scripture as Communication: Introducing Biblical Hermeneutics*, 2nd ed. (Baker Academic, 2021), 130–131.
6. Longman, *Confronting Old Testament Controversies*, 18.
7. See Hebrews 1:1-2 and 2 Peter 1:20-21.
8. This combined approach is called the historical-grammatical method of interpretation. See Adonis Vidu, "Hermeneutics," in *Evangelical Dictionary of Theology*, 3rd ed., ed. Daniel J. Treier and Walter A. Elwell (Baker Academic), 196, 730. See also Anthony C. Thiselton, *Hermeneutics: An Introduction* (Eerdmans, 2009), 22; Friedrich Schleiermacher, *Hermeneutics: The Handwritten Manuscripts*, ed. Heinz Kimmerle, trans. James Duke and Jack Forstman (Scholars Press, 1977), 104.

9. Gordon D. Fee and Douglas Stuart, *How to Read the Bible for All Its Worth*, 3rd ed. (Zondervan, 2003), 26.
10. These questions are adapted from Adonis Vidu, "Hermeneutics," in *Evangelical Dictionary of Theology*, ed. Daniel J. Treier and Walter A. Elwell (Baker Academic, 2017), 380. Also see Howard G. Hendricks and William D. Hendricks, *Living by the Book: The Art and Science of Reading the Bible* (Moody Publishers, 2007), 133; Kenneth Berding, *Bible Revival: Recommitting Ourselves to One Book* (Lexham Press, 2013), 52.
11. Eric J. Bargerhuff, *The Most Misused Verses in the Bible: Surprising Ways God's Word Is Misunderstood* (Bethany, 2012), 72.
12. Michael J. Gorman, *Apostle of the Crucified Lord: A Theological Introduction to Paul and His Letters*, 2nd ed. (Eerdmans, 2017), 12–13.
13. Sherwood G. Lingenfelter and Marvin K. Mayers, *Ministering Cross-Culturally: An Incarnational Model for Personal Relationships* (Baker Book House, 1986), 37–51, 81–94.
14. A great example of this type of transaction/exchange is found in the story of Jesus' encounter with the Syrophoenician woman found in Mark 7:24-30. For explanation of how the honor-shame dynamic works in this encounter, we highly recommend Ched Myers, *Binding the Strong Man: A Political Reading of Mark's Story of Jesus* (Orbis Books, 1988), 204. We also discuss this dynamic and passage in chapter 12.
15. Werner G. Jeanrond, "Interpretation, History of: History of Biblical Hermeneutics," in *The Anchor Bible Dictionary*, Anchor Yale Bible Dictionary, vol. 3, ed. David Noel Freedman (Doubleday, 1992), 439.
16. See Acts 1:6. See also Mark 9:12-13; Luke 17:20.
17. See Matthew 26:14-16; Luke 22:3-6; John 12:1-8; John 13:2, 27.
18. The only verse that might provide some support that Judas had other motives besides greed is Matthew 27:3. In this passage Judas has second thoughts about his actions and admits he has betrayed innocent blood. We believe the inclusion of these words does not suggest any messianic disillusionment but rather shows that Judas was fully aware that his actions were ignoble and disgraceful.
19. E. Randolph Richards and Brandon J. O'Brien, *Misreading Scripture with Western Eyes: Removing Cultural Blinders to Better Understand the Bible* (IVP Books, 2012), 213.
20. C. S. Lewis, *Reflections on the Psalms* (HarperCollins, 2017), 115.
21. Richard Dawkins, *The God Delusion* (Houghton Mifflin, 2006), 51.
22. Eugene H. Merrill, *Deuteronomy*, The New American Commentary, vol. 4 (B&H, 1994), 294; Peter C. Craigie, *The Book of Deuteronomy*, The New International Commentary on the Old Testament (Eerdmans, 1976), 216. See Psalm 78:8; Jeremiah 5:23.

23. Wilhelm Gesenius, *Gesenius's Hebrew and Chaldee Lexicon to the Old Testament Scriptures*, trans. Samuel Prideaux Tregelles (Wiley & Sons, 1893), 246.
24. Edward J. Woods, *Deuteronomy: An Introduction and Commentary*, Tyndale Old Testament Commentaries (IVP Academic, 2011), 235.
25. See Exodus 32:13; 34:9; Leviticus 20:24; 25:46; 27:28; Numbers 18:20-26; 26:53-56; 27:7-11; 32:32; 34:2, 13-18; 35:2, 8; 36:2-4, 7-9, 12; Deuteronomy 1:38; 4:20-21, 38; 10:9; 12:9-12; 14:27-29; 15:4; 16:20; 18:1-2; 19:10, 14; 20:16; 21:16, 23; 24:4; 25:19; 26:1; 29:8. The verses here only include those passages from the Pentateuch (the first five books of the Bible) where "inheritance" is mentioned. There are countless similar verses scattered throughout the Old and New Testaments, especially in the book of Joshua.
26. The phrase "hear and fear" found at the end of this passage in Deuteronomy 21 is used in three other places (see Deuteronomy 13:5, 10-11; 17:11-13; 19:18-20). Each of these instances reveals that rebellious living was on par with idolatry, contempt, and murder. Why? Because all these endangered Israel's very existence. This punishment was designed specifically to "purge the evil" (see Deuteronomy 22:21-24; 24:7, which also has implied "inheritance" ramifications).
27. J. Dyneley Prince, review of *The Code of Hammurabi, King of Babylon About 2250 BC*, ed. and trans. Robert Francis Harper, *American Journal of Theology* 8, no. 3 (1904): 604, https://www.jstor.org/stable/3153895?seq=1.
28. "The place of the judicial hearing was the gate, that is, the broad plaza just outside the gate where matters of public interest were conducted (for example see Deuteronomy 22:15, 24; 25:7; Ruth 4:1, 11; Psalm 69:12; Proverbs 31:23, 31; Jeremiah 17:19)." Merrill, *Deuteronomy*, 294.
29. Woods, *Deuteronomy*, 236. The same can be said about other severe laws elsewhere (e.g., Deuteronomy 22:21).
30. See Deuteronomy 21:22-23, which immediately follows the "rebellious son" law, and which *prophetically* points to Christ hanging on a tree (see Galatians 3:13) as the faithful Son who pays the price and takes on the curse and shame of humankind's rebellion in order to rescue all God's children and protect their future inheritance.
31. This is a common theme found throughout the wisdom books of the Bible. For example, see Proverbs 10:19; 12:18; 15:28; 18:2; 29:20; Ecclesiastes 3:7; also, contrast Job 2:11-13 with Job 16:1-5.
32. Michael F. Bird, *Seven Things I Wish Christians Knew About the Bible* (Zondervan Reflective, 2021), 96.

CHAPTER 9: DOING THE RIGHT THING

1. Richard Dawkins, *The God Delusion* (Houghton Mifflin, 2006), 51.
2. Douglas Stuart, *Old Testament Exegesis: A Handbook for Students and Pastors*, 5th ed. (Westminster John Knox Press, 2022), appendix 2.
3. Bart D. Ehrman, *Jesus, Interrupted: Revealing the Hidden Contradictions in the Bible (and Why We Don't Know About Them)* (HarperOne, 2009), 281.
4. Chris Colvin, "How NOT to Preach the Old Testament," *Influence*, January 8, 2019, https://influencemagazine.com/Practice/How-NOT-to-Preach-the-Old-Testament.
5. See Psalm 107:23-32, where the Lord (Yahweh) is extolled as the one who is in control of the wind and sea.
6. Ludwig Koehler et al., *The Hebrew and Aramaic Lexicon of the Old Testament*, vol. 2, ed. and trans. M. E. J. Richardson (E. J. Brill, 1995), 707; Francis Brown, Samuel Rolles Driver, and Charles Augustus Briggs, *Enhanced Brown-Driver-Briggs Hebrew and English Lexicon* (Clarendon Press, 1977), 654–655.
7. The word *na'ar* appears in the following passages and refers to various people depending on context. For "baby," see Exodus 2:6; "young man," see 2 Samuel 14:21; 18:5; "young servant," see Genesis 22:3; "armor-bearer," see Judges 9:54; "king's official," see 2 Kings 19:6; "priest," see 1 Samuel 2:17; "construction workers" and "warrior," see Nehemiah 4:16.
8. Paul R. House, *1, 2 Kings*, The New American Commentary, vol. 8 (B&H, 1995), 260.
9. See Genesis 9:24; 27:15, 42; 29:16, 18; Judges 15:2; 1 Samuel 14:49; 16:11; 17:14; 1 Chronicles 24:31; Ezekiel 16:46, 61.
10. See 1 Kings 3:7; 11:17. Although Solomon describes himself as a "little child" (*na'ar qatan*), he is old enough to marry and govern Israel (see also 1 Kings 3:1, 9). Later, Hadad is also called a "little child" (*na'ar qatan*), yet he is an adversary (i.e., a rival) of Solomon (see 1 Kings 11:14) and is old enough to be given a house and a portion of land (see 1 Kings 11:18).
11. R. K. Harrison, "Bethel, Bethelite (City)," in *Baker Encyclopedia of the Bible*, vol. 1 (Baker Book House, 1988), 286–287; Donald J. Wiseman, *1 and 2 Kings: An Introduction and Commentary*, Tyndale Old Testament Commentaries, vol. 9 (IVP Academic, 1993), 211. See 1 Kings 12:28-33 and Hosea 13:1-3. Perhaps they were even descendants of those false prophets that Elijah had executed after the contest on Mount Carmel (see 1 Kings 18:40), which would also help explain their disdain for Elisha (his disciple).
12. See Eric J. Ziolkowski, "The Bad Boys of Bethel: Origin and Development of a Sacrilegious Type," *History of Religions* 30, no. 4 (1991): 331–358, https://www.journals.uchicago.edu/doi/10.1086/463245.

13. The story of Elijah's departure occurs earlier in the same chapter (see 2 Kings 2:1-18).
14. See Isaiah 15:1-3; 22:12; Jeremiah 16:6; Ezekiel 7:18; 27:31; Amos 8:10; Micah 1:16.
15. In Genesis 28:10-22, Jacob names the place Bethel ("House of God") and consecrates it to Yahweh.
16. House, *1, 2 Kings*, 260–261. See 1 Kings 18:20-40.
17. David J. Hesselgrave and Edward Rommen, *Contextualization: Meanings, Methods, and Models* (William Carey Library, 2000), 148.
18. Daniel Castelo and Robert W. Wall, *The Marks of Scripture: Rethinking the Nature of the Bible* (Baker Academic, 2019), 160.
19. See 2 Timothy 3:16 and Hebrews 4:12-13.
20. Jeannine K. Brown, *Scripture as Communication: Introducing Biblical Hermeneutics*, 2nd ed. (Baker Academic, 2021), 237.
21. Haddon W. Robinson, *Biblical Preaching: The Development and Delivery of Expository Messages*, 3rd ed. (Baker Academic, 2014), 58; Brown, *Scripture as Communication*, 255.
22. Scott B. Rae, *Doing the Right Thing: Making Moral Choices in a World Full of Options* (Zondervan, 2013), 157.
23. Elliott Johnson, *Expository Hermeneutics: Advancing the Discussion* (Wipf and Stock, 2023), 48, 125–126. See Romans 4:23-24; 15:4; 1 Corinthians 9:9-10; 10:6.
24. Michael F. Bird, *Seven Things I Wish Christians Knew About the Bible* (Zondervan Reflective, 2021), 150.
25. S. I. Hayakawa and Alan R. Hayakawa, *Language in Thought and Action*, 5th ed. (Harcourt Brace Jovanovich, 1993), 84–85.
26. Obviously, Paul did not use Hayakawa's ladder of abstraction. We mean this in a purely retrospective sense.
27. Eugene H. Merrill, *Deuteronomy*, The New American Commentary, vol. 4 (B&H, 1994), 298.
28. With special thanks to Ken Edwards.
29. See Luke 7:38, 45; 15:20; Acts 20:37.
30. See Luke 7:44-48. See also C. S. Keener, "Kissing," in *Dictionary of New Testament Background*, ed. Craig A. Evans and Stanley E. Porter (InterVarsity Press, 2000), 628–629; Linda L. Belleville, *2 Corinthians*, The IVP New Testament Commentary Series (InterVarsity Press, 1996), 336–337. "*Kiss* (*philēma*) comes from the Greek word for 'friend' (*philos*)—a person to whom one is under a basic obligation."
31. Moyer V. Hubbard, "2 Corinthians," in *Zondervan Illustrated Bible Backgrounds Commentary: Romans to Philemon*, vol. 3, ed. Clinton E. Arnold (Zondervan, 2002), 258; Robert J. Banks, *Paul's Idea of Community*, rev. ed. (Hendrickson, 1994), 85.

32. Dio Chrysostom, "The Euboean Discourse," *Discourses 1–11*, trans. J. W. Cohoon, Loeb Classical Library 257 (Harvard University Press, 1932), 319.
33. David W. J. Gill, "1 Corinthians," in *Zondervan Illustrated Bible Backgrounds Commentary: Romans to Philemon*, vol. 3, ed. Clinton E. Arnold (Zondervan, 2002), 100–105.
34. "Understanding the Kiss: Reverence in Orthodox Christianity," Orthodoxy Christianity 101, March 25, 2024, https://www.orthodoxchristianity101.com/post/understanding-the-kiss-reverence-in-orthodox-christianity; Emmanuel Stamatiou, "The Kiss," Saint Anna Gold Coast, Greek Orthodox Parish-Community, accessed March 12, 2025, https://gocstanna.org/the-kiss/.
35. Simon J. Kistemaker, *Exposition of the Second Epistle to the Corinthians*, New Testament Commentary (Baker Books, 1997), 459.
36. Or "brothers and sisters." Not unlike the word *hermanos* in Spanish, in Greek, the plural *adelphoi*, depending on context, may mean either "brothers" or "brothers and sisters."
37. What Paul labels a *holy* kiss, Peter calls a kiss of *agape* (see 1 Peter 5:14). *Agape* means something different from a friendly or romantic kiss. *Agape* was a key theological word for early Christians, specifically associated with God's abundant love for humankind. It refers to a godly (covenantal) love.
38. Joseph H. Hellerman, *The Ancient Church as Family* (Fortress Press, 2001), 36.
39. For example, Cicero writes to his younger brother, Quintus, the following words: "When I miss you, am I feeling the absence only of a brother? No, I miss a brother who is, in charming companionship, like a friend, in obedience like a son, in wisdom like a father. What pleasure did I ever have without you, or you without me?" Marcus Cicero, *Letters to His Brother Quintus* 1.3.3, as quoted in Jo-Ann Shelton, *As the Romans Did: A Sourcebook in Roman Social History*, 2nd ed. (Oxford University Press, 1998), 23–24.
40. See 1 Corinthians 1:10-13; 3:1-4; 11:18; 12:25; 14:20.
41. See also Galatians 3:25-29; Colossians 3:11-15; Murray J. Harris, *The Second Epistle to the Corinthians*, New International Greek Testament Commentary (Eerdmans, 2005), 936.
42. David E. Garland, *2 Corinthians*, The New American Commentary, vol. 29 (B&H, 1999), 554.
43. See 1 Thessalonians 1:6; 2:14; 3:3-4; Mark A. Seifrid, *The Second Letter to the Corinthians*, The Pillar New Testament Commentary (Eerdmans, 2014), 495.
44. Gustav Stählin, "The Kiss of Judas," in *Theological Dictionary of the New Testament*, ed. Gerhard Kittel and Gerhard Friedrich, trans. Geoffrey W. Bromiley, 10 vols. (Eerdmans, 1964), 140–141.

45. For a discussion on biblical ethics, we highly recommend the following books by Scott B. Rae: *Doing the Right Thing: Making Moral Choices in a World Full of Options* (Zondervan, 2013) and *Moral Choices: An Introduction to Ethics*, 4th ed. (Zondervan, 2018).
46. "Pope Quotes Gandhi to Encourage Bible Reading," Matters India, February 28, 2016, https://mattersindia.com/2016/02/pope-quotes-gandhi-to-encourage-bible-reading/.

CHAPTER 10: BEHIND THE TIMES

1. "Egyptian Jurists to Sue 'the Jews' for Compensation for 'Trillions' of Tons of Gold Allegedly Stolen During Exodus from Egypt," Special Dispatch, no. 556, MEMRI, August 22, 2003, https://www.memri.org/reports/egyptian-jurists-sue-jews-compensation-trillions-tons-gold-allegedly-stolen-during-exodus. See Exodus 3:22; 11:2; 12:35-36; 35:4-36.
2. "Jots & Tittles: Moses & Co. on Trial," *Bible Review*, December 2003, 12.
3. "Egyptian Intellectuals Warn Against Suing 'the Jews,'" Special Dispatch, no. 575, MEMRI, September 19, 2003, https://www.memri.org/reports/egyptian-intellectuals-warn-against-suing-jews.
4. René Pache, *The Inspiration and Authority of Scripture*, trans. Helen I. Needham (Sheffield, 1969), 128.
5. Robert Dick Wilson, *A Scientific Investigation of the Old Testament* (Sunday School Times, 1926), 5. To this day, skeptics and higher critics have not answered his groundbreaking investigations, and rather than attempt to address them, they simply choose to ignore them. See Brian Nicks, "Life and Work of Robert Dick Wilson," *The Master's Seminary Journal* 19, no. 1 (2008): 106.
6. "W. M. Ramsay," Christian Classics Ethereal Library, accessed March 13, 2025, https://www.ccel.org/ccel/ramsay.
7. W. M. Ramsay, *The Bearing of Recent Discovery on the Trustworthiness of the New Testament*, 2nd ed. (Hodder and Stoughton, 1915), 81.
8. Ramsay, *Bearing of Recent Discovery*, 222.
9. Ramsay was educated in the Tübingen school of thought, founded by F. C. Baur, which doubted the reliability and historicity of the New Testament. See W. Ward Gasque, *Sir William M. Ramsay: Archaeologist and New Testament Scholar; A Survey of His Contribution to the Study of the New Testament* (Baker Book House, 1966), 23; W. M. Ramsay, *St. Paul the Traveller and the Roman Citizen*, 3rd ed. (Putnam's Sons, 1898), 7–8. Ramsay testifies to the following: "I may fairly claim to have entered on this investigation without any prejudice in favour of the conclusion which I shall now attempt to justify to the reader. On the contrary, I began with a mind unfavourable to it, for the ingenuity and apparent completeness of the Tübingen theory had at one time quite convinced me. It did not

lie then in my line of life to investigate the subject minutely; but more recently I found myself often brought in contact with the book of Acts as an authority for the topography, antiquities, and society of Asia Minor. It was gradually borne in upon me that in various details the narrative showed marvellous truth."

10. Ramsay, *Bearing of Recent Discovery*, 85.
11. "Dr. Nelson Glueck Dead at 70; Archaeologist and College Head," *New York Times*, February 14, 1971, https://www.nytimes.com/1971/02/14/archives/dr-nelson-glueck-dead-at-70-archeologist-and-college-head-president.html.
12. Nelson Glueck, *Rivers in the Desert: A History of the Negev* (Farrar, Straus and Cudahy, 1959), 31.
13. National Museum of Natural History–Smithsonian Institution, "The Bible as History," accessed March 13, 2025, https://csnradio.com/wp-content/uploads/2019/12/SmithsonianLetter-o.pdf; also see Margaret Hunter, "15 Historical Proofs of the Bible," Amazing Bible Timeline with World History, April 29, 2013, https://amazingbibletimeline.com/blog/q9_historical_proof_bible/.
14. John Blanchard, *Why Believe the Bible?* (EP Books, 2004), 16–17; special thanks to Blanchard for inspiring this section.
15. This is what both Carl Sagan and Richard Dawkins suggest in their respective books. See Carl Sagan, *The Demon-Haunted World: Science as a Candle in the Dark* (Ballantine Books, 1997), 207; Richard Dawkins, *Outgrowing God: A Beginner's Guide* (Random House, 2019), 13.
16. John N. Oswalt, distinguished professor of Old Testament at Asbury Theological Seminary, defines history like this: "A history is a narrative of a series of events revolving about human beings acting in time and space. Existing for the purpose of human self-knowledge, it purports to be an accurate account of all significant elements in the series and includes an attempt to evaluate the relative importance of these elements for the eventual outcome." John N. Oswalt, *The Bible Among the Myths: Unique Revelation or Just Ancient Literature?* (Zondervan, 2009), 113.
17. R. G. Collingwood, *The Idea of History* (Oxford University Press, 1946), 9–10.
18. Oswalt, *Bible Among the Myths*, 112.
19. Glueck, *Rivers in the Desert*, 31.
20. Mark W. Chavalas, "New Perspectives in the Study of Ancient Israel's Past," *Ashland Theological Journal* 23 (1991): 64–65, https://biblicalstudies.org.uk/pdf/ashland_theological_journal/23-1_62.pdf.
21. Mark Water, *Hard Questions About the Bible Made Easy* (Hendrickson, 2000), 12.
22. International Council on Biblical Inerrancy, *The Chicago Statement on*

Biblical Inerrancy (1978), article 13, https://library.dts.edu/Pages/TL/Special/ICBI_1.pdf; Mark Ellingsen, "The Great Debate on Biblical Authority and Biblical Hermeneutics: Are Baptists Really as Divided as They Think?," *Faith and Mission* 10, no. 1 (1992): 57, https://www.galaxie.com/article/fm10-1-03.

23. Carl F. H. Henry, *God, Revelation and Authority*, vol. 1 (Word Books, 1976), 232.
24. V. Philips Long, *The Art of Biblical History*, Foundations of Contemporary Interpretation, vol. 5 (Zondervan, 1994), 27–57.
25. Chad Bird, *The Christ Key: Unlocking the Centrality of Christ in the Old Testament* (1517 Publishing, 2021), 2–3; David C. Steinmetz, "Uncovering a Second Narrative: Detective Fiction and the Construction of Historical Method," in *The Art of Reading Scripture*, ed. Ellen F. Davis and Richard B. Hays (Eerdmans, 2003), 54.
26. Steinmetz, "Uncovering a Second Narrative," 54–65.
27. For example, see Numbers 12:8; Psalm 49:4; 78:2; Proverbs 1:6; Ezekiel 17:2; 24:3; Daniel 2:18-19, 27-30, 47; 5:12; Hosea 12:10; Matthew 13:10-13; 13:35; Mark 4:11, 33-34; Romans 11:25; 16:25; 1 Corinthians 4:1; 13:2; 14:2; 15:51; Ephesians 1:9; 3:3-9; 5:32; 6:19; Colossians 1:26-27; 2:2; 4:3; 1 Timothy 3:9, 16; Revelation 1:20; 10:7; 17:5-7.
28. Tremper Longman III, "Christotelic Approach," in *Five Views of Christ in the Old Testament: Genre, Authorial Intent, and the Nature of Scripture*, ed. Brian J. Tabb and Andrew M. King, Counterpoints: Bible and Theology (Zondervan Academic, 2022), 82–83.
29. Craig A. Carter, "Premodern Approach," in *Five Views of Christ in the Old Testament: Genre, Authorial Intent, and the Nature of Scripture*, ed. Brian J. Tabb and Andrew M. King, Counterpoints: Bible and Theology (Zondervan Academic, 2022), 249; Long, *Art of Biblical History*, 13, 57, 71–73.
30. J. C. Ryle, *Expository Thoughts on the Gospel of Luke*, rev. ed. (Aneko Press, 2020), 508.
31. According to most commentators, there were essentially two reasons for a census-taking in the biblical world. The first was to levy taxes (see Exodus 30:12-13; Numbers 3:40-51) and the second was to register adult males for military service (see Numbers 26:1-4). The nature of Joab's report to David suggests that the objective of this census was the latter (see 1 Chronicles 21:5). If this is the case, it would suggest that David's sin was a lack of trust in the Lord to protect him from his enemies. Perhaps this was Israel's sin as well. See Andrew E. Hill, *1 & 2 Chronicles*, The NIV Application Commentary (Zondervan, 2003), 293.
32. For the census numbers, see 2 Samuel 24:9 and 1 Chronicles 21:5. For the price David paid, see 2 Samuel 24:24 and 1 Chronicles 21:25.

33. For example, in 2 Samuel the number of Judahites is listed as 500,000 (see 24:9); the chronicler puts the number at 470,000 (see 1 Chronicles 21:5). It seems clear in this example that both authors are rounding off, but the author of 2 Samuel is rounding the number to the nearest hundred thousand while the author of 1 Chronicles is rounding off to the ten thousand. As for the other set of numbers, it seems to include the sum total, minus the Levites and the tribe of Benjamin. Roddy L. Braun, *1 Chronicles*, Word Biblical Commentary, vol. 14 (Thomas Nelson, 1986), 217–218.
34. "The discrepancy between the 'six hundred shekels of gold' in 1 Chronicles 21:25 and 'fifty shekels of silver' often has been explained on the basis of the different objects in view. Chronicles gives this as the price of 'the site,' which included land for the whole temple complex, whereas the fifty shekels of silver covered only the threshing floor and the oxen." J. A. Thompson, *1, 2 Chronicles*, The New American Commentary, vol. 9 (B&H, 1994), 103. Also, remember, chronology is only a minor concern to the biblical author; the purchase of the full site may have been made at a later time or perhaps in installments.
35. "While the Hebrew noun *satan* can refer to a human 'adversary' (1 Kings 5:4; 11:14, etc.) or an angelic adversary (Numbers 22:22, 32), it can also refer to the accuser in God's heavenly court, known as Satan (Job 1:6, 7, 8, 9, 12; 2:1, 2, 3; Zechariah 3:1-2)." Carol M. Kaminski, *1 & 2 Chronicles*, ed. Tremper Longman III and Scot McKnight, The Story of God Bible Commentary (Zondervan Academic, 2023), 210. Some scholars suggest there is no reference to Satan in this passage, only an unidentified adversary. I (Shawn) do not fall into this camp. The lack of a defined enemy, Joab's response, the supernatural flavor of the entire account, the Persian influence of duality, and the connection with Temple worship all lead me to believe the chronicler is referring to Satan.
36. Martin J. Selman, *1 Chronicles: An Introduction and Commentary*, Tyndale Old Testament Commentaries, vol. 10 (IVP Academic, 1994), 211.
37. See Job 1:12; 2:3, 6; Hill, *1 & 2 Chronicles*, 293.
38. V. Philips Long, *1 and 2 Samuel: An Introduction and Commentary*, Tyndale Old Testament Commentaries, vol. 8 (IVP Academic, 2020), 468.
39. See Matthew 4:1-11; Luke 13:10-17; 22:3, 31; 2 Corinthians 12:7; 1 Thessalonians 2:18; Revelation 12:3–13:10; 20:1-10.
40. See 2 Samuel 24:15; 1 Chronicles 21:14.
41. See Josephus, *Jewish Antiquities* 7.318. The literary context of Exodus 30:11-16 associates the census with the Day of Atonement (verse 10) and the Tabernacle (verses 17-20), emphasizing its great religious importance. If connected, the plague that strikes Israel appears to be a direct result

of Israel as a nation failing to remember the Lord. When a census was given, each person twenty years and older was to give a half shekel for the "ransom" for their lives (verse 12). The purpose was to "bring the people of Israel to remembrance before the LORD, so as to make atonement for your lives" (verse 16). As king of Israel, David would have been responsible for leading in this symbolic act. This means, because the Tabernacle was located in Gibeon (see 1 Chronicles 21:29-30), David and the people were not faithfully keeping the Day of Atonement. If this intertextual interpretation is correct, it would explain why the Lord led David to "raise an altar to the LORD on the threshing floor of Ornan the Jebusite" (1 Chronicles 21:18), which becomes the foundation for the future Temple that Solomon built (see 2 Chronicles 3:1; i.e., Mount Moriah). Certainly not by chance, it is also the place where in the past Abraham had offered Isaac but the Lord provided a sacrifice instead. In the future, it was where Christ would sacrifice himself by dying on the cross to atone for the sins of the world.

42. See Romans 16:25; Ephesians 3:4; Colossians 2:2; 4:3; Michael F. Bird, *Seven Things I Wish Christians Knew About the Bible* (Zondervan Reflective, 2021), 190.
43. Long, *Art of Biblical History*, 43, 167.
44. Michael McAfee and Lauren McAfee, *Not What You Think: Why the Bible Might Be Nothing We Expected yet Everything We Need* (Zondervan, 2019).
45. Charles H. Spurgeon, "Christ Precious to Believers," sermon no. 242, Blue Letter Bible, March 13, 1859, https://www.blueletterbible.org/comm/spurgeon_charles/sermons/0242.cfm. .
46. Hans Boersma, *Scripture as Real Presence: Sacramental Exegesis in the Early Church* (Baker Academic, 2017), 114.

CHAPTER 11: IT'S NOT ROCKET SCIENCE

1. Aaron Tabor, "How Science Almost Ruined My Faith," BioLogos, December 17, 2014, https://biologos.org/personal-stories/how-science-almost-ruined-my-faith.
2. Ryan Burge, "Can You Ever Really Leave Religion Behind?," Graphs About Religion, January 4, 2024, graphsaboutreligion.com, https://www.graphsaboutreligion.com/p/can-you-ever-really-leave-religion.
3. "Six Reasons Young Christians Leave the Church," Barna, September 27, 2011, https://www.barna.com/research/six-reasons-young-christians-leave-church/.
4. "Atheism Doubles Among Generation Z," Barna, January 24, 2018, https://www.barna.com/research/atheism-doubles-among-generation-z/.
5. J. P. Moreland, *Christianity and the Nature of Science: A Philosophical Investigation* (Baker Academic, 1999), 59–103.

6. Geoffrey Burbidge, "Why Only One Big Bang?," Scientific American, February 1992, 120.
7. W. Wayt Gibbs, "Profile: George F. R. Ellis," Thinking Globally, Acting Universally, *Scientific American*, October 1995, 55.
8. SubtractOneMore, "Science and religion are irreconcilable not because of the claims," reply to r/DebateReligion, "Science and Bible contradict each other," Reddit, February 7, 2024, https://www.reddit.com/r/DebateReligion/comments/1al9mcr/science_and_bible_contradict_each_other/?rdt=49127.
9. "#343 Concordism," Questions and Answers with Dr. William Lane Craig, Reasonable Faith, November 11, 2013, https://www.reasonablefaith.org/question-answer/P10/concordism; Johnny V. Miller and John M. Soden, *In the Beginning . . . We Misunderstood: Interpreting Genesis 1 in Its Original Context* (Kregel, 2012), 37.
10. John H. Walton, *Ancient Near Eastern Thought and the Old Testament: Introducing the Conceptual World of the Hebrew Bible* (Baker Academic, 2006), 165–178. It should be noted that while many evangelical scholars agree with Walton, some point out that we do not know for certain that the Israelites *believed* the cosmos was structured as Walton and others claim. As far as we are aware, all scholars agree that the Israelites *described* the cosmos as consisting of a dome stretched over a flat, circular earth, resting on pillars, surrounded by water. The question is, did the Israelites hold to that conceptual framework or simply use it to express their views? We suspect, given the Israelites' embeddedness in the thought world of the ancient Near East, they likely did assume the way they described the world reflected the world as it is.
11. Christy Hemphill et al., "From the Mailbag: Why Would God Allow Scientific Errors in the Bible?" BioLogos, September 15, 2016, https://biologos.org/articles/from-the-mailbag-why-would-god-allow-scientific-errors-in-the-bible.
12. John H. Walton and D. Brent Sandy, *The Lost World of Scripture: Ancient Literary Culture and Biblical Authority* (IVP Academic, 2013), 55.
13. John H. Walton, *The Lost World of Genesis One: Ancient Cosmology and the Origins Debate* (IVP Academic, 2009), 18.
14. Walton, *Lost World of Genesis One*, 19.
15. Johnny V. Miller and John M. Soden, *In the Beginning . . . We Misunderstood: Interpreting Genesis 1 in Its Original Context* (Kregel, 2012), 149.
16. Miller and Soden, *In the Beginning*, 101, 104.
17. Miller and Soden, *In the Beginning*, 148.
18. Along with our belief that Genesis 1 and 2 are not teaching science is our belief that the first three chapters of Genesis are not written to report history in a way that would be reflected if the events were recorded with

a video camera. We do not think Genesis is Hebrew poetry, but neither do we think it should be read as literal history. Rather, we agree with C. John Collins's description of the early chapters of Genesis as exalted prose: It's prose, and as such makes truth claims about the world. It's exalted in that it is not ordinary narration but extends beyond straightforward information. It uses rhetorical and literary techniques to communicate a worldview. We, like Collins, believe there was a real, historical couple who gave in to temptation and sinned, constituting what theologians call the fall. See C. John Collins, "Response from the Old-Earth View," in *Four Views on the Historical Adam*, ed. Matthew Barrett and Ardel B. Caneday (Zondervan, 2013).

19. Miller and Soden, *In the Beginning*, 149.
20. Encyclopedia.com, "Textbooks," updated June 11, 2018, https://www.encyclopedia.com/history/united-states-and-canada/us-history/textbooks.
21. For example, we have heard several well-meaning (but misled) pastors teach something similar to this: "Romans 5:12-14 tells us that sin is passed down genetically through males; therefore, this is why, as we find in Matthew 1:20-21, it was necessary for Jesus to be born of a virgin." We purposely have not referenced them here.
22. "Attention to the Bible's statements bearing on the physical sciences . . . will enable its readers to avoid many misconceptions to which empirical inquiry remains ongoingly vulnerable." Carl F. H. Henry, *God, Revelation and Authority*, vol. 1 (Crossway, 1999), 232.
23. John C. Lennox, *Seven Days That Divide the World: The Beginning According to Genesis and Science* (Zondervan, 2011), 30.
24. Augustine, *The Literal Meaning of Genesis*, vol. 1, trans. John Hammond Taylor, Ancient Christian Writers (Paulist Press, 1982), 42–43.
25. See Romans 1:20.
26. Amy Plantinga Pauw, *Proverbs and Ecclesiastes*, Belief: A Theological Commentary on the Bible (Westminster John Knox Press, 2015), 41; Duane A. Garrett, *Proverbs, Ecclesiastes, Song of Songs*, The New American Commentary, vol. 14 (B&H, 1993), 96; Tremper Longman III, *Proverbs*, Baker Commentary on the Old Testament Wisdom and Psalms (Baker Academic, 2006), 172; Gary Anderson, "What Happens When the Queen Ant Dies?," EcoGuard Pest Management, April 1, 2022, https://www.ecoguardpestmanagement.com/pest-resources/what-happens-when-the-queen-ant-dies.
27. Lennox, *Seven Days*, 27–35.

CHAPTER 12: TRUTH, JUSTICE, AND A BETTER TOMORROW

1. United Press International, "National Guard Moves into Gary," *Daily Banner*, July 29, 1968, Hoosier State Chronicles; Raymond A. Mohl,

"Gary, IN," in *Encyclopedia of Chicago*, ed. Janice L. Reiff, Ann Durkin Keating, and James R. Grossman (Chicago Historical Society, 2005), http://www.encyclopedia.chicagohistory.org/pages/503.html.

2. See, for example, Exodus 22:21-22; 23:9; Leviticus 23:22; Deuteronomy 14:29; Jeremiah 7:5-7; Ezekiel 22:29.
3. See Psalm 82:3; Proverbs 22:22; Isaiah 1:17; Zechariah 7:8-10; Malachi 3:5.
4. In this section, for brevity's sake, we do not explore the biblical concern about the poor in depth. Nonetheless, the God of the Bible is equally concerned about the poor and the other groups (see, for example, Exodus 22:25; 23:11; Leviticus 19:10; 25:35, 39; Deuteronomy 15:9-11; Psalm 72:4, 12; Proverbs 14:31; 19:17; 31:20; Isaiah 41:17; 61:1; Matthew 11:5; Mark 10:21; Luke 4:18; 2 Corinthians 9:9; Galatians 2:10; James 2:1-7, 14-17; 5:1-6; 1 John 3:17-18).
5. See Numbers 15:14; Deuteronomy 16:14.
6. See Mark 12:40; Luke 7:12-14; 21:2-3. See also Acts 6:1; 9:39-41; 1 Timothy 5:3-16; James 1:27. The fatherless were often associated with widows for obvious reasons and were specifically noted as needing special protection (see Job 29:12; Psalm 10:14-18; 68:5; 82:3; Hosea 14:3; John 14:18).
7. See Matthew 4:24-25; 12:18-21. For the centurion's servant, see Matthew 8:5-13. For the Syrophoenician woman's daughter, see Mark 7:24-30. For healing and feeding in the region of the Decapolis, see Mark 7:31–8:10.
8. See John 3:16-17; 4:42; 12:47; 1 John 2:2; 4:14.
9. See Acts 1:8; 8:1-40; 10:1–11:30.
10. See Acts 9:15; 13:46-48; 14:27; 15:1-21; 21:19; 26:23; 28:28; Romans 1:13-17; 3:29; 9:1–11:36; 15:8-21; Ephesians 3:7-8; Colossians 1:27; 1 Thessalonians 2:16; 1 Timothy 2:7; 2 Timothy 4:17.
11. See Revelation 5:9; 7:9; 21:24-26; 22:2.
12. See Matthew 27:4; Mark 14:55-59; Luke 23:47; Hebrews 4:15; 5:2; 7:26. See also Isaiah 53:3-4, 7-9; George Lindbeck, summarized in *The Nature of Confession: Evangelicals and Postliberals in Conversation*, ed. Timothy R. Phillips and Dennis L. Okholm (InterVarsity Press, 1996), 19–20.
13. Carl F. H. Henry, "Responsibility Toward Victims' Rights," in *God and the Victim: Theological Reflections on Evil, Victimization, Justice, and Forgiveness*, ed. Lisa Barnes Lampman (Eerdmans, 1999), 64.
14. Some have noted how Superman has often represented social justice ideals and has marked the evolution of the movement since his appearance in the spring of 1938. In the fall of 2021, Jim Lee, the chief creative officer of DC Comics, announced that Superman would be "evolving." No longer would he be fighting for "Truth, Justice and the American Way" but instead for "Truth, Justice and a Better Tomorrow." A press statement explained the company's rationale. Their decision was meant

"to better reflect the storylines that we are telling across DC and to honor Superman's incredible legacy of over 80 years of building a better world." This was not the first or only time his motto had changed. The original motto, including the words "the American Way," started in the 1940s, during World War II, "as a way to cheer on American military efforts" and continued through the 1950s during the Cold War. In the 1960s, during the heat of the Civil Rights Movement, the Man of Steel's motto changed. He was then fighting for "Truth, Justice and Freedom." During the 1990s, he fought for simply "Truth and Justice." It is interesting to see how his mottoes have changed with each passing generation. So it is, for the current generation, he is no longer fighting for the "American way" but for a "better tomorrow." The question remains: What exactly does that "better tomorrow" look like? Adam B. Vary, "Superman Changes Motto to 'Truth, Justice and a Better Tomorrow,' Says DC Chief," *Variety*, October 16, 2021, https://variety.com/2021/film/news/superman-new-motto-dc-fandome-1235090712.

15. F. A. Hayek, *Law, Legislation, and Liberty: A New Statement of the Liberal Principles of Justice and Political Economy*, ed. Jeremy Shearmur, The Collected Works of F. A. Hayek, vol. 19 (University of Chicago Press, 2021), 3–4.
16. For example, see Isaiah 11:1-10; 65:17-25; Ezekiel 34:11-31; Hosea 2:18-20; Micah 4:1-7; Zechariah 14:6-11; 2 Peter 3:13; Revelation 21–22.
17. "Social Justice," *Britannica*, last updated February 5, 2025, https://www.britannica.com/topic/social-justice; *Catechism of the Catholic Church*, 2nd ed. (USCCB, 2019), section 1928.
18. Nicholas P. Wolterstorff, *Journey Toward Justice: Personal Encounters in the Global South* (Baker Academic, 2013), 176.
19. See Luke 4:18-19. See also Matthew 18:23-35; Ephesians 4:25-32.
20. Martin Luther King Jr., *Strength to Love* (Beacon Press, 2019), 7.
21. For Jesus' teaching on humility and sacrificial love over revenge, see Matthew 5:38-39. For fiercely defending the vulnerable and oppressed, see Matthew 18:1-6; Mark 10:13-16; 11:15-18; Luke 5:12-16, 29-32; 7:36-50; 8:43-48; 13:10-17; John 4:7-9, 27-30, 39-42; 8:1-11. These examples highlight how Jesus stood up for the marginalized, offering them dignity, healing, and grace, often in defiance of social and religious norms.
22. For Paul's teaching on obedience to governing authorities, see Romans 12:19–13:7 (see also Proverbs 20:22; 24:29; 1 Thessalonians 5:15; 1 Peter 3:9-17). For Peter and John on obeying God rather than corrupt authorities, see Acts 5:29. While it is improper to assume every action performed by the apostles is instructive, in this case, the context of the narrative suggests their actions are to be considered exemplary.
23. For the Bible permitting self-defense, see Exodus 22:2-3, which establishes

that self-defense is permissible when facing an immediate and unknown threat; and Nehemiah 4:7-23, which positively recounts a time when a community of Israelites stood up to defend themselves from their oppressors. For turning the other cheek, see Luke 6:29-30; Romans 12:17.

24. E. Randolph Richards and Brandon J. O'Brien, *Misreading Scripture with Western Eyes: Removing Cultural Blinders to Better Understand the Bible* (IVP Books, 2012), 52–69.
25. David M. Goldenberg, *The Curse of Ham: Race and Slavery in Early Judaism, Christianity, and Islam* (Princeton University Press, 2003), 200.
26. Miroslav Volf, "Original Crime, Primal Care," in *God and the Victim: Theological Reflections on Evil, Victimization, Justice, and Forgiveness*, ed. Lisa Barnes Lampman (Eerdmans, 1999), 26–30.
27. See, for example, Edward Ullendorff, *Ethiopia and the Bible: The Schweich Lectures of the British Academy, 1967* (Oxford University Press, 1968), 8; D. S. Margoliouth, "Ethiopian Woman," in *A Dictionary of the Bible: Dealing with Its Language, Literature, and Contents, Including the Biblical Theology*, vol. 1, ed. James Hastings (Charles Scribner's Sons, 1908), 790–791.
28. Margoliouth, "Ethiopian Woman," 791.
29. Flavius Josephus, *The Works of Josephus: Complete and Unabridged*, updated ed., trans. William Whiston (Hendrickson, 1987), 70.
30. David Goldenberg, "Why Do Miriam and Aaron Criticize Moses for Marrying a Kushite Woman?," TheTorah.com, accessed March 20, 2025, https://www.thetorah.com/article/why-do-miriam-and-aaron-criticize-moses-for-marrying-a-kushite-woman.
31. See Genesis 10:8-9; Psalm 68:30-31; 87:4-6; Isaiah 45:14; Jeremiah 46:9; Nahum 3:8-9; Zephaniah 3:9-10. See also Goldenberg, *Curse of Ham*, 33–37.
32. Goldenberg, *Curse of Ham*, 32–38. Still, some skeptics appeal to Song of Solomon 1:5 and Jeremiah 13:23 to show that Israelites despised or scorned dark-skinned people. This is unfortunate, for there is nothing in these verses that should cause us to come to this conclusion—that is, unless we are reading into them our own cultural influences. A straightforward reading of these verses has no hint of negative sentiment toward those with dark skin. Solomon mentions the skin as a distinguishing feature, and Jeremiah simply uses the Cushite's black skin as a metaphor for that which is unchangeable. Neither verse implies that dark skin is undesirable or a curse, unless we think the tents of Kedar and leopard spots were equally despised.
33. Exodus 34:16; Deuteronomy 7:3-4; Joshua 23:12-13; 1 Kings 11:2; 16:31; Ezra 9–10. See also Ruth 1:22; 2:6; 4:10-13.
34. This story both assumes and exposes "the ethnic, cultural, and sociopolitical hostility between Jews and their Gentile neighbors" at the time, but, as we

will see, this does not necessarily entail that Jesus has adopted them. Ched Myers, *Binding the Strong Man: A Political Reading of Mark's Story of Jesus* (Orbis Books, 1988), 204.

35. For example, see John 4:9, 27.
36. It is interesting to note that the children of Israel have *literally* already been fed (Mark 6:42; translated *satisfied*, the same Greek word used here in verse 27). Later Jesus will repeat the miracle, only in a more Gentile location and presumably for a more Gentile crowd (see Mark 8:4, 8). The same Greek root word is used in each of these passages.
37. David E. Garland, *Mark*, The NIV Application Commentary (Zondervan, 1996), 288.
38. Maryknoll Missioners (@MaryknollFrsBrs), "Jesus was part of his culture: prejudiced against Canaanites. But he allowed a foreign woman to expand his views. Do we?," Twitter (now X), August 19, 2017, https://x.com/maryknollfrsbrs/status/899036678102237184.
39. "Whoever eats together with an idol worshiper is like one who eats together with a dog; as the dog is uncircumcised, so also is the idol worshiper uncircumcised." Garland, *Mark*, 289.
40. See 1 Samuel 17:43; 24:14; 2 Samuel 3:8; 9:8; 16:9; 2 Kings 8:13; Proverbs 26:11; Ecclesiastes 9:4; Isaiah 56:10-11.
41. See John 3:16; Hebrews 4:15. See also 2 Corinthians 5:21; 1 Peter 2:22; 1 John 3:5.
42. See Romans 3:1-2. See also Deuteronomy 4:8; Psalm 147:19-20; John 4:22; Garland, *Mark*, 288.
43. See Acts 1:8; 3:26; 13:4, 14, 46; Romans 1:16; 2:9-10; 11:28-29.
44. Myers, *Binding the Strong Man*, 204.
45. Perhaps it even prepared Peter for his heavenly vision near Caesarea (see Acts 10:1–11:18) and his confrontation with the apostle Paul (see Galatians 2:11-14).
46. See Acts 2:17-18, 38-39; Galatians 3:28; Colossians 3:11; Titus 3:4-6.
47. Even the household codes found in the New Testament that instruct wives to submit to their husbands are countercultural and subversive. Peter instructs wives to "be subject to your own husbands, so that even if some do not obey the word, *they may be won* without a word by the conduct of their wives, when they see your respectful and pure conduct" (1 Peter 3:1-2, emphasis added). When wives respond this way, they are following Christ's supreme example (see 1 Peter 2:21-23).
48. Darrell L. Bock, *Ephesians: An Introduction and Commentary*, Tyndale New Testament Commentaries, vol. 10 (IVP Academic, 2019), 192.
49. G. B. Caird, *Paul's Letters from Prison* (Oxford University Press, 1976); John R. W. Stott, *The Message of Ephesians*, The Bible Speaks Today (InterVarsity Press, 1979), 255; Albert A. Bell Jr., *Exploring the New*

Testament World: An Illustrated Guide to the World of Jesus and the First Christians (Thomas Nelson, 1998), 191–197; Marleen Boudreau Flory, "Family and Familia: A Study of Social Relations in Slavery" (PhD diss., Yale University, 1975), ProQuest Dissertations & Theses.

50. Wayne A. Meeks, *The First Urban Christians: The Social World of the Apostle Paul*, 2nd ed. (Yale University Press, 2003), 20–25.
51. Bruce J. Malina, *The New Testament World: Insights from Cultural Anthropology*, 3rd ed. (Westminster John Knox Press, 2001), 66, 157; Stott, *Message of Ephesians*, 255.
52. Aristotle, *Nicomachean Ethics*, trans. H. Rackham, 5.6.1134b9.
53. Miroslav Volf, *Captive to the Word of God: Engaging the Scriptures for Contemporary Theological Reflection* (Eerdmans, 2010), 80; Klyne Snodgrass, *Ephesians*, The NIV Application Commentary (Zondervan, 1996), 324; Tony Merida, *Exalting Jesus in Ephesians* (Holman Reference, 2014), 163.
54. "O Holy Night," by Placide Cappeau, trans. John S. Dwight, 1847, Hymnary.org, https://hymnary.org/text/o_holy_night_the_stars_are_brightly_shin.
55. Russ Dudrey, "'Submit Yourselves to One Another': A Socio-Historical Look at the Household Code of Ephesians 5:15–6:9," *Restoration Quarterly* 41, no. 1 (1999), 27–44; Stott, *Message of Ephesians*, 254–255. These seeds become blatantly obvious when Paul's household codes are contrasted with Aristotle's household codes. Aristotle's *Politics* 1.1254b3–1.257b25. See also Merida, *Exalting Jesus in Ephesians*, 164.
56. See Ephesians 2:1–3:21.
57. See Acts 17:30-31. See also Psalm 96:13; 98:9.
58. "Bibles on the Front Lines: Difficult. Dangerous. Illegal.," The Voice of the Martyrs, accessed March 20, 2025, https://www.persecution.com/bibles/.
59. See Revelation 6:10-11. See also Exodus 23:4-5; 2 Kings 6:22; Proverbs 25:21-22; Luke 6:27; Romans 12:17-21.
60. See Revelation 20:12. See also Genesis 18:25; Psalm 58:11; Ecclesiastes 12:14; Romans 2:16; 14:10, 12; 1 Corinthians 4:5. See also Scott David Allen, *Why Social Justice Is Not Biblical Justice: An Urgent Appeal to Fellow Christians in a Time of Social Crisis* (Credo House, 2020), 38–39.

Discussion Guide

1. The authors describe the assumptions we bring to the Bible as "lenses" that affect (and can distort) our vision (see pages 9–10). Think of how you approach the Bible. What assumptions do you bring to it? Have you ever brought to the text any of the eight faulty assumptions on page 12? Which ones?

2. What do people today say about the Bible? What surprised you about the authors' description of the Bible (see pages 20–24)? How would you answer the question "What is the Bible?"

3. What comes to your mind when you think of the legacy of the Bible? In your experience, has the Bible been more of a positive or negative force? How has reading this chapter reshaped your view of it?

4. The authors write, "When evaluating or interpreting a work of art, it's wise to first consult those who are genuine experts on it" (page 51). Do you agree with this principle?

Why or why not? In what ways is the Bible "the church's book"? In what ways would it benefit a person considering the Bible's claims to consult Christian experts?

5. In what ways do "social imaginaries" (see pages 81–85) inform the ways in which we see the world? What social imaginaries affect the way people read the Bible today? How might living in another time or place (with its own set of social imaginaries) change the way you read it?

6. What is the doctrine of inerrancy? Why do the authors not advocate an all-or-nothing approach to inerrancy? What does it mean that the Bible is highly reliable?

7. What does the doctrine of the "perspicuity [clarity] of Scripture" reveal about how we can understand the Bible? How does the doctrine of Scripture's clarity intersect with passages that are difficult to understand? How are modern readers at a disadvantage when it comes to understanding Scripture? What advantages do modern readers have?

8. In what ways is the interpretation of Scripture both a science and an art? How are the goals of hermeneutics (the science of interpretation) and forensics similar? Which of the eight rules of interpretation found on pages 122–128 stood out to you the most? Why?

9. What does it mean that "the Bible was written *for* us, it was not written *to* us" (page 151)? In what ways is reading the Bible like visiting another culture? Why is it important to understand the historical context of the Bible's original audience?

10. Many people think of the Bible as an ancient rule book. Why is this a false assumption? What does it mean to universalize, spiritualize, and moralize a passage of Scripture? Why is this a dangerous way to interpret the Bible?

11. What do the authors mean when they say that the Bible "is not a formal history book" (page 185)? What expectations do you have when you think of a history book? In what ways does the Bible meet or not meet those expectations?

12. How would you have characterized the relationship between the Bible and science before reading chapter 11? How do you see their relationship after reading the chapter? Did anything change? Why or why not?

13. What are the differences between biblical justice and social justice? How does reconciliation guide the Bible's approach to justice? How does "clearing the mechanism" affect your reading of challenging passages like the ones presented in chapter 12?

14. What questions do you still have about the Bible? Which of the interpretive methods presented in the book might help you to better discover answers to your questions? What faulty assumptions might be standing in your way?

About the Authors

John Marriott is a faculty affiliate of the Human Flourishing Program at Harvard University's Institute for Quantitative Social Science. He is the former research and program coordinator for the Biola University Center for Christian Thought and teaches part-time in the department of philosophy at Talbot School of Theology. A former pastor, he holds a PhD from the Cook School of Intercultural Studies. His dissertation focused on deconversion from Christianity to atheism.

Shawn Wicks is a pastor, author, and ministry leader in Southern California. He serves as vice president of the Southern California Bible Conference, directing camps and retreats at Verdugo Pines Bible Camp. A graduate of Talbot School of Theology (MDiv), he coauthored *Before You Go: Uncovering Hidden Factors in Faith Loss*. Shawn has served as a youth minister and cross-cultural ministry trainer. He lives in Orange County with his wife, Dawnita, and their four children.